THE ROAD TO PEACE

Ray Jones

Dec. 23.

THE ROAD TO PEACE

*Edited by Ernie Regehr
and Simon Rosenblum*

James Lorimer & Company, Publishers
Toronto 1988

Cover illustration: Geoff Butler

Canadian Cataloguing in Publication Data:

Main entry under title:
The Road to Peace
Includes index.
ISBN 1-55028-041-4 (bound) ISBN 1-55028-039-2 (pbk.)
1. Nuclear disarmament. 2. Canada - Military policy. I. Regehr,
Ernie, 1941- . II. Rosenblum, Simon.
JX1974.7.R62 1988   327.1'74.   CBB-093675-4

James Lorimer & Company, Publishers
Egerton Ryerson Memorial Building
35 Britain Street
Toronto, Ontario M5A 1R7
Printed and bound in Canada
6 5 4 3 2 1 88 89 90 91 92 93

In memory of
Margaret Laurence

Contents

Contributors

AL BANNER has a background in remote sensing imaging, with a particular focus on arms-control verification.

JOHN BARRETT is the deputy director of the Canadian Centre for Arms Control and Disarmament.

DON BATES, professor in the history of medicine at McGill University, is a member of Physicians for Social Responsibility and chairman of the McGill Study Group for Peace and Disarmament.

LEONARD JOHNSON retired from the Canadian Armed Forces in 1984. A member of Generals for Peace and Disarmament, and the author of *A General for Peace*, he now lives in Westport, Ont.

GARY MARCHANT is a geneticist currently studying public policy on science and technology.

ERNIE REGEHR, author of *Arms Canada: The Deadly Business of Military Exports* and the research director of Project Ploughshares, lives in Waterloo, Ont.

BILL ROBINSON is a researcher with Project Ploughshares.

SIMON ROSENBLUM is the author of *Misguided Missiles* and co-editor, with Ernie Regehr, of *Canada and the Nuclear Arms Race*. He is the political affairs coordinator for Project Ploughshares.

Acknowledgements

We would like to acknowledge our debt to the many people who helped produce this volume. Most important, of course, have been the writers. Their willingness to contribute their time and expertise to produce entirely new essays for the book is greatly appreciated. All have done so without remuneration, and all have agreed to assign the proceeds from the book to Project Ploughshares.

We are also indebted to our friends and colleagues at Project Ploughshares for their support and assistance. In particular, we have benefited from the help and advice given by Bill Robinson in reviewing and checking substantial portions of the manuscript, as well as from the assistance of Eleanor Moyer, who typed the initial draft and corrected the subsequent ones.

Our indebtedness to our editor, Curtis Fahey, deserves special mention. Without his persistence, patience and critical piloting of the manuscript to its final form, this important set of essays would not have become available to Canadians and to the ongoing public campaign for disarmament.

The encouragement of our friends and families has been indispensable to the completion of this book, as it is to all our work.

Ernie Regehr
Simon Rosenblum
May 1988

Introduction

The hands of the doomsday clock of the *Bulletin of the Atomic Scientists*, for forty years a reminder of the imminent threat of nuclear war, recently moved back from three minutes to six minutes before midnight. The journal's editors, the keepers of the clock, attributed this modest retreat from Armageddon to the Reagan-Gorbachev signing of the INF Treaty and the general improvement in Soviet-American relations. It was the first time in sixteen years that the *Bulletin* clock had been moved back from midnight, rather than steadily toward it.

The value of the INF Treaty is in its unique achievement of eliminating a class of state-of-the-art nuclear weapons held by the superpowers. The agreement has raised the hope that the nuclear arms race can be stopped and actually reversed. With the Soviets and Americans now seriously discussing deep cuts in strategic (long-range) nuclear weapons, concrete steps are finally being taken in the right direction.

But the INF Treaty will become a symbol of false hope if the momentum for disarmament and the fires of public opinion that produced it are not maintained. Whether the positive change in the political atmosphere created at the 1987 summit will in fact lead to a real and sustained shift in priorities depends largely on the continued engagement of concerned people throughout the world.

In the meantime, most of the painful nuclear realities remain. Even with strategic arsenals cut in half, a goal that might well be realized by the early 1990s, the world will not have abandoned its capacity for Armageddon. But reality also resides in the public mind, and it is that reality which has undergone the most dramatic change. While nuclear weapons still have their sponsors, powerful sponsors with more than their fair share of influence over public policy, disarmament has its own champions — not vested interests or powerful elites, but people the world over who have come to understand that security cannot be found in the means to destruction. These are the people who cheered when Mikhail Gorbachev and Ronald Reagan shook hands in Washington; indeed, these are the people who brought the two together in the first place. The point that has been grasped by the public mind is, not that the superpowers cannot be trusted to disarm, but rather that they cannot be trusted with nuclear arms. For forty years we have been told that our security requires the preservation of nuclear arms. It is an old lie that is now losing its power.

A reassessment of our continuing struggle with nuclear weapons, which is the preoccupation of this book, needs to begin with a review of the current state-of-the-art. In chapter one, Simon Rosenblum reviews the strategic nuclear arsenals that are the subject of current negotiations, as well as the major talking points in those negotiations. Len Johnson, in chapter two, examines the doctrines and ideologies that sustain those arsenals. He dissects a nuclear-weapons doctrine that is evolving, not toward a more stable deterrent, but toward a nuclear war-fighting capacity, albeit at lower levels of arms. Despite reductions in numbers of weapons, currently envisioned agreements would still preserve an unconscionable overkill capacity and, more disturbing, a new generation of weapons and weapons-infrastructure designed ultimately for *use*.

Chapter three, by Donald Bates, addresses the question of whether reduced levels of nuclear weapons and "limited war" scenarios mean that the threat of nuclear war in this more limited form is tolerable. Can we risk a limited nuclear war in the pursuit of military-security objectives? The evidence shows that our understanding of the environmental effects of nuclear war has become much more sophisticated in the post-Chernobyl era. There is no threshold under which the environmental costs of using nuclear weapons for military ends would be tolerable. Any use promises extraordinary and unacceptable risks. The point is that we must get rid of nuclear weapons. We cannot tolerate merely lower levels.

Chapter four, by Gary Marchant and Al Banner, addresses one of the chief obstacles to real disarmament — the fear that one side or the other will cheat. This chapter reviews verification capabilities and concludes that disarmament agreements can indeed be verified and that it is time to call the nuclear powers to account on this point — verification is no longer an excuse for avoiding disarmament. Chapter five, occupying the mid-point of the book, is John Barrett's review of

Canada's traditional approach to disarmament, as well as some of the opportunities in the current arms-control environment that are available to Canada.

The final four chapters look at the road ahead. What is the new disarmament agenda that Canada ought to be promoting? In chapter six, Ernie Regehr argues that disarmament must now be pursued in the context of a new understanding of the basis of security. The concept of common security provides a critical guide to security objectives that are consistent with the genuine security needs of individuals, states and the environment. It also has particular implications for Canadian security policy — security policy which includes, but is not exclusive to, the pillars of disarmament and defence. This chapter reviews the defence/disarmament implications for Canada and offers some basic principles to guide Canadian policy.

Bill Robinson's chapter seven examines what may be the single greatest threat to current arms-control progress — the increasing possibility of the "weaponization of space." This chapter examines the current military uses of space, the agreements that currently control the military use of space, and the prospects for the dangerous weaponization of space (these dangerous prospects include the introduction into the space environment of weapons that will create pressures toward the greater weaponization of earth, including the Canadian North, and that will increase the likelihood of nuclear war). The chapter concludes with suggestions about the practical steps that Canada can take to prevent the weaponization of space — steps that have implications for Canada's continued participation in NORAD.

In chapter eight the editors examine the problem of Europe, the site of the world's greatest military arsenal today and throughout history. If war, anywhere on the globe, comes to involve the military forces of the superpowers, it is inevitable that the fighting will move quickly to the theatre which has been prepared for it — Europe. Hence Canadian and world security interests are linked to disarmament in Europe. This chapter assesses the prospects for European disarmament. The book concludes, in chapter nine, with a discussion of the concept of a nuclear-weapon-free-zone as a framework for Canada's approach to nuclear disarmament, and indicates the policy changes that would be necessary for Canada to become such a zone.

The publication of a book about disarmament testifies that true hope is sustained, not so much by utopian visions in technicolor, but by debate followed by action — concrete measures to reorganize the world's security system. A disarmament book published in Canada for Canadians is also testimony to the belief that nuclear disarmament is not best left to the superpowers. Superpowers left to their own devices are not inclined toward disarmament, but superpowers challenged by their own people and their allies do some surprising things — they start talking about ridding the world of nuclear weapons. The Canadian government, no less than superpower governments, derives its will to act imaginatively and creatively for disarmament from its people, and this book is offered as part of the public discussion and action that, if sustained, can bring urgency and persistence to the disarmament agenda.

We dedicate this volume in grateful memory to Margaret Laurence, whose persistent urging of disarmament action is eloquently reflected in her declaration that disarmament is "the most pressing practical, moral and spiritual issue of our time."

1

Farewell to Arms?: The Strategic Nuclear Arms Race and the Possibilities of Disarmament

Simon Rosenblum

After the December 1987 summit during which President Reagan and General Secretary Gorbachev signed the INF Treaty (governing intermediate-range nuclear forces) there was much speculation that an agreement on strategic (long-range) offensive forces could be reached early enough in 1988 to permit its signature at a summit in Moscow. The fact that a genuine disarmament agreement has at last been concluded opens up expectations hitherto quite unknown in almost twenty years of nuclear negotiations.

Yet the question remains whether the United States is still prepared to "sacrifice arms control on the altar of SDI [Strategic Defense Initiative]," as U.S. Rear Admiral (Ret.) Eugene Carroll expressed it, or whether a so-called "grand compromise" is possible in which the U.S. restrains its strategic defence program in return for strategic arms reductions. Though the United States and the Soviet Union have discussed a commitment not to withdraw from the ABM (Anti-Ballistic Missile) Treaty for a set period of time, they continue to remain divided over what sort of research, development and testing should be permitted during that period, and what should happen once the period ends.

This chapter will review the spiralling arms race that led up to the Washington summit and that, despite the agreement signed there, still continues. It will then assess the significance of the INF agreement, the threat SDI poses to the arms-control process, and the prospects for — and desirability of — deep cuts in the superpowers' nuclear arsenals.

On the Edge

Until the signing of the INF Treaty, the Reagan administration had been primarily responsible for a dramatic escalation in the nuclear arms race. On November 28, 1986, the United States deliberately violated the SALT II Treaty — unratified but largely observed by the superpowers — with its announcement that it intended to ignore all numerical limits on U.S. and Soviet missiles and bombers carrying nuclear warheads. The Reagan administration's decision on SALT II was based on alleged Soviet violations of the agreement. These charges were part of a continuing campaign to portray the Soviet Union as engaged in a "pattern of non-compliance" with all arms-control agreements.

While Soviet activities have raised some questions, the formal charges of Soviet violations of SALT II were based on ambiguous treaty provisions and uncertain monitoring information. Moreover, Washington's charges are inconsistent. For example, the Reagan administration claims that the throw weight, (the size or yield of the warhead plus aiming devices in the warhead), of the Soviet SS-25 missile is greater than that of its predecessor, the SS-13, by more than the 5 per cent that is permitted by the provisions of SALT II. The Americans also charge the Soviets with interfering illegally with the ability of the U.S. to collect data from Russian flight tests. While the Soviets may, in fact, be stretching the rules, any claim that Moscow has impeded (the technical term is "encrypted") flight-test verification would appear to be undercut by the detailed charges the U.S. has levelled concerning the SS-13 and SS-25 throw-weight comparisons, since precise data is certainly required to make such a judgement.[1] Objective assessments indicate that the overall Soviet compliance record has actually been good and has served U.S. security interests well.[2]

At the same time, the Reagan administration develops and deploys highly accurate multiple-warhead missiles, such as the MX and the Trident II (D-5), which are capable of destroying Soviet land-based missiles and thus threaten the Soviet Union with increased American first-strike capabilities. These U.S. nuclear war-fighting capabilities are not being acquired to deter a Soviet bolt-out-of-the-blue nuclear attack, but rather to increase American military options world-wide. The theory is that, under the U.S. nuclear umbrella, all levels of American military force can be used without risking a direct military response from the Soviets. This theory is premised on "limited nuclear war" scenarios — the claim that a nuclear war could be managed in such a way as not to escalate to global war and to allow America to "prevail" (win) in the end. The threat to use nuclear weapons is, therefore, not viewed as an intention to resort to nuclear war, but part of a process of controlled threat escalation which, even though it risks nuclear war, is intended to deter military action by othrt nations at all levels.[3]

The notion of limited nuclear war is also partly based on an assessment of one's own strengths and the other side's weaknesses. Studies have revealed, for example, that there would be a substantially greater number of American warheads remaining after an American first-strike. Calculations by the Washington-based Coalition for a New Foreign and Military Policy estimate that, in 1985, 3,600 Soviet strategic warheads would have survived a U.S. surprise attack; by January 1995 the number could drop to 700. The United States, on the other hand, will continue to have 4,500 survivable warheads. This imbalance is attributed to the greater accuracy of U.S. nuclear weapons and to the different ways in which the two superpowers have shaped their strategic arsenals. The United States has 18 per cent of its strategic warheads in land-based missiles (ICBMs), 39 per cent in bombers and 43 per cent in less vulnerable submarine-launched ballistic missiles (SLBMs); the Soviets, in contrast, have 61 per cent in ICBMs, 10 per cent in bombers and 29 per cent in SLBMs. (See Table.) Hence the increased willingness of the U.S. to engage in nuclear war-fighting strategies, and the resulting pressure on the Soviets to adopt a "launch on warning" practice (launching land-based missiles as soon as an attack on them is detected, so that the attacking missiles will find only empty silos to destroy).

The search for nuclear "superiority" is primarily dependent on technology. In testimony before the United States Congress in support of the administration's 1987 budget requests, the Pentagon listed twen-

Strategic Nuclear Forces of the U.S. &U.S.S.R.
(December 31, 1987)

Type	Name	Launchers		Warheads	
United States					
ICBMs					
LGM-30F	Minuteman II	450		450	
LGM-30G	Minuteman III				
	Mk-12	220		660	
	Mk-12A	300		900	
LGM-118A	MX-Peacekeeper	30		300	
Total		1,000	(50%)	2,310	(18%)
SLBMs					
UGM-73A	Poseidon C-3	256		2,560	
UGM-96A	Trident I C-4	384		3,072	
Total		640	(32%)	5,632	(43%)
Bombers/weapons					
B-1B		64		1,614	
B-52G/H		241		1,140	
FB-111A		56		2,316	
Total		361	(18%)	5,070	(39%)
Grand Total		**2,001**		**13,012**	
U.S.S.R.					
ICBMs					
SS-11	Sego				
M2		184		184	
M3		210		630	
SS-13 M2	Savage	60		60	
SS-17 M3	Spanker	139		556	
SS-18 M4	Satan	308		3,080	
SS-19 M3	Stiletto	360		2,160	
SS-24	Scalpel	5		50	
SS-25	Sickle	126		126	
Total		1,392	(56%)	6,846	(61%)
SLBMs					
SS-N-6 M3	Serb	272		544	
SS-N-8 M1/M2	Sawfly	292		292	
SS-N-17	Snipe	12		12	
SS-N-18 M1-3	Stingray	224		1,344	
SS-N-20	Sturgeon	80		560	
SS-N-23	Skiff	48		480	
Total		928	(37%)	3,232	(29%)
Bombers/weapons					
Tu-95	Bear A	30		120	
Tu-95	Bear B/C	30		150	
Tu-95	Bear G	40		240	
Tu-95	Bear H	55		660	
Total		155	(6%)	1,170	(10%)
Grand Total		**2,475**		**11,248**	

ALCM —air-launched cruise missile; AS—air-to-surface missile; ICBM—intercontinental ballistic missile, range of 5,670-15,360 kilometers; MIRV—multiple, independently targetable reentry vehicles; MRV—multiple reentry vehicles; SLBM—submarine-launched ballistic missile; SRAM—short-range attack missile. Names of Soviet weapons are codenames assigned by NATO. (Source, Bulletin of the Atomic Scientists, January/February 1988)

ty areas of basic research in the two countries. In fourteen of these, the United States was described as superior to the Soviet Union, and in six they were equal.[4] Not surprisingly, then, American proposals for nuclear weapons reductions do not contain a freeze on future weapons modernization, but instead seek to protect American advantages and new programs. Insofar as nuclear weapons superiority proves to be elusive, improved U.S.-Soviet relations and progress in arms control are likely to be accompanied by calls from Cold War strategists for enhanced U.S. conventional weapons capabilities and for greater forcefulness in responding to "low intensity conflicts" in the Third World.[5]

The Tale of Two Summits

Historically, arms limitation treaties have not prevented either side from obtaining the weapons it sought. The SALT I treaty was little else but an agreement to perpetuate and even intensify the nuclear arms race. SALT II has had essentially the same effect; it has been observed mainly because it has permitted virtually every new weapon that either the United States or the Soviet Union could develop and deploy during the treaty's term. Indeed, the nuclear arms race has escalated and intensified through all the years of negotiations about arms reductions. As Nobel Peace Prize winner Alva Myrdal observed, the function of nuclear arms limitations talks has been to help "institutionalize the arms race," providing the superpowers with a forum for constant discussions about the weapons each side would be developing and deploying.[6] It has been an ideal format for the two sides to reach limited agreements on often unwanted weapons and to create the impression that the arms race was under control.

In recent years, the superpowers missed a magnificent opportunity to achieve genuine progress in arms control. At Reykjavik, Iceland, in October 1986, the leaders of the two superpowers walked right up to the edge of a breath-taking agreement encompassing a schedule for ridding the world of the scourge of nuclear weapons. Seeking to outdo each other in their commitment to reducing nuclear arms, they were reported to have agreed on the goal of eliminating all nuclear weapons within ten years. Other versions of the proposed agreement indicated that it called only for the elimination of ballistic missiles (missiles propelled by rockets). Whatever the case, when the chips were down, Ronald Reagan could not bring himself to surrender his vision of Star Wars — SDI — and the meeting ended in disarray without final agreement on anything.

Yet beyond the failure of Reykjavik remains the reality that the two leaders came astonishingly, tantalizingly, close to an arms deal on a scale that has never been even remotely approached in four decades of superpower nuclear rivalry. After all the years of fruitless talk about arms control and of bureaucratic fencing over details, we learned from Reykjavik that the two superpowers might be able to reach a disarmament agreement in the broadest terms. We learned that the numbers of nuclear weapons need not go on endlessly climbing — they can be drastically reduced — and that lesson won't soon be forgotten.

While the Washington summit of December 1987 did not match the daring proposals set out at Reykjavik, it did produce the INF agreement which may yet lead to the very thing that the Reykjavik summit came so close to achieving — real disarmament. Progress was made not only in regards to the INF treaty but also concerning reductions in strategic nuclear weapons. At the end of the three days, Reagan said the meeting had "lit the sky with hope for all people of goodwill," and Gorbachev declared the summit a "major event in world politics."

Both sides agreed to a reduction of strategic nuclear delivery vehicles (SNDV) to 1,600 and to a limit of 6,000 on strategic warheads. In an effort "to ensure that the reductions enhance strategic stability," agreement was reached on a sub-limit of 4,900 warheads on the aggregate number of ICBM and SLBM warheads within the 6,000-warhead ceiling. The Soviets also undertook to limit warheads on "heavy missiles" to 1,540 cruise missiles, and the U.S. finally agreed that some limits on sea-launched cruise missiles are acceptable, although their nature and the means to verify them must still be resolved.

Because the warhead limit would count all bombs and short-range attack missiles on an individual bomber as a single warhead and since sea-launched cruise missiles are to be dealt with outside the 6,000-warhead limit, the actual reductions from current strategic force levels would be closer to 25 per cent than to the claimed 50 per cent reduction. If these weapons were added to the 6,000-warhead aggregate, U.S. and eventually Soviet strategic arsenal levels would be closer to 9,000 and could grow even higher if, as might be anticipated, both sides devote their energies to increasing those elements of the strategic forces omitted from the 6,000-warhead aggregate. The outstanding difficulty is in the area of sub-limits within the agreed categories. The United States tabled an additional sub-limit of 3,300 on ICBM warheads, but the Soviet Union has resisted such a constraint on land-based missiles, the primary leg of its strategic triad. Moscow has proposed instead to permit no more than 3,600 warheads on any one leg of the triad: ICBMs, SLBMs and long-range bombers. Also among the issues that have not been settled is the question of mobile ballistic missiles. Negotiations on sub-limits and other matters continue in Geneva, leading up to a projected third Reagan-Gorbachev summit in the late spring of 1988.

On the central issue of the ABM Treaty and ballistic missile defences, the two sides remain deadlocked. The only agreement reached was to cloak the impasse in ambiguous language, thereby avoiding a repetition of the acrimonious collapse of the Reykjavik summit. The joint communique sidestepped the divisive SDI issue by deferring it. It instructed the negotiators of both nations "to work out an agreement that commits the sides to observe the ABM Treaty, as signed in 1972, while conducting their research, development and testing as required, which are permitted by the ABM Treaty, and not to withdraw from the ABM Treaty for a specified period of time." The language of the communique carefully avoided the issue of whose interpretation of the treaty is right. American officials use that fact to support their case that the U.S. can pursue SDI experiments under the broad interpretation of the treaty. However, back in Moscow, Gorbachev warned that any move by the U.S. to speed up the development of space-based defence systems would undermine the progress being made in disarmament talks.

The SDI Impasse

The conflict over SDI revolves around differing interpretations of the ABM Treaty. For years a "strict" interpretation of the pact has prevailed. Article V says that neither side will "develop, test or deploy ABM systems or components which are sea-based or mobile land-based." A passage called Agreed Statement D says that systems based on new "physical principles" — such as lasers and particle beams —

would be "subject to discussion" in order to "ensure fulfillment of the obligation not to deploy ABM systems."[7] In 1985 the Reagan administration formulated its controversial "broad" interpretation, which would make it possible to proceed with Star Wars testing in space without renegotiation of the treaty. Reagan has insisted on converting the ABM Treaty, intended initially to be of unlimited duration, into a totally different agreement that would permit SDI testing and would last for only ten years, after which a full-scale deployment of a nation-wide ABM defence would be allowed.

Gorbachev rejects, as a precondition to deep cuts in strategic nuclear weapons, the U.S. vision of a revised ABM treaty. The Soviets seek a long (up to fifteen years) moratorium on strategic defence research outside the laboratory and hence on development and deployment of strategic defences. That would be the death of what President Reagan calls "my baby," death by suffocation in the cradle. Meanwhile, the Reagan administration is moving towards early deployment of SDI in order to lock the next administration into a commitment to strategic defences. SDI has thus become, in the words of a letter to the editor of the New York *Times*, "a leakproof defense against improved U.S.-Soviet relations and against arms control."[8]

Reagan's enthusiasm notwithstanding, the overwhelming consensus within the scientific community is that Star Wars is not viable if what is intended is an invulnerable shield.[9] If SDI is so problematic, why does it bother Moscow so much? Besides the distinct possibility of eventually using SDI laser technology for direct offensive purposes,[10] strategic defences could enhance existing offensive nuclear-weapons capabilities. The International Institute of Strategic Studies in England describes SDI as a dangerous risk to peace, noting that "even if strategic defences were to prove feasible, they could damage stability rather than strengthen it." The greatest danger in strategic defence is the temptation it produces for a pre-emptive strike. While it is highly unlikely that a defensive system could be constructed which would be adequate to deal with the first strike of a determined opponent, it might be considered to be adequate to deal with the missiles of that opponent which are left after one's own first strike against them. Strategic defence is a leaky umbrella which offers little protection in a downpour but which might be quite useful in a drizzle.

The Soviet leader knows what President Reagan, in his insistence that the SDI is "purely defensive," cannot seem to grasp. The thesis was developed long ago in the Lyndon Johnson administration by Secretary of Defense Robert S. McNamara: a defensive system can add to a nation's offensive capacity. As Richard Nixon once put it, if two gladiators are fighting with swords, and one is handed a shield, the shield is not just a defensive instrument but an aid to the offensive ability of the gladiator who possesses it. It was an appreciation of this fact that caused Prime Minister Mulroney to urge that: "Extreme care must be taken to ensure that [strategic] defences are not integrated with existing forces in such a way as to create fears of a first strike." In almost any scenario the existence of large-scale defensive systems would make it more attractive for both sides to strike first — including in such a strike, of course, attacks on the defensive systems of the other side.

The first-strike threat is to some extent exaggerated since even the side with the less developed strategic defence system should be able to use its ABM infrastructure to protect its missile silos and — assuming that its command, control and communication facilities had not been rendered inoperable — thereby release a substantial retaliatory response. The immensely destructive consequences of nuclear war on the global environment — the so-called nuclear winter effect — would also help to deter against any first-strike, no matter how "successful." Yet, given the irrational nuclear war-fighting strategies drawn up in the Pentagon, the instabilities introduced by strategic defences — especially in a crisis situation — cannot be discounted.

What the Soviets want is an assurance that the United States will not be aggressively developing defensive systems — that would permit American forces to strike first and cripple the Soviet retaliatory capability — at the same time that the Soviet Union and the United States are reducing their nuclear forces by 50 per cent. That would mean the end of deterrence for the Soviet Union but not for the United States. Former Defense Secretary Caspar Weinberger's testimony can only increase these Soviet fears:

> If we can get a system which is effective and which we know can render their weapons impotent, we would be back in a situation we were in, for example, when we were the

only nation with the nuclear weapon and we did not threaten others with it.[11]

If, as Robert McNamara has declared, "it can be said without qualification [that] we cannot have both Star Wars and arms control," can there be any legitimate rationale for strategic defenses? President Reagan justifies SDI as an "insurance policy" against cheating when all nuclear weapons have been destroyed: "I likened it [SDI] to our keeping our gas masks even though the nations of the world have out-lawed poison gas after World War I."[12] Putting aside the fact that the offensive capabilities of SDI make it somewhat less benign than a gas mask and that, for a transitional period at least, strategic defenses would be deployed alongside nuclear weapons, is SDI a useful and necessary "insurance policy"?

It is true that there would be immense difficulties in verifying the total abolition of nuclear weapons, which leads to the proposition that SDI could defend against the few nuclear weapons that might be developed without detection. But if this is the rationale, a space-based strategic defence system is unnecessary. Princeton University physics professor Freeman Dyson has written about a modest ground-based ballistic missile defence system capable of protecting against the danger of one side cheating on an elimination of nuclear weapons pact and having a small nuclear arsenal.[13] Although not perfect, a multi-layered ground-based defence is a technical task well within the realm of possibility. Such a minimal defensive system would be totally inef-fective against a significant number of nuclear weapons; however, it would be able to protect the major population centres at greatest risk of an attack by a small number of ballistic missiles that might remain hidden. Thus, in the context of nuclear weapons being radically reduced but not eliminated, it would not pose the destabilizing (first-strike) dangers that are presented by a larger, more capable space-based defensive system.[14] The Federation of American Scientists (FAS) ar-gues that, not only are the technical requirements for such a modest system elementary for both superpowers, but also that such a "com-promise" should be acceptable to the United States.[15] It should be kept in mind, however, that there is no absolute "technical fix" against even a limited number of nuclear weapons. Nuclear weapons can be delivered by means (for example, in suitcases) that, while more risky than ballistic missiles, are much less susceptible to defences.

Sam Nunn, the U.S. Senate's leading Democratic expert on the military, has proposed that SDI be transformed into a "Sensible Defense Initiative," an extremely limited defence against an accidental missile launch. Unfortunately, the Reagan administration has not indicated any willingness to reduce the scope of SDI and continues to pursue what strategic analyst William Kaufmann has called "the last Nuclear Arcadia" of total American strategic superiority. Even though the Joint Chiefs of Staff believe that "a deployment decision is premature" since the "military utility of what is proposed has not been properly assessed",[16] Reagan is pushing SDI along as far and as fast as he can. In this context the American proposal on the ABM Treaty is a transparently self-serving arrangement to abolish the treaty on a timetable consistent with an optimistic assessment of SDI. Many observers remain confounded over how a nonexistent system can come between two superpowers that otherwise would agree to reduce and perhaps even eliminate nuclear missiles.

The Soviet Union, for its part, is softening its stance on SDI and now appears willing to allow some space-based testing as long as specific limits are negotiated and the ABM Treaty as a whole remains intact. Moscow is suggesting bilateral negotiations both on a list of devices not to be put into space and on "performance thresholds" designed to control tests conducted in space. The "thresholds" would establish limits on such things as the size of mirrors, the brightness of lasers, the power of space-based reactors and the speed of interceptors so that, when the devices became sufficiently powerful to play an anti-ballistic missile role, they would be banned.[17] Given that there are currently questions over what is considered an ABM "component" or what constitutes "development" — terms that are central to the ABM Treaty — the Federation of American Scientists recommends "threshold limits" since they could provide less ambiguous operational definitions and are verifiable.[18] Such limits would still allow developments on the "learning-curve" of Star Wars technologies but for the foreseeable future would block any space-based defence deployment. Despite the advocacy of Paul Nitze, special arms-control adviser to President Reagan, this proposal has been, so far, rejected by the United States.

If an agreement on the ABM Treaty cannot be reached, the Soviet Union would be well advised to separate progress on strategic reductions from Star Wars—what in Moscow is being called the "Sakharov" approach. Soviet scientist and human rights activist Andrei Sakharov has recommended that, failing an accommodation on the ABM Treaty, the Soviet Union should circumvent the Star Wars issue by agreeing to strategic reductions without further ado about SDI, and by coupling this policy with a unilateral statement that it would withdraw from the agreement if the United States proceeded too far with work on deployment of a space-based ABM system.[19] Because of the myriad technical, budgetary and political constraints that confront SDI, and the momentum of a deep reductions agreement, it could very well be that SDI will not survive the Reagan presidency. If SDI were subsequently to progress, Moscow could simply reverse its course on reductions. This approach has the merit of holding Star Wars hostage by putting the world on the disarmament road and letting the resulting political atmosphere deal with SDI. There are, in fact, preliminary indications from Soviet officials that they are indeed moving toward this position.

Deep Cuts and Beyond

Currently proposed strategic reductions are not the final answer. It is, in fact, possible to have fewer overall strategic nuclear weapons but a less stable situation because of the nature of the residual forces. Reductions must be properly designed to ensure the invulnerability of the reduced forces. Deep cuts might exacerbate strategic instabilities by worsening cost-exchange ratios (increasing the number of weapons an attacker could destroy with a single warhead and thereby raising the value of the target and the incentive to destroy it).[20] Reductions should maintain a bias against those nuclear weapons considered to be most destabilizing: accurate systems with short flight-times or short detection times, necessary for nuclear war-fighting strategies, and accurate multi-warhead missiles.

The problem of first-strike vulnerability will remain as long as modernized nuclear weapons are exempted from the reductions.[21] A recent study by the Canadian Institute for International Peace and Security[22] has demonstrated that the implementation of both U.S. and

Soviet reductions proposals could — with ongoing modernization — sharply increase the first-strike pre-emption capabilities of both of the superpowers. After modernization and with reductions, the United States in particular would possess highly destabilizing, increased first-strike capabilities. Because of this advantage, it is the Reagan administration which resists incorporating a flight test ban on new nuclear weapons delivery systems — as advocated by Pierre Trudeau in his "strategy of suffocation" — into a reductions agreement.

A more far-reaching, yet achievable extension of deep cuts is "minimum deterrence." If it can be accepted that nuclear weapons can serve no rational purpose — with the possible exception that small numbers of invulnerable nuclear weapons may be necessary for some time to deter direct nuclear attack from a nuclear-armed adversary in times of crisis — then a relatively small number of nuclear weapons — a few hundred perhaps — is sufficient. Minimum deterrence requires only a second-strike capability. This means that the remaining nuclear weapons should not be accurate enough to disarm an opponent's nuclear forces. When rival states are secure in the knowledge that each has a second-strike capability — sufficient numbers of survivable nuclear weapons to threaten unacceptable damage to the other side even after suffering a nuclear attack — greater strategic stability or mutual deterrence exists. Former U.S. Defense Secretary Robert McNamara has recently proposed such a minimum deterrence system which would rely at least in part on less vulnerable submarine-launched ballistic missiles with single warheads.[23] Others have recommended minimum deterrence with different numbers and force configurations.[24] A stabilizing influence on any minimum deterrent force structure would be the establishment of large "submarine sanctuaries" for each superpower where the attack submarines of the opposing superpower would not be allowed to operate. By physically separating the opposing ballistic missile and attack submarines, a safety net would be placed on what could otherwise be a hair-trigger for nuclear war. Central to the minimal deterrence model is the recognition that nuclear warheads are weapons that cannot be used to fight and win wars and that foreign policies based upon nuclear intimidation are unacceptable. As McNamara concludes: "I do not believe we can avoid the serious and unacceptable risk of nuclear war until we recognize — and until we base all our military plans, defense budgets, weapons deployment, and arms registrations on the recognition — that nuclear weapons serve no military purpose whatsoever. They are totally useless — except to deter one's opponent from using them."

Minimum deterrence, while considerably less provocative and destabilizing, is still, however, not without dangers given the possibilities of accident, or error or miscalculation, particularly in times of crisis. As Freeman Dyson writes, the abolition of nuclear weapons is an essential part of a more hopeful future for humanity:

> Too few of us believe that negotiating down to zero is possible. To achieve this goal, we shall need a worldwide awakening of moral indignation pushing the governments and their military establishments to get rid of these weapons which in the long run endanger everybody and protect nobody. We shall not be finished with nuclear weapons in a year or in a decade. But we might, if we are lucky, be finished with them in a half century, in about the same length of time that it took the abolitionists to rid the world of slavery. We should not worry too much about the technical details of weapons and delivery systems. The basic issue before us is simple. Are we, or are we not, ready to face the uncertainties of a world in which nuclear weapons have been negotiated all the way down to zero? If the answer to this question is yes, then there is hope for us and for our grandchildren.[25]

British disarmament leader E.P. Thompson has lamented: "In a world better designed and run we could destroy all existing nuclear weapons and dismantle facilities for their production. But today no such treaty can be verified or enforced." Even if the superpowers, along with the British, French, Chinese and other "near-nuclear" nations, could be persuaded to destroy their nuclear weapons, the fear of cheating would be great. The destruction of existing nuclear weapons could be verified but the knowledge of how to make them would remain. Governments would have an incentive to stockpile bombs secretly, assuming that others were doing the same. It is not, of course, that the vision of a non-nuclear world is undesirable, but that it is not feasible under existing circumstances. Unless it becomes possible to develop technologies and procedures to detect steps toward building nuclear weapons, an agreement for total nuclear disarmament could degenerate into an unstable rearmament race.

Anti-nuclear author, Jonathan Schell, has described a detailed disarmament approach in which the final step is labeled "weaponless deterrence".[26] He would have nuclear nations sign a disarmament pact and scrap their weapons, but keep mobile-warhead factories poised to resume production. Leaders would know that, even if by cheating they had a few weapons and launched them at a rival, retaliation would eventually follow. Among the problems with Schell's proposal is that these factories might become lightning rods, tempting an adversary to make a pre-emptive strike. As Gwynne Dyer, the Canadian military analyst and internationally syndicated columnist, noted at the international physicians congress in Moscow: "Let us suppose that today by a resolution of this conference we could magically abolish all the nuclear weapons in the world. If we make all the nuclear weapons vanish, and did not change the international political structures and the psychological assumptions which produced them, how long do you think it would be before we got back to the present situation, with thousands of nuclear weapons in the hands of the great powers?"[27]

Such difficulties notwithstanding, the elimination of all nuclear weapons would not necessarily make the world — as we know it at present — a safer place either. If the superpowers felt they had less to fear from the dangers of escalation because of the abolition of nuclear weapons, the probability of war might actually go up in regions where the superpowers have conflicting interests and the risks of direct confrontation are high. In order, then, to abolish nuclear weapons, we must create conditions in which a conventional war among the major powers is just as unthinkable as a nuclear one. Nations will not give up their "ultimate deterrent" until their leaders believe the world has become safe enough to do so.[28]

American foreign policy analyst Richard J. Barnet notes that total nuclear disarmament implies far-reaching changes in the composition and deployment of non-nuclear forces and new understanding of the role of force in international politics.[29] The term "common security" has been widely used of late to provide an alternative to nuclearism, militarism and interventionism. The concept was initially developed by the Independent Commission on Disarmament and Security Issues, chaired by the late Swedish Prime Minister, Olof Palme,[30] and it is discussed in the Canadian context by Ernie Regehr in chapter six. Amongst the major elements of a common security regime would be: a restructuring of national military forces so that they pose less of a threat to others;[31] an end to military intervention by the major powers in the Third World;[32] strengthened international and regional institutions of peacekeeping and co-operation, including the United Nations and the World Court; a greater international commitment to global economic justice and removing what the United Nations, in its International Conference on the Relationship Between Disarmament and Development (August 24-September 11, 1987), now calls "the non-military threats to security"; and an end to the Cold War.[33]

Ronald Reagan is said to have suggested to Mikhail Gorbachev at the 1985 Geneva summit that, if Martians were suddenly to land, Russians and Americans would settle their differences very quickly. It must be emphasized that a new international code of conduct for nation states is crucial now so as to prevent the aliens (nuclear weapons) from landing and to create the conditions for their abolition. The last words appropriately belong to Andrei Sakharov:

> A nuclear-free world is a desirable goal, but it will be possible only in the future as the result of many radical changes in the world. The conditions for peaceful development now and in the future are settlement of regional conflicts; parity in conventional arms; liberalization, democratization and greater openness of Soviet society; observance of civil and political rights; a compromise solution on the issue of antimissile defenses without combining it in a package with other questions of strategic weapons. Convergence — a rapprochement of the socialist and capitalist systems — offers a real and lasting solution to the problem of international security.[34]

2

A Mad, Mad World: The Evolution of Nuclear War-fighting Strategies

Leonard V. Johnson

In its 1987 White Paper on defence, the Government of Canada reaffirmed its commitment to collective defence based ultimately on nuclear weapons. The consequences of this policy for Canadian security can be determined only from an understanding of the technologies and strategies of nuclear war. When these are understood, it becomes evident that a defence policy based on nuclear deterrence is anything but beneficial to Canada.

Since the mid-19th century, the technological growth of the Industrial Revolution has transformed war. From what had been skirmishes fought between small regular armies and navies for limited political objectives, war became global conflict involving millions of combatants and the economic power of large and small industrial states fighting for unlimited and nebulous political objectives. These conflicts destroyed the empires of the 19th century and left the United States and the Soviet Union contending for hegemony in the world. This rivalry led in its turn to permanent mobilization for war, an arms race with high technology conventional and nuclear weapons, a permanent state of nuclear terror, the growth of powerful technocracies not accountable to populations, the consequent erosion of democratic values and practices, and the sacrifice of economic and social well-being.

By the mid-1960s, there were four nuclear powers — the U.S.A., the U.S.S.R., the United Kingdom, and France — and technology had overwhelmed an international security system modelled on a 19th-century balance of power, rendering it incapable of providing security. Technology had made war too destructive, and too indiscriminate in its effects, for it to serve any conceivable political purpose. Thus, while technology exponentially multiplied the destructive power of weapons, it made warfare an obsolete instrument of policy. The nuclear and conventional arms races of the present day are manifestations of failure to come to terms with this one inescapable fact, and of an inability to curb the growth of powerful human institutions which find their purposes in preparations for a final war — a war which cannot be won and which must never be fought. If the preparations continue, science, technology and strategy may well make final war inevitable.

Technology and War

Once the initial reluctance of the military to embrace technological change was overcome, military research and development proceeded rapidly. Each new development has affected military strategy and tactics, often in unintended ways. In the late 19th and early 20th century, new explosives, stronger metal alloys, and new machine tools produced rifled artillery and breech-loading, magazine-fed rifles and machine guns with unprecedented fire-power. Steamships, railways, automobiles, and aircraft gave strategic and tactical mobility to armies and provided the means to supply them from homelands secure from attack. The telegraph, telephone, and radio replaced the dispatch rider on horseback, giving commanders and staffs better means to control large forces in the field. At sea, armoured steam-driven warships fought battles with batteries of rifled guns; the diesel engine and lead-acid storage batteries found applications in submarines, and reconnaissance aircraft with cameras gave new eyes to navies and armies. At home, new manufacturing technology produced weapons and ammunition in the vast quantities needed, and propaganda, transmitted by newspapers and other mass media, generated public support for the war effort. War became total, demanding mobilization of the entire fighting potential of nations.

The lethal nature of battlefields dominated by new technology immobilized troops in the tunnels and trenches of the First World War, creating a stalemate broken only by the invention of the armoured fighting vehicle and the decisive intervention of fresh troops from the United States of America. This intervention permanently changed the balance of power in Europe, with political and military consequences that persist to this day.

The development of the airplane led to strategic bombing, which pointed the way to indiscriminate attacks on civilian populations and later gave rise to nuclear deterrence. Until 1915, when a German zeppelin airship bombed London, civilians and troops beyond the range of artillery were safe from direct attack. Only seven people were killed in history's first aerial bombing, but panic and rioting broke out. Further raids led to civilian demands for protection and for retaliation against German cities. The zeppelins were defeated, but the Gotha bomber appeared by the end of the year. On the sunny morning of July 7, 1917, twenty-one of them bombed London before the eyes of millions of citizens, humiliating the defenders.

In August, Lieutenant-General Jan Christian Smuts of South Africa, who had been named as a committee of one to report on aerial home defence, reported that an air service:

> ...can be used as an independent means of war operations....As far as can at present be foreseen, there is absolutely no limit to the scale of its future independent war use. And the day may not be far off when aerial operations with their devastation of enemy lands and destruction of industrial and populous centres on a vast scale may become the principal operations of war, to which the older forms of military and naval operations may become secondary and subordinate.[1]

Smuts' predictions gave hope to a War Cabinet anxious to break the bloody stalemate in France. It promptly authorized the establishment of an air ministry and the Royal Air Force, formed from the Royal Flying Corps and the Royal Naval Air Service.[2] A new bomber force, under the command of Major-General Sir Hugh Trenchard, soon carried the war to German soil with attacks on industrial targets in the

Rhine and Moselle valleys, but the effort was dispersed, sporadic, and costly in aircraft and crews. With the technology available, strategic bombing could not live up to the extravagant expectations of it, but its proponents were not disposed to objective criticism of the new force. The war ended with the world's first independent air force committed to an independent role without tested doctrine to guide it.

In 1921, the Italian General Giulio Douhet published his vision of future war in his treatise, *The Command of the Air*: "First would come explosions, then fires, then deadly gases floating on the surface and preventing any approach to the stricken area. As the hours passed and night advanced, the fires would spread while the poison gas paralyzed all life."[3] Widespread panic would set in as word of the horror spread, immobilizing civilians with terror, breaking the social structure and causing the victims to demand an end to the war before armies and navies could even be mobilized.

Although Douhet seems to have been concerned about the moral implications of this strategy, he justified it as preferable to long wars of attrition like the one just ended. The utilitarian concept that ends determine the morality of means survives in the logic of nuclear deterrence, where the risk of general nuclear annihilation is deemed preferable to that of a Soviet invasion of West Germany, for example.

The doctrines of Douhet and other air-power apostles flew in the face of the code of military honour. This code required a declaration of war and not surprise attack, prohibited "attacking those who have surrendered, causing 'unnecessary suffering' and the use of weapons that cause it, treachery, taking of hostages, and a series of acts called war crimes."[4] Although there was concern about the moral implications of strategic bombing in the Second World War, moral considerations seldom, if ever, prevailed over operational expediency. This was reflected in the strategic bombing policy adopted at the Casablanca Conference of January 1943: "Your primary object will be the progressive destruction of the German military, industrial and economic system, and the undermining of the morale of the German people to a point where their armed resistance is fatally weakened."[5]

History has judged the strategic bombing offensive a costly means to a marginal military end. The destruction of cities was limited by the inability to deliver — in spite of attrition inflicted on determined defenders — vast tonnages of high explosive and incendiary bombs.

In addition, strategic bombing did not, as the theorists had predicted, break civilian morale and cause them to demand surrender. Until the atomic bomb made morale irrelevant in nuclear war, bombing civilians strengthened their will to resist and was in that sense counter-productive. Diversion of scarce resources to the bombing campaign may even have prolonged the war and certainly hastened the postwar decline of the United Kingdom.

All this changed with Hiroshima and Nagasaki. The new atomic bomb was a quantum leap in the technology of destruction that promised to validate Douhet's predictions. At the same time, in the hands of the American air force, army, and navy, which soon saw their own futures dependent on nuclear weapons, nuclear technology offered the means to dominate the Soviet Union in any contest for influence in what the U.S. saw as its economic domain.

Despite scientific opinion to the contrary, U.S. leaders expected their country's monopoly on atomic weapons to endure for at least fifteen years, and believed they would maintain decisive technological superiority indefinitely.[6] As it turned out, the monopoly ended in 1949. The American technological lead still exists, but it no longer confers any usable margin of superiority.

The arms race that began in 1949 is driven by the economic and bureaucratic interests of what President Eisenhower termed the "military-industrial complex," by Soviet response to U.S. developments, by the tendency of planners on both sides to inflate threats and plan for the worst possible case, and by the delusion that one more development will achieve a decisive and permanent advantage.[7] This is accompanied by bellicose rhetoric to demonize and intimidate the opponent, terrorize populations into supporting military spending, maintain hegemony over allies, and secure access to resources in the name of national security.

Although no nuclear war has occurred since 1945, the U.S. has used the threat of nuclear weapons on at least twenty-two specific instances in international crises.[8] These include the Berlin Blockade in 1948, China in 1950-53, Indo-China in 1954, and the Arab-Israeli war in 1973. Soviet leaders have also rattled the nuclear sword several times, but their attempted deployment of missiles to Cuba in 1962 failed when it provoked confrontation with the United States. Having failed to mount a direct, Cuban-based threat to the U.S., the Soviets embarked on a drive for nuclear and conventional parity with the U.S. Regarding this drive as an attempt by the Soviets to attain superiority, the U.S. began modernizing its strategic weapons and improving the state of its conventional forces, including those in NATO. The Soviets matched U.S. developments five to seven years after each of them appeared, and the arms race continued, piling up more and more unusable weapons at ever-increasing cost and risk.

The Evolution of Nuclear Doctrine

Massive Retaliation, 1949-61

There has always been a close relationship between nuclear weapons and delivery systems on the one hand, and nuclear doctrine on the other. The characteristics of the weapons have determined the doctrine in fashion. So far, experience has demonstrated that whatever is feasible will be developed and whatever is developed will be deployed to rationalize the development.

The first nuclear "strategy" was the doctrine of massive retaliation, which threatened an all-out nuclear response to any Soviet use of nuclear weapons. It was also seen as a strategy that could be adopted in the last resort to prevent defeat in Europe. Appropriate to U.S. nuclear monopoly and decisive superiority, this doctrine lost credibility when the Soviets achieved the means to attack the United States. After that, nobody could seriously believe that the U.S. would invite its own destruction, even to save Europe from being overrun. The U.S. bomber force was vulnerable to surprise attack, which led to fears that the Soviets would destroy it in a pre-emptive first-strike if war seemed imminent and unavoidable. Radar early-warning systems, of which there were three in Canada, rapid-reaction alert postures, dispersal plans, active air defences, and other measures evolved to ensure that sufficient bombers would survive attack to devastate the Soviet Union in a so-called second strike. These measures preserved the ability to destroy the U.S.S.R., but limiting nuclear weapons to retaliation after a Soviet first-strike did nothing to limit damage to the U.S., nor did it permit nuclear weapons to be employed offensively since any such use could prove suicidal. Although it appeared that nuclear weapons could be effective in deterring an all-out nuclear attack, only such an attack could justify the threat of massive retaliation. It was intolerable to military planners that such powerful weapons should be unusable in war.

Flexible Response, 1961-65

President John F. Kennedy and Robert S. McNamara, his Secretary of Defence, saw the inflexibility and incredibility of the all-or-nothing policy of massive retaliation. Their solution was flexible response, a range of options to respond to any contingency from sub-conventional insurgency in the U.S. economic domain to general nuclear war. This required comprehensive war-fighting doctrines covering the spectrum of conflict elaborated by Herman Kahn and others, improvements to command-control communications and intelligence, and new families of weapons to diversify the nuclear and conventional arsenals.

The weapons developed in the 1950s had to be powerful to compensate for the inaccuracies of delivery systems, and the inability to hit small military targets made it necessary to aim the weapons at cities. Attacks on cities were too indiscriminate and destructive to be satisfactory, however, and the destruction of cities would leave the Soviets no incentive to ask for terms. As an alternative, military planners suggested counterforce attacks on Soviet nuclear weapons to blunt the capacity for retaliation, city-avoidance to offer an incentive to terminate the war before populations were attacked directly, shelters to protect people from radioactive fallout, and concrete silos, blast protection and other passive measures to shield the offensive weapons.

Within a short time, the limitations of flexible response had become apparent. These included the inability to avoid cities because of the proximity of military targets and the high-yield, low-accuracy weapons available to attack them with, and the dispersion and diversification of Soviet forces, which made them too costly and difficult to locate and attack. Another problem was the Soviet refusal to play by the rules of flexible response — if a nuclear war is to be limited there must be some agreement about how to conduct it. The Soviets promised only that any attack whatsoever would be met with a massive response, terminating the contest in the manner of a chess player sweeping all his opponent's pieces off the board in his opening move.

Still another objection was that flexible response encouraged each side to strike first, and massively, thereby limiting damage to itself.

Mutual Assured Destruction, 1965-74

The so-called doctrine of mutual assured destruction (MAD) was less deliberate policy than recognition of the fact that each side possessed the capability to destroy the other, even after suffering a pre-emptive first-strike. One of its attractions to Defense Secretary McNamara was its simplicity — it made it possible to define what constituted unacceptable destruction, and thus to estimate what forces would be necessary to achieve it. McNamara defined sufficiency as the ability to destroy a fifth to a third of the Soviet population (55-90 million people) and half to three-quarters of its industrial capacity. He calculated that 400 nuclear weapons would do that and still leave a margin of overkill to hedge against uncertainty. This ceiling gave him arguments to use against new development proposals that would only waste resources on redundant weapons. The prospect of curbing development of profitable new weapons systems like multiple independently targetable re-entry vehicles (MIRV), cruise missiles, manned bombers, and more lethal warheads was, needless to say, unacceptable to defence contractors and to politicians whose electoral prospects would be harmed by closing defence industries. To the military departments, curbing new development threatened vital bureaucratic interests, and military leaders were dissatisfied with a strategy that accepted vulnerability. McNamara could not prevail over his opponents, and so the arms race continued without restraint.

There were other problems with assured destruction. For one thing, the Soviets did not accept it. Seeing themselves innocent of any intention to strike first, they thought it reasonable to build shelters for their population and disperse their industries while also planning for damage-limiting attacks on U.S. offensive forces. U.S. leaders, also professing innocent intent, used similar arguments.

Assured destruction suffers as well from logical incoherence: why retaliate after deterrence has failed, inflicting revenge for no good purpose? And how can nuclear weapons deter conventional attack in Europe or prevent loss of a conventional war anywhere when the only available response would lead to an all-out nuclear exchange?

Mutual assured destruction was unstable, moreover: fears that strategic nuclear forces would become vulnerable to attack led each side to seek means to limit damage to their forces by concealment, mobility, dispersion, and blast shelters and by destroying the opponent's forces before they could be used. These concerns led eventually to integration of command-control and warning systems, automation of decision-making, launch-on-warning policies, pre-planned hair-trigger responses to impending attack, and to new counterforce weapons suitable only for a pre-emptive first-strike. These developments helped to lead the way into the next stage of strategic evolution, a doctrine which rationalized them.

Selective Options and Nuclear War-fighting, 1974-

In 1974, James Schlesinger, Secretary of Defense in the second Nixon administration, revived flexible response under a new term, "selective options, limited nuclear war." Multiple warheads, improved accuracy, and smaller weapons had renewed hopes of city-avoidance and counterforce attacks with reduced blast damage to nearby cities. The new doctrine required large and diversified nuclear forces capable of selective operations: warning shots to demonstrate resolve, attacks against selected military targets, selective assistance to conventional forces, and pre-emptive attacks on Soviet nuclear forces. The aims of this limited nuclear war strategy are to intimidate the Soviets into early termination of hostilities by holding forth the prospect of worse to come if they continue, and to attain superiority at some level of conflict short of all-out war, thus inhibiting the Soviets from raising the ante. To do this, it is thought essential to achieve escalation dominance — superiority at each increasing level of nuclear violence.

A major problem with the new strategy is that a defensive nuclear war-fighting posture could be mistaken for preparation for a pre-emptive first-strike intended to disarm the opponent. Thus, though selective options or limited nuclear war strategies are still purportedly defensive, intended to deter attack only, it does not appear that way to Soviet planners. Instead of deterring the Soviets from attacking the United States, it gives them the incentive to fire first if nuclear war seems imminent and unavoidable. In those circumstances there would be a compulsion to avert the imminent loss of their own weapons and to blunt the coming attack by destroying as many American warheads as possible before they could be launched.

Although the development of Soviet counterforce capabilities had encouraged U.S. planners to hope that the Soviets would also be willing to play the limited nuclear war game, thus permitting a war of nuclear tit-for-tat till the Soviets threw in the towel, the Soviets refused again. Soviet doctrine still calls for all-out response to attack, and still assumes there would be much to be gained by firing first.

In 1975 the Soviets deployed their first multiple-warhead missiles, closing a "gap" created by American deployments in 1970. This gave the Soviets the same advantage the Americans had — the ability to destroy several missile silos with one attacking missile. Because the single-shot kill probability of a single-warhead missile against a hardened silo was, say, 0.5 at best, at least two missiles had to be fired to destroy one missile silo and the attacker would have run out of missiles before he had destroyed all the targets, an unfavourable exchange ratio. With up to ten warheads on each missile, the MIRV offered the prospect of destroying up to five missile silos with each missile fired, making the exchange ratio more favourable. As might have been foreseen, the Soviet's development of MIRVs caused headaches about the survivability of American land-based missiles and hence their vulnerability to pre-emptive attack. Elaborate schemes were devised to protect the new MX missile, including a multiple protective shelter with thirty-six shells to hide the missile under and a transporter-erector to move it from one shell to another under cover. This turned out to be impracticable, and so the MX has been deployed in vulnerable Minuteman silos and will remain there until someone devises a better basing mode. In the meantime, submarine-launched missiles maintain the invulnerability of strategic nuclear forces.

In addition to counterforce war-fighting against strategic nuclear forces, the concept of limited nuclear war envisaged attacks against Soviet command centres, communications nodes, and other infrastructure. The Pershing II missile, which was under development, was found eminently suitable for the purpose and deployed in the Federal Republic of Germany, from which it could reach targets in the Soviet Union. This weapon, seen as "strategic" by the Soviets, obliterated the "firebreak" between theatre and strategic nuclear forces, making escalation more certain. A small, first step toward safety was taken with the 1987 agreement to withdraw Pershing II and other intermediate-range nuclear forces from Europe.

In 1976, President Jimmy Carter and Defense Secretary Harold Brown took office. They had doubts about the feasibility of limited nuclear war, but could not stop the preparations for it in face of growing Soviet counterforce capabilities, political setbacks in Iran, Afghanistan, and Poland, and shrill accusations of military neglect coming from Republicans and the Committee on the Present Danger. (This ultra-conservative organization listed Ronald Reagan and most of the prominent members of his administration among its members.)

The military-industrial complex triumphed again, illustrating the extent to which private interests have taken control of the U.S. government. Instead of changing the strategy, as Carter perhaps intended, he reaffirmed it in July, 1980, with Presidential Directive 59. Among other things, this directive reaffirmed the American commitment to extended deterrence, "...the dangerous notion that nuclear weapons can do more than deter the use of nuclear weapons by others."[9] This is what PD-59 said:

> Deterrence must restrain a far wider range of threats than just massive attacks on U.S. cities. We seek to deter any adversary from any course of action that could lead to general nuclear war. Our strategic forces must also deter nuclear attacks on smaller sets of targets in the U.S. military forces, and be a wall against strategic coercion of, or an attack on, our friends and allies. And strategic forces, in conjunction with theatre nuclear forces, must contribute to deterrence of conventional aggression as well.[10]

The directive also enunciated a "countervailing" strategy, the key element of which was the elimination of Soviet leadership and command systems to prevent them from maintaining control of their forces. There would be nobody left to surrender, or to prevent escalation to general nuclear war.

The Reagan administration has pursued war-fighting preparations with new vigour, modernizing and expanding the nuclear arsenals with 17,000 new weapons promised by 1990. The Strategic Defence Initiative, known as "Star Wars," can be seen only as a system to defend nuclear weapons or to provide a partial defence against Soviet forces surviving an American pre-emptive attack. With the deployment of the 131st cruise-missile-armed B-52 bomber in November 1986, the administration abrogated the unratified SALT II Treaty, and it is trying to find a way to reinterpret the Anti-Ballistic Missile (ABM) Treaty so as to legitimize ballistic missile defences. The U.S. suspended negotiations on a Comprehensive Test Ban (CTB) in 1981 despite an obligation under Section VI of the Nuclear Non-Proliferation Treaty to achieve one; and it refused to respond to a long unilateral Soviet test moratorium. The recently concluded intermediate-range nuclear force agreement and the promise of more to come marks a sharp discontinuity in the Reagan administration's opposition to arms control.

To implement its war-fighting strategy and to achieve strategic superiority over the Soviet Union, the Reagan administration has a long shopping list:

- 100 MX ICBM in Minuteman silos with 10 MIRV warheads each and continued production planned
- 100 B-1B bombers with up to 30 air-launched cruise missiles (ALCM) each
- Trident submarines at a deployment rate of one or more per year, each with 24 Trident I MIRV missiles with eight warheads each, totalling 192. After 1989, more accurate Trident II missiles will be deployed with up to 14 warheads each.
- More than 150 B-52 bombers are being modified to carry 12-20 air-launched cruise missiles each.
- Up to 4,000 ship-launched cruise missiles will be deployed on surface ships and attack submarines by 1990.
- "Stealth" bombers and supersonic cruise missiles invisible to radar are being developed.

In addition to the offensive forces listed above, the U.S. is developing air defence, anti-submarine warfare, and ballistic missile defences as components of a comprehensive strategic defence program.

The linchpin of this program, the Strategic Defence Initiative (SDI), has serious implications. It will not, as President Reagan announced in 1983, make nuclear weapons "impotent and obsolete," but will provide a limited defence against only ballistic missile attack, leaving the door open to cruise missiles and submarine-launched missiles. Because the Soviets see its purpose as offensive — the means to counter Soviet missiles surviving a U.S. first-strike — they will be forced to build more missiles to saturate the defences and diversify their nuclear forces with more weapons immune to ballistic missile defences. Moreover, in the unlikely event that SDI does work, giving the Americans the strategic superiority they strive for, the Soviets will have to embark on an anti-ballistic missile program of their own. This will produce a costly, destabilizing and uncontrollable arms race in space which neither side can afford.

American plans to build up their nuclear arsenal are matched by Soviet ones. According to the International Institute of Strategic Studies,[11] the Soviet Union will:

- replace the SS-11 ICBMs with the same number of SS-19 missiles;
- MIRV older missiles; and
- continue production of the Backfire medium-range bomber;
- replace the SS-N-18 submarine-launched ballistic missile with the SS-NX-23 and replace older submarines with the Typhoon class.

Although a new manned bomber (NATO designation "Blackjack") has been developed, it is not yet in service. The propeller-driven Bear "H" is in production as a cruise missile carrier, however.

The Soviets are undoubtedly engaged in ABM research to avoid technological surprise arising from U.S. research, but it is extremely unlikely that they could build and deploy an ABM system unknown to the Americans, or that they could deprive the U.S. of its capacity to destroy their country if they did.

The Balance Sheet

Deterrence of Aggression?

No military conflict has occurred between nuclear-armed powers, leading some to assert that nuclear weapons have kept the peace since 1945. While there is no doubt that these weapons have made leaders more cautious when crises arose, there is no proof that war would have broken out had there been no nuclear weapons. Indeed, so-called conventional war has become too destructive to serve any conceivable political purpose, and this fact alone necessitates a policy of war avoidance. It was not nuclear war the United Nations resolved to abolish in a Charter drafted and signed before the atomic bomb had even been tested — it was conventional war.

Even if it could be conceded that nuclear weapons have prevented war between the U.S. and the U.S.S.R., the Cuban missile crisis took them to the brink of war and threatened to sweep them over it. Since then, the stability of assured destruction has been eroded by technology and strategy, and especially by first-strike counterforce weapons and nuclear war-fighting doctrines. While nuclear war is no less irrational than it ever was, rational behaviour will not prevent it if decision-making is delegated to failure-prone technology. Using analytical models, scientists have predicted that there is almost a 50 per cent chance of a war-threatening false alarm of some type occurring during a protracted crisis.[12] One study presents a statistical argument predicting an accidental missile exchange by 2012 if preparations for it continue.[13]

Extended Nuclear Deterrence

Extended nuclear deterrence, long the keystone of NATO military planning, is intended to prevent conventional war. It originated in the doctrine of massive retaliation, when the United States had a nuclear monopoly over the Soviet Union, and it became a part of the strategy of flexible response, current NATO policy. This strategy requires: direct defence to defeat attack or place the burden of escalation on the other side; deliberate escalation by NATO to nuclear weapons; and general nuclear response.[14] Its justification is the claim that conventional forces of the Warsaw Treaty Organization are "overwhelmingly superior" to those of NATO. When the military situation in Europe is objectively analyzed, the justification for extended deterrence evaporates.

Extended deterrence rests on the declared intention to resort to nuclear weapons to prevent defeat by Warsaw Pact conventional forces. Only by the twisted logic of nuclear deterrence is it believable that responsible politicians could seriously contemplate a suicidal act that would destroy all that they are committed to defend, and only by this macabre logic is nuclear annihilation preferable to any other conceivable outcome. Americans are expected to be willing to die by the scores of millions in a nuclear war for the sake of some limited military objective in Europe, the achievement of which would be irrelevant in the ensuing holocaust. Since politicians, bureaucrats, generals, journalists, scientists, academics and members of the general public are all presumed to be rational individuals, one can only conclude that they are collectively irrational, or that they are so complacent about nuclear deterrence that they have not thought through the implications of the doctrine. Public acquiescence is maintained by propaganda, fear and hatred of the supposed enemy, false patriotism, ignorance of reality, misuse of language and the misplaced trust accorded "experts" in defence and foreign policy establishments.

Nuclear Hegemony

Nuclear deterrence is extended to other countries of the "free world" to which the U.S. has given explicit or implicit security guarantees. These include Israel, Japan, Canada, Australia, the Philippines, and other countries declared vital to U.S. security interests. The "protection" this affords is described by a comforting euphemism, "nuclear umbrella," under which its supposed beneficiaries "huddle." The price of this protection is willingness to help hold the handle of the umbrella — that is, support of and acquiescence to American strategic policy.

This example illustrates how language is misused to legitimize the immoral and irrational. Words are the tools of thought, but the language of nuclear deterrence is the language of smoke and mirrors, of illusion and deception, the enemy of clear thinking and of safety. In the case of nuclear deterrence, they mask the realities — that the nuclear umbrella is a system of global annihilation; that the obligations referred to are commitments to co-operate in self-destruction; that willingness to do so is the definition of a loyal ally; that there is no such thing as a collective decision where U.S. "interests" are involved; that there is no defence against nuclear weapons; and that the U.S.-led nuclear arms race is a greater threat to security and democracy than the Soviets ever were by themselves.

Since the military threats to U.S. protectorates generally exist only in the minds of paranoiacs, extended nuclear deterrence is intended to keep U.S. allies committed to U.S. war planning and to secure the use of their territories for military purposes. The strong U.S. reaction to New Zealand's refusal to permit visits by nuclear-armed warships was a calculated response to prevent other allies from emulating New Zealand's example, not because New Zealand is of great strategic importance.[15]

Arms-control negotiations, which — despite the INF agreement — have still done almost nothing to reduce the nuclear danger, have been mostly conducted to pacify populations afraid of nuclear war. At the alliance level, demands for solidarity are made to prevent allies from asserting their own interests in arms control, as in the intermediate-range nuclear force negotiations at Geneva between 1980 and 1983. The threat of failure due to lack of alliance unity compelled European governments to agree to cruise-missile deployments despite public opposition. Nuclear politics are totalitarian politics.

When the ostensible purposes of nuclear strategy are analyzed, it becomes apparent that the negligible political and military utility of nuclear weapons does not justify the costs and risks that come with them. What does justify them to nuclear decision-makers is the profit and prestige that they bring. The strategic modernization programs, Star Wars, and every other development that gets funded and deployed, preserve the power of elected politicians, keep scientists employed, earn profits for defence contractors, and preserve the military and civilian bureaucracies which depend on them for their justification. Extended deterrence and the idea that strong conventional forces would delay resort to nuclear weapons employ fear of nuclear war to gain public support for conventional armaments.

Nuclear weapons are a potent source of bureaucratic, political, and economic power, and that, finally, is what drives the arms race. The evolution of nuclear strategy is only the history of attempts to make nuclear weapons usable weapons of war, and to rationalize the use of what technology provides.

Whither Canada?

Technology and strategy have made Canada's postwar defence policies obsolete. The policy of resort to nuclear weapons in Europe, which would probably escalate to a nuclear exchange between the U.S. and the U.S.S.R., is a potential death sentence to millions of Canadians. It is not in Canada's security interest to participate in this collective suicide. As a condition of membership in NATO, Canada should insist that the alliance adopt a policy of no nuclear first-use and establish a non-offensive defence posture capable of containing and terminating war in Europe.

There is no likelihood whatever that either the U.S. or the U.S.S.R. would destroy the other intentionally and without provocation. What is ultimately likely is that each will destroy the other through accident or miscalculation. In the latter case, apprehension of imminent nuclear war will cause one or the other to launch a pre-emptive first-strike intended to destroy as many as possible of the attacking weapons before they can be launched. There are two possibilities.

If the Soviet Union attacks first, it seems likely that the North Warning System, the CF-18 interceptor bases, NORAD headquarters, the maritime air bases, and the command-control system will be struck before any Soviet bombers arrive. The air defence system will be destroyed before it is engaged. On the other hand, if the United States strikes first, anti-submarine and air defence forces will be deployed to attack Soviet missile-firing submarines before they can fire their missiles. They will also be able to defend against Soviet retaliation with surviving bombers and cruise missiles. Canada will become the nuclear killing ground in an air battle fought to defend remaining U.S. strategic nuclear forces. In either case, the Canadian government will have no control over the initiation or the conduct of a war fought between the opposing nuclear forces of the U.S. and the U.S.S.R.

After the Second World War, the U.S. Joint Chiefs of Staff put into place the geographic elements of a forward strategy intended to keep potential enemy forces at the maximum possible distance from the United States. This strategy required military base rights and air transit privileges in Canada, which lies astride the Arctic air approaches to the U.S. Canada willingly co-operated on the premise that what was good for the U.S. was good for Canada, with the proviso that Canada, unlike the United States, reserved the right to limit military co-operation in its own interests. But defence, the original aim of the partnership, has been rendered impotent by the overwhelming destructiveness of nuclear weapons. Its successor, nuclear deterrence, has evolved into technologies and strategies of nuclear war-fighting, and Canada has been drawn into a partnership preparing to fight nuclear war. In failing to recognize changes wrought by technology and strategy, and in their failure to recognize the prudent limit of military co-operation, Canada's military planners are failing the country they serve.

3

How Our Vision of Nuclear War Has Changed

Don Bates

Major turning-points in history are often as much the culmination of the old as they are the introduction of the new. Certainly that was true when the first atomic bomb was dropped on Hiroshima in August 1945.

In some ways, this "big bomb" was indeed a culmination of the old. The number of immediate deaths in Hiroshima was roughly the same (about 80,000) as it was in an intensive fire-bombing of Tokyo during the preceding March.[1] And, in both cases, the city was ravaged by a firestorm shortly after the attack. In other words, the immediate effects of the atomic bomb were consistent with the upper range of damage that could be inflicted by conventional bombing raids. What was new was that all that damage was done with a single, 9,000 pound bomb.[2]

Although the absolute numbers of deaths in the two attacks were roughly equal, there were many fewer injured survivors in Hiroshima. The ratio of dead to injured (about half and half) was much higher than in the case of the conventional attack on Tokyo, where only ten to twenty per cent of the injured died.[3] One of the main reasons for this difference was probably the presence of something else that was new — radiation. The direct exposure of a large population to high doses of radioactivity had never happened before. The following discussion will explore what the cases of Hiroshima and Nagasaki have taught us regarding the probable effects of a nuclear war, and how our vision of such a war has recently changed as a result of other events and a growing body of scientific knowledge.

Radiation

The first scientist to confirm to the Japanese authorities that the Hiroshima bomb was atomic was the man charged with building Japan's atomic bomb, Yoshio Nishina, who noted on August 10th that stored photographic film had been exposed, clear evidence that radiation had accompanied the blast.[4] Over the next two or three weeks there were many cases of radiation sickness. When an epidemic of leukemia appeared among survivors a few years later, Japanese doctors mapped out the location where their patients had been at the time of the bomb. The result was a doughnut-shaped ring surrounding the original circle of complete mortality. Within this ring, radiation exposure had been high, but, until now, not fatal.[5]

Over many more years, long-term effects of radiation among the Japanese survivors gradually made their appearance. Excess numbers of various kinds of cancers ten, twenty, and more than thirty years after August 1945 proved conclusively that humans exposed to high levels of radiation can show effects long afterwards.

Sadly, a number of factors conspired to make the suffering of Japanese radiation victims less useful to posterity than one would have hoped. First, the efforts of the Japanese themselves to observe and study the effects systematically were halted after a year and a half, largely owing to an Allied policy which forbade any Japanese from publishing A-bomb data. This meant that most of the work was left to the U.S. Atomic Bomb Casualty Commission. Then, in 1955, it was clear that the ABCC's efforts to survey the exposed population had been severely hampered by the secrecy surrounding the investigations and by the poor relations that existed between the American occupational forces and Japanese residents. As a result, the research efforts of ABCC had to be started afresh, more than ten years after the original attack.[6]

Finally, the effects that were recorded were largely those that arose from exposure to direct radiation coming from the explosion itself.

Very much less was learned about radiation effects on those who were exposed indirectly from fallout (the contaminated particles that fall back to earth, downwind from the blast, mostly in the first twenty-four hours after an explosion). This was partly because the Hiroshima and Nagasaki bombs were airbursts that caused relatively small amounts of fallout, and partly because people migrated into and out of the affected areas in the hours and days during which the fallout would have affected them. This made later surveys difficult.

Unfortunately, it is a knowledge of the radiation effects from fallout, not from direct exposure, that is most relevant to us now. With today's much bigger bombs, anyone exposed to the direct kind of radiation that was experienced in Hiroshima would be killed immediately by the blast and thermal wave. Furthermore, many explosions in any future nuclear exchange would occur at ground level, in attacks on missile silos and other "hardened" military targets, and these would give rise to vast quantities of fallout.

The past four decades have given us some answers to the question of fallout. Atmospheric testing in the 1950s and early 1960s demonstrated that fallout from even a single explosion contaminates milk and other foods, in small but detectable amounts, all around the world.[7] In addition, one U.S. test on a Pacific atoll in 1954 yielded an explosion two-and-a-half times what scientists had calculated it would be.[8] This explosion carried debris far higher than expected into the atmosphere, and above the zone for which meteorological data about wind direction had been gathered. At that height, an unexpected wind shear carried radioactive ash to four other atolls to the east of the test site, where Marshallese Islanders were living, and onto the crew of a Japanese fishing boat, ironically called the "Lucky Dragon." From this fallout, victims were exposed not only externally through the skin, but also internally through contaminated food, a double exposure that is more closely similar to what would happen in a future nuclear war. Nevertheless, the lessons learned from the experience have been limited. Some of the results are still a matter for dispute among scientists. And, in any event, the circumstances surrounding this isolated occurrence, such as the fact that the exposed population was evacuated within forty-eight to seventy-two hours and given U.S. naval medical care, are obviously very different from those that would prevail after a nuclear war.[9]

As the years have gone by, other events have provided more detail but, in the main, have added only marginally to our basic knowledge of the impact of radiation on the human body. In the more than one hundred U.S. trials at Yucca Flat in Nevada, soldiers participating in the tests and people who lived down-wind, in the areas of Nevada, Arizona and especially southern Utah, were chronically exposed to low doses. The consequences of this experience are still being investigated.[10]

The scientific facts are hard enough in themselves to evaluate, but these difficulties are greatly compounded by political and vested interests which make an independent scientific analysis of the evidence all but impossible. Other tests, by the British in Australia and the French in Polynesia, have been attended by the suppression of information by government authorities.[11] And, again because of secrecy, we may never know all that we could about the medical consequences of an enormous, accidental nuclear explosion that apparently occurred in the Urals in the winter of 1957-58.[12]

Two years have passed since another terrible nuclear tragedy in the Soviet Union, at Chernobyl. A disastrous release of radioactivity from a nuclear power-plant explosion has caused widespread contamination in the U.S.S.R. and neighbouring European countries. It is still too early to tell precisely what this experience will add to our knowledge of the effects of radiation. Indeed, in view of the very long time it takes for some of the effects to show up, it could be years before the current epidemiological studies of the exposed populations produce any important new insights. Meanwhile, serious radio-active contamination has turned up in everything from reindeer in Lapland to tea and hazelnuts in the Soviet Union.[13] Perhaps the greatest value to be derived from the Chernobyl disaster has been to emphasize to experts, government leaders and the public alike how unpredictable, how uncontrollable, how invisible and how disrupting such contamination of the environment can be.

The Chernobyl accident may shed some light on the question of what constitutes a lethal dose of radiation for human beings. Figures have ranged from 350 to 600 rads, the most common being 450 rads (a "rad" being a unit of the energy absorbed from radiation). This dose is called the "LD50," meaning a dose that is lethal for fifty per cent of an exposed population. The 450 figure was established, not on the basis of Hiroshima and Nagasaki, but on fatal accidents with patients receiving radiotherapy for the treatment of cancer.

The main reason why evidence from the Japanese bombings has not so far been used in research is that it was thought to be impossible to separate deaths caused by radiation from deaths caused by blast and heat. In addition, there have been as yet unresolved disputes over the exact composition of the two bombs and the doses of radiation that people received at various distances from the point of detonation, or "ground zero" as it is normally called.[14] Revised estimates of these doses are now becoming available and have inspired a British scientist, Dr. Joseph Rotblat, to re-examine the data. Arguing that deaths from radiation can indeed be distinguished from those owing to other causes, he has calculated the LD50 for the victims of Hiroshima and finds it to be 220 rads.[15] One of the reasons why this figure is so much lower than the conventional one may be that the victims were living under wartime conditions, in contrast to the victims of treatment accidents living in peacetime and surrounded by high-level medical care. There is evidence that the people of Hiroshima were suffering from malnutrition both before and after the attack. As well, medical care, so important in saving radiation victims, was obviously inadequate. However, because these or other adverse conditions would also afflict the victims of a nuclear war, Rotblat's figure is perhaps more realistic than one based on accidents with radiation therapy or the experience at Chernobyl. Other recent studies, not based on Hiroshima, have also suggested a lower figure.

When the issue of what constitutes a lethal dose of radiation is finally settled, the casualty estimates of nuclear war will change. In fact, says one expert, "dropping the LD50 from the usual 450-rad value to 250 rads would approximately double the number of fatalities due to the fallout from an attack on U.S. strategic nuclear targets."[16]

Fire

Clearly, there are strategic implications to these assessments of casualties but, before any conclusions can be reached, it is necessary to say something about another kind of calculation that has also been revised lately. This has to do with casualties from burns.

Unlike radiation, which was a totally new feature of the bomb dropped on Hiroshima, fires and injuries from burns were not new. As has been mentioned, the March 1945 fire-bombing of Tokyo had created a deadly firestorm. From the perspective of a world emerging from World War II, the Hiroshima bomb was the culmination of an historical evolution. People thought of it in terms of a bigger bomb, with a bigger bang. Not surprisingly, then, it was the blast element of the first atomic bomb that formed the basis of calculations about casualties: how many people would be dead or injured at various distances from ground zero, based on the strength at that distance of the concussion from the blast?

This method of calculating casualties has been named the "overpressure" model because the strength of the shockwave is measured in terms of the number of pounds per square inch of pressure that it produces, over and above normal atmospheric pressure. In contrast to the overpressure model, a "conflagration" model has recently been proposed.[17] This alternative approach is based on the fact that, in the case of modern nuclear warheads, the dynamics of blast and heat would be quite different in their impact on mortality from the effects of the Hiroshima bomb.

When the energy in a nuclear warhead is released by detonation a thermal wave radiates out from the fireball at the speed of light, setting fires throughout a large circle around ground zero. Although the blast that would follow behind it might blow out many of these initial fires, its destructive effects, coupled with the earlier thermal pulse, would leave fires burning over a wide area. Within a short time small fires would coalesce into larger ones, leading to "superfires," such as a conflagration (a wall of fire marching with the wind on a very broad front) or a firestorm (a giant circular fire that widens at the base as it draws fierce winds into its centre at ground level and shoots them high into the air).

Admittedly, such a fire developed in Hiroshima too, but today the circumference of the circle of flame and the area that would be involved would be much larger. Those in this area, even if not injured, would not have time to get out because of the distance they would have to go to get free of the flames, and because of the enormous obstacles in their way from the rubble. As a result, within the large "burn area" the mortality rate would be 100 per cent. On the strength of the conflagration model, then, it is believed that fires "might result in two to four times as many fatalities as that predicted by standard government blast scaling rules [the overpressure model]."[18]

The Synergistic Effects

A third factor arising from a nuclear explosion that has never been satisfactorily incorporated into casualty estimates (because it is so difficult to do so without the actual experience of a nuclear war) is the "synergistic" effect of differing kinds of assault on the human body — injury, burns, radiation, malnutrition, infections and infectious diseases. "Synergistic" means that these effects, when occurring together, are greater than the mere sum of their effects taken separately.

Recently, new insight into synergistic effects has been gained from looking at the body's own defences — its immune system.[19] In the blood, there are various kinds of white cells that contribute to the body's defence. In particular, there are two types that are in a critical balance with each other when the system is working properly. On the one hand, there are the "Helper T lymphocytes" that stimulate an immune response to virus-infected cells, and reject foreign elements in the body, like tumours. On the other hand, there are "Suppressor T lymphocytes" that prevent the activation of Helper T cells. These prevent the body's defences from becoming overly sensitive or "trigger-happy."

Any one of a number of factors can tip the delicate balance between these two types of cells. In particular, radiation, malnutrition, burns and stress (including depression and bereavement), all factors that might readily exist in some combination after a nuclear war, can cause the ratio of these cells to reverse so that the suppressor cells get the upper hand and reduce the body's immune response. Moreover, if most of these factors were working at the same time, the body's immune system could become so depressed as to behave much as it does in Acquired Immune Deficiency Syndrome or AIDS. In fact, in that invariably fatal disease, precisely the same blood picture is seen — Helper T cells are greatly reduced in number, and the balance tips strongly in favour of the Suppressor T cells. Thus, our estimates of the number of injured and burned people who would die may be far too low, considering that their natural capacity to recover from their wounds would have been severely impaired by other factors, working synergistically.

The combination of a lowered LD50 for radiation, the higher figures for casualties from the "conflagration" model, and the synergistic effects of wounds, burns, radiation, infection and malnutrition have given rise to substantially higher estimates of the effects of certain kinds of nuclear attack on populated areas.

It might be argued that such refinements of our vision of nuclear war add very little to the end result. After all, "an all-out attack on the U.S. population or economic targets involving thousands of megatons would be relatively insensitive to the casualty-model used. The degree of overkill would be so high that...the calculations would find that virtually the entire U.S. urban population would die of fallout-caused radiation illness, and most of the remainder would die of starvation and disease."[20] But despite this gloomy prediction, there are good reasons for examining casualty estimates closely. In fact, they have considerable strategic significance.

Take, for example, the subject of "limited" nuclear war, which is brought up repeatedly to justify various new nuclear weapon systems. The rationale behind the concept is that if the Soviet Union could manage to cripple the American capacity to retaliate, and at the same time do little damage to the U.S. civilian population, then the Soviets could still threaten the U.S. with a second blow, should the latter be tempted to retaliate with its much reduced forces. Such a gamble, however, is just not believable, unless the U.S.S.R. has the ability to mount a clean-cut or "surgical" strike that does major damage to military forces, yet little "collateral damage" to civilian targets and populations. Otherwise, if casualties were high, the U.S. would have little reason not to retaliate massively.

In 1974, when then Secretary of Defense James Schlesinger made his budget requests to Congress for the coming fiscal year, he argued that the United States required additional nuclear options to be able to respond in case of a "limited attack on military targets that caused relatively few civilian casualties."[21] When he was asked at a hearing what "relatively few casualties" meant, he responded, "I am talking here about casualties of 15,000, 20,000, 25,000...." His point was that the United States needed the capacity to respond to a "minor" attack without provoking a full-scale nuclear war in which the civilian casualties would then be very high. (Later on, at the end of President Carter's term of office, the same argument began to be heard in support of the "window of vulnerability" concept. It was claimed that the Soviets might attempt a "surgical strike" on U.S. land-based missiles, thereby creating a decisive nuclear edge for the U.S.S.R. without causing massive casualties.)

Schlesinger's estimates of casualties in 1974 were not, however, accepted. Even at the time they were put forward, Congress challenged them and the Department of Defense was obliged to come up with more careful estimates. DOD's new answer was that 1 to 1.5 million civilians might be killed but, as Schlesinger pointed out, this figure was still "minor" compared to the 95 to 100 million U.S. deaths that he believed would result from an all-out Soviet nuclear attack on the United States. These newer estimates were also challenged and a final estimate in 1975 suggested that there would be between 3.2 to 16.3 million deaths in a limited attack.

There the matter stood until recent recalculations took into account the conflagration model, various values for the LD50 of radiation, and, to some extent, possible synergistic effects. The result is that, for an attack of the sort that Schlesinger had envisaged, the estimates now range between 13 and 34 million deaths with 25 to 64 million total casualties. Moreover, when doing its estimates, the DOD did not include attacks on some very likely targets, such as potential bomber dispersal bases (frequently civilian airports near large population areas). Taking such attacks into account would make the estimates higher still.

It is clear that a considerable amount of what passes for "expert" strategic analysis does not withstand careful and realistic examination of the possible effects of even a limited nuclear war. As Frank von Hippel puts it: "If nuclear weapons policy-makers understood these results, they would also understand that attacks on strategic weapons systems are no more thinkable than attacks on cities. This would reduce both paranoia and fantasies on both sides."[22]

Another area where an increased knowledge of the effects of nuclear war has affected the public debate is in the realm of civil defence. In the 1950s, there was little public objection, and a good deal of docile acquiescence, to the advice of civil defence "experts." A whole generation of Americans and Canadians can remember their classroom exercises of "duck and cover" whereby they were to protect themselves from a nuclear explosion by diving under their desks and hiding their faces. But now that a more realistic assessment of the effects of nuclear war has been widely publicized, civil defence training films from that era have become laughable. Today, showing the film "Eleven Steps To Survival," produced by the National Film Board for Emergency Planning Canada, usually elicits guffaws of derision. When Canada's Public Works Department brought out a manual on how to build a fallout shelter in one's own home, the media met its appearance with amusement and ridicule.[23]

In 1962, when Canadians were asked whether they would choose nuclear war or a communist takeover, 65 per cent preferred nuclear war, only 11 per cent chose communist rule and 24 per cent were undecided. In 1987, on the other hand, the number with no opinion had dropped to 7 per cent and the number who would choose nuclear war to 33 per cent. But the number who would accept communist rule, if they had to, had risen to 60 per cent![24]

Of course, the question used in these opinion polls has itself become an anachronism. Canadians do not want either communist rule or nuclear war, and there is no reason to believe today that those are our only options. But the 1987 poll does demonstrate that the fear of nuclear war is now greater than the fear of dealing with the Soviets. Undoubtedly, an improved public awareness of the consequences of such a war has contributed to this profound change in attitude.

The Global Environment

So far we have been considering the more direct effects of nuclear war and how our estimates of them have been gradually escalating over the forty years since Hiroshima.[25] During the last twenty years, however, scientific and public attention has been increasingly focused on the indirect effects — the impact on the environment and, through that, on peoples and countries that are far from the areas of initial destruction.

The first real indication that there might be large-scale effects in the global environment, apart form radioactive contamination, appeared in the early 1970s and arose because of increased scientific attention to the ozone layer.[26]

The ozone layer can be thought of as a blanket of oxygen, in a special form, that surrounds the globe high up in the stratosphere. Ozone is an unstable substance and uncommon form of oxygen in which atoms of the element combine loosely with other atoms of the same element. Closer to earth, oxygen combines much more commonly, and much more stably, with other substances such as nitrogen to form nitrous oxide or nitrogen dioxide. If, therefore, chemicals such as nitrogen are introduced into the cloud of ozone, the ozone breaks up and releases its oxygen to form stable compounds with these other substances. When powerful nuclear weapons, say one megaton or more, are exploded, the mushroom cloud rises high into the stratosphere. Carried up with it are large amounts of nitrogen compounds. The result is ozone depletion.

As sunshine approaches the earth, the ozone normally shields it from much of the harmful part of ultra-violet light, known as UV-B radiation. If even a small increase in the amount of these harmful rays reaches the earth's surface, it could decrease the productivity of terrestrial plants and also of plankton, which is the beginning of the food chain for all marine life, and cause the suppression of the immune system (in the same way that radiation from nuclear explosives does) as well as other forms of physiological stress and blindness. These effects, in turn, increase susceptibility to disease among humans and mammals.[27]

Originally, scientific preoccupation with ozone depletion was directed at civilian sources: fluorocarbons, coming from spray cans, and nitrous oxides from supersonic jets. But by the time the U.S. National Academy of Sciences (NAS) published its report, *Long-Term Worldwide Effects of Multiple Nuclear-Weapons Detonations* (Washington, 1975), atmospheric chemists had come to appreciate that here was another potential cause.

The mere fact that a connection between nuclear detonations and ozone depletion had been recognized marked a new trend in thinking about the much broader consequences of a nuclear conflict. As the title of the NAS report suggests, 1975 was the beginning of scientific interest in the atmospheric and climatological impact of a nuclear exchange, and out of this interest would come new insights of even more profound significance. But the route to these wider implications continued to be through the further study of ozone.

The man who had first pointed to the destructive potential of nitrogen oxides on the ozone layer was Paul Crutzen of the Max-Planck-Institut in West Germany, and he continued his studies through the late 1970s and early 1980s.[28] He realized that, if a proper assessment were to be made of the impact of nuclear explosions on the stratospheric ozone, two other factors needed to be taken into account.

One was that nuclear warheads were getting progressively smaller. That would mean more warheads would be used and more explosions would occur, but each explosion would be smaller. Much less nitrogen would be lofted into the stratosphere. The other factor was that, in the presence of sunlight and many fires, nitrogen and other chemicals would interact to *produce*, not destroy ozone, nearer the ground. In 1982, along with another atmospheric chemist, J. Birks, Crutzen published his research, concluding that, rather than the depletion of ozone in the stratosphere, the problem might be the toxic production of it as photochemical smog in the air we breathe. Our post-nuclear future was shifting from overly strong sunlight to potentially serious air pollution![29]

One factor argued against the production of photochemical smog, however. Crutzen thought that so much smoke might be produced from the fires that the sunlight would be diminished and, with it, the production of smog. This prompted an interest in smoke that soon overtook the concern about smog. The interesting question had become: would there be enough smoke to blot out the sun and so affect the climate?

Even in the 1975 NAS report it had been observed that dust from volcanoes, lofted into the stratosphere, could spread around the world and shield it from some of the sun's heat, thereby causing cooler weather on earth. Over the next decade, space science learned what dust clouds do to the climate on Mars. From yet another field, the study of ancient rocks and fossils raised the possibility that the earth has periodically undergone episodes of catastrophic climate change, either from dust or smoke clouds that have cooled the land and caused mass extinctions of plant and animal life. And, finally, the infant science of global-climate modelling with giant computers was beginning to make possible the testing of various hypotheses that had been constructed to explain these phenomena.[30]

In the early 1980s, scientists from various fields of study joined together to see if a nuclear war, with all the dust that it could kick up and all the smoke that it could produce, might, in fact, give rise to some of the large-scale changes that had been observed on other planets and, in aeons past, on our own. Their work resulted in the formulation of the now familiar concept of "nuclear winter."

The possibility that nuclear winter would follow an all-out nuclear war was first announced to the public in the fall of 1983.[31] The initials of the last names of the five authors of the report on this phenomenon make an anagram that has become the customary way of referring to the "TTAPS" report.[32] The basic argument of this study was that, after a nuclear war, the burning of cities, oil storage depots, and forests would create a thick pall of smoke over the northern hemisphere that could have dramatic climatic effects. In particular, because of its optical properties, the smoke would create a one-way street, allowing the heat of the earth, given off as infrared rays, to pass up through the cloud, but acting as a barrier to prevent heat and light of the sun from reaching the earth's surface. The net result would be abnormal cold and little or no sunlight for weeks or months, a phenomenon that Richard Turco dubbed "nuclear winter."[33]

Although the authors had consulted scientists from many countries, including the Soviet Union, before publishing their results, the TTAPS report stirred up a lot of controversy. Scientists not involved in the original study have pointed out that the one-dimensional computer model used by TTAPS was quite primitive. In particular, because it did not allow for any movement of the wind during simulation, the moderating effects of the oceans upon the land were not taken into account. In addition, many guesses had to be made about the size of the smoke particles, the amount of smoke that would be produced, the amounts of nuclear explosives that would be used, and the kinds of targets at which they could be directed. There was (and still is) a great deal that is unknown — for example, the specific optical properties of smoke as a barrier to light and heat under the conditions considered likely in a nuclear war.[34]

It is no wonder, then, that some of the conclusions in the TTAPS report have been questioned. For instance, the notion that the whole human race might die out as a result of nuclear winter has been rejected. The extent to which the temperature could drop is now thought to be much less. The notion that there is a "threshold" of numbers of nuclear weapons, above which a nuclear winter would likely be triggered, and that this "threshold" would be very low (possibly 100 megatons) is no longer believed. The data and the analyses are just too imperfect to make precise predictions possible.

Since the TTAPS report appeared, more information about smoke emission and its optical properties has been gathered, and a number of laboratory and field experiments have been done. More standardization of the kinds of attacks, amounts of nuclear explosions and other variables has also been achieved, thus providing some uniformity and comparability in the experiments being carried out. (No one can say, though, how closely these conventions reflect what would actually happen in a nuclear war.) Most important, the modelling of climate is now carried on with much more sophisticated, three-dimensional, computer simulations.

Of the several major studies that have been done since the TTAPS report appeared, one of the most authoritative was again sponsored by NAS and is entitled *The Effects on the Atmosphere of a Major Nuclear Exchange*.[35] It comes to the conclusion that there are still such great uncertainties about so many of the factors that we "cannot subscribe with confidence to any specific quantitative conclusions." Nevertheless, the authors believe that, to the best of their knowledge to date, "long-term climatic effects with severe implications for the biosphere could occur." Even moderate-sized attacks (that is, with substantially fewer numbers of warheads than presently exist in nuclear arsenals) could lead to temperature drops in the northern hemisphere. A study still more recent than that of NAS concludes that, in the spring or summer, there could be a drop in temperature in the order of 10 to 12 degrees Celsius, a "nuclear fall."[36] How long this would last, and how much light deprivation would accompany the drop is less certain, but the changes would be great enough to do serious harm to living things.

This brings us to the real issue behind nuclear winter. Questions about how much the temperature would drop and how dark it would be for how long are only important insofar as they tell us something about the impact these changes would have on life on earth.

Because scientists cannot say with any degree of certainty just how great the climatic effects would be, those charged with looking into the consequences of climatic changes decided to change the question around. Instead of asking what the damage would be for a given temperature drop or period of light loss, they asked of their data: how much climatic change would it take to bring about important consequences for the biosphere? From this approach came the realization that growing things are sensitive to even minor changes in climate.[37]

The reason for the sensitivity is that there is a narrow range within which a complicated set of conditions must exist if plants are to grow adequately for harvesting. And there is also an absolute level of temperature — usually the freezing point — below which everything is lost, even if that freezing temperature lasts only for a very short time.

Crops require a minimum number of days for full maturation, a minimum temperature at all times, a minimum amount of light over the growing period, a minimum amount of heat, and a minimum amount of water. There can be small, but only small, trade-offs. If the amount of light is reduced, then the minimum growing season must be lengthened. But, in general, *all* of these conditions must be met if there is to be a crop to harvest at all, and they must be more than met if the crop is to reach an average yield.[38]

If a nuclear war occurred in the spring or summer, temperature drops that are well within the more conservative estimates of nuclear "fall" could be devastating. Take Canadian wheat, for example. If the average mean temperature for the wheat growing areas of the west was reduced by one degree Celsius, the area that could grow crops would be reduced by about thirty per cent. If there was a two-degree drop, wheat growing in Canada would be virtually wiped out. Moreover, even modest drops in temperature could bring the weather system close to the freezing point, and even a very brief period of frost would destroy the entire crop.[39]

Another result of climatic changes after a nuclear war might be the alteration of the pattern of monsoons in India and East Asia. These seasonal winds bring water to the land from the oceans, assuring the growth of vast quantities of food in that part of the world. Changes in wind patterns, as a result of the smoke cloud, could result in the failure of these monsoons or in a very great decrease in the precipitation that usually accompanies them. Here, too, small changes in the climate could result in large changes in the production of food.

Thus, arguments over the exact amount of climatic change that might result from nuclear winter are not as crucial as they have sometimes appeared. As long as there is a possibility of even a small drop in temperature, or sudden patches of frost, or changes in precipitation from the monsoons, the impact on agriculture during the growing period would be severe.

Whereas concern over harm to the ozone layer drew attention to smoke, and studies of the effects of smoke drew attention to climatic effects, so studies of climatic effects have underlined the vulnerability of crops. In the same way, the recognition of the vulnerability of crops to climatic changes has, in its turn, brought further insights about food in a post-nuclear world. Following this newest lead will bring us full circle by connecting the long-term climatic effects with the acute phase of destruction by blast and fire.[40]

In nuclear war the world's food supply would not be jeopardized just by climatic changes. There are other, perhaps more serious, consequences to be considered. For example, the natural carrying capacity of the earth — the number of people it can feed without agriculture — is about 50 million, or 1 per cent of the number alive today. How do we make up the difference? By the application of energy. For centuries this meant, essentially, the energy of peasant labour and draft animals, but now it means diesel oil, gasoline and, above all, fertilizers for the soil. With huge subsidies of energy have come the hundred-fold increase in the yield from the earth.

But, after a nuclear war, a serious depletion of energy would occur. Chemical fertilizers, farm machinery and refined fuels are the products of the industrial northern hemisphere and would be lost in the general devastation. Without them, agriculture would be severely hampered, even in those countries relatively untouched by the destruction.

There is also the problem of food storage. Parts of Europe and countries like Canada, the United States and Australia, which are responsible for much of the world's food production, have supplies on hand that could keep their surviving populations alive for about a year. Some of the supplies, of course, would be destroyed and there might be wholly inadequate means for getting the remainder from where it is kept to where the people are. This is especially true for Canada, where distances are vast and where the very existence of our country, in practical terms, depends upon our capacity to transport and communicate easily.

Many countries, however, have only a few months to a few weeks of supplies, depending upon the time of the year relative to local harvests. These countries, many of them the developing countries of the

Third World, depend heavily upon the importation of food from the northern hemisphere for their survival. The combination of low supplies, and few if any imports from the war-torn north, would mean that starvation in India and Africa following a nuclear war would cause more deaths than those caused by the war itself in all of North America, Europe and the U.S.S.R. combined.

On the strength of this projection, a major international study of the environmental effects of nuclear war has suggested that more people world-wide would die from the indirect effects of nuclear war (famine) than from the direct effects (burns, wounds etc.). It concludes, therefore, that "rather than reflecting images of Hiroshima and Nagasaki, a modern nuclear war would, for most people of the world, much more resemble current images of Ethiopia and the Sudan."[41]

The End of History?

From ecological and environmental studies has come perhaps the most important insight of all — the fact that the consequences of nuclear war could not be limited to the combatants, but would result in a global disaster. Consequently, those countries that maintain a posture of nuclear deterrence, and which do not couple it with the utmost effort to negotiate the ultimate removal of nuclear weapons, are not just holding each other's populations hostage. They are threatening the whole of humanity. They are not protecting their allies under a "nuclear umbrella." They are risking all societies in the hope that they will save their own.

In all the wars of history, it is probably true that most of the victims were neither the cause nor the beneficiaries of the conflict itself. But at least the harmful effects of such upheavals were largely localized to the areas where the conflict occurred. In this sense, the effects of a nuclear war would be so different that it really should not be called a "war" at all. To use this term is an understandable habit but at the same time invokes an inappropriate analogy. It would not really be "World War III." True, its causes would be historically familiar — but its results would not. What would happen would be a holocaust caused, not by "weapons," but by instruments of genocide. Unlike Hiroshima, it would not just link the past with some things that are new. It would be an entrance-way into a world that was utterly, utterly different.

4

Verification: Promise, Politics and Prospects

Gary Marchant and Al Banner

When the United States and Soviet Union sit down at the bargaining table to negotiate an arms-control treaty, they face two challenges. First, they must agree on what weapons and activities are to be banned or limited. Second, they must also agree on whether and how compliance with these limits or bans can be satisfactorily determined. Although the first requirement involves most of the substantive issues and goals of arms control, in reality it is the second requirement — adequate verification provisions — that frequently proves to be the stumbling block in disarmament negotiations. Often the two sides will agree, or at least claim to agree, on a specific arms-control goal, and yet disagree on how to verify the measures being discussed. As a result, problems of verification often put serious limitations on the types of arms control which are politically possible.

There is abundant evidence that verification plays a critical role in both international negotiations and domestic debates regarding arms control. Disagreements over issues such as a comprehensive nuclear test ban often become focused on the question of verification. Verification is also frequently the major sticking point in East-West arms-control negotiations. For example, only 15 per cent of the 1979 SALT II Treaty dealt with substantive issues, while the remaining 85 per cent was concerned with verification issues, according to U.S. SALT II negotiator Ralph Earle.[1] The U.S. Arms Control and Disarmament Agency calls verification "*the* critical element of arms control",[2] while the Canadian government is of the opinion that "no single issue is likely to be of greater significance in international arms control and disarmament negotiations than verification."[3]

There are obvious reasons why verification is so central to arms control. The two superpowers do not trust each other, and therefore are not prepared to entrust their national security to the other side's good faith. While both sides recognize and accept this reality, verification remains contentious because of the very different perspectives of East and West bloc nations. The Soviet Union and its allies have much more closed societies than do Western nations. As a result, the Soviets can learn a great deal about American military programs simply by reading the *New York Times* or *Aviation Week & Space Technology*, while no comparable sources of information are available in the Soviet Union. This important asymmetry, combined with other fundamental political and cultural differences, leads the United States to demand more stringent and intrusive verification standards than the Soviets are often willing to accept.

These differences in perspective are reflected in the different priority the two sides have traditionally given to verification during arms-control talks. The Soviet negotiators want to reach "agreement in principle" on substantive issues first and then talk about verification, while American negotiators usually want to discuss verification at the outset. In an atmosphere of distrust, the Americans accuse the Soviets of propaganda because they seem interested only in disarmament without verification. The Soviets suspect that the U.S. is more interested in espionage than arms control because American officials seem to want verification without disarmament.

Despite the obvious importance of verification in arms control, the general public rarely understands the specifics of verification capabilities or activities. One reason for this lack of understanding is the complex nature of many verification technologies. Needless to say, there are very few dinner-table discussions on "the intercept capabilities of electronic intelligence satellites" or "the spatial resolution of synthetic aperture radars." Another obstacle to public knowledge is that verification capabilities are highly classified, in part because of the large overlap between sensors used for verification and those used for strategic intelligence gathering. For example, the satellites used to verify Soviet treaty compliance are also used to identify targets for U.S. nuclear war-fighting plans. Verification technologies are also kept secret to increase the adversary's uncertainty about the extent to which their activities are known.

Because of this lack of public understanding, verification can be used as a smoke-screen to mask opposition to arms control. For instance, the Soviet Union has often put forward sweeping disarmament proposals that included no provisions for verification, thus making the proposal totally unacceptable to the Americans. Unverifiable proposals do not help bring about arms-control agreements, but they may appear to be worthy and credible peace initiatives to a public which is uninformed about verification. Conversely, in the West there is often a tendency for officials to use alleged problems with verification as a pretext for blocking a treaty they actually oppose for other reasons. A politician can always justify a vote against an arms-control proposal by citing verification concerns, regardless of whether they are legitimate or not. Sydney Graybeal, the former U.S. Commissioner to the Standing Consultative Commission which deals with U.S.-Soviet compliance issues, recently warned that "verification is becoming a shield for those not interested in arms control to hide behind."[4]

Recent Soviet arms control initiatives under General Secretary Mikhail Gorbachev have been much more forthcoming on verification. In announcing his comprehensive proposals for the elimination of nuclear weapons by the year 2000, Gorbachev said on January 15, 1986: "Verification of the destruction of limitation of arms should be carried out by both national technical means and through on-site inspections. The USSR is ready to reach an agreement on any other additional verification measures."[5]

Given the significant potential for verification issues to be abused, it is important that the public be capable of distinguishing when concerns about verification are spurious and when they are legitimate. Despite the very real impediments to public understanding, it is possible for the public to make informed judgements about verification issues. Enough information has been disclosed through congressional testimony and leaks to give a general sense of what is possible with sophisticated new monitoring technologies. Furthermore, most controversies about verification are of a political rather than technical nature, and common sense more than technical expertise is required to assess the relative validity of the arguments.

The Tools

An understanding of verification activities and capabilities must begin with the basic tools. These are known as "national technical means" and consist of remote sensors stationed on a variety of platforms that operate outside the borders of the nation being observed. The best known, and probably most important, national technical means of verification are photo-reconnaissance satellites. The main U.S. satellites of this type are the Keyhole series: the current generation is known as the KH-11. These satellites circle the earth at an altitude of 150 to 400 kilometres, with powerful telescopes trained on the ground below the satellite's path. The images collected by the satellites are digitally transmitted to the ground where the signal is converted to television pictures and photographs.

The exact capabilities of the most powerful photo-reconnaissance systems is a closely guarded secret, and the subject of much speculation. There are stories from reputable sources that the satellites can read licence plates on cars in Moscow, or distinguish whether a man perusing a newspaper in a northern Soviet town is reading *Pravda* or *Izvestiya*.[6] These claims are probably exaggerated, as the most commonly accepted figures are that the satellites can detect objects as small as ten to twenty centimetres under optimal conditions.

The KH-11, using multispectral sensors, records images in different spectral wavebands simultaneously. Many techniques exist to enhance the interpretation of images acquired by satellite sensors. Images can be combined to form "false colour" photographs which make particular features more apparent. For example, a combination commonly used for analysing data from civilian systems such as LANDSAT makes green leaves appear bright red but green paint appear blue. This combination would be useful for identifying camouflaged objects.

The photo-reconnaissance satellites constantly move in relation to points on the earth's surface. Hence, they do not provide a continuous image of the entire Soviet Union, but "snapshots" of regions they pass over. It usually takes about one week for a KH-11 to cover the entire territory of the Soviet Union. The United States normally has several photo-reconnaissance satellites in orbit potentially to provide coverage of suspicious activities every few days.

The KH-11 is scheduled to be replaced by a new KH-12 satellite. The new satellite will significantly improve U.S. monitoring capabilities. One of the key improvements the KH-12 will provide is that it will carry thermal infrared scanners that will provide coverage at night. The new scanners may also be useful to detect underground activity or construction by changes in the surface temperature. The KH-12 will have more extensive manoeuvering capabilities, allowing it to appear over an area of interest in an unpredictable fashion. Currently, the Soviets can predict when a U.S. photo-reconnaissance satellite will be overhead, and so they can conceal certain activities they do not wish to be observed. There are plans to have four KH-12 satellites in orbit at any time, which will make it possible to view any area of interest within twenty minutes.

Whereas reconnaissance satellites can observe only a relatively small section of the Soviet Union at any one time, early-warning satellites keep a vigilant watch over the Soviet Union at all times. The Defence Support Program satellites which perform this function are in a geostationary orbit at an altitude of about 35,000 kilometres. Satellites orbiting at this specific altitude travel at the same speed as the earth's rotation, and thus remain stationary with respect to the earth's surface. Although their main function is early warning of an enemy attack, these satellites assist verification by detecting test flights of Soviet ballistic missiles.

Photo-reconnaissance and early-warning satellites serve as the "eyes" for verification. Electronic intelligence satellites act as the "ears." These satellites intercept many types of military electronic and radio communications in the Soviet Union and elsewhere. They also pick up telemetry — signals transmitted by Soviet missiles during tests — which contain important information about the missile's performance and characteristics. Although this telemetry is produced for the purpose of helping the testing nation assess and improve a new missile, it also provides important data for verification and other purposes to an eavesdropping nation. The key U.S. electronic intelligence satellites are in geostationary orbits. The earlier versions were named

Rhyolite; they are now being replaced by newer models known as *Chalet* and *Magnum*. The U.S. also has smaller electronic intelligence satellites in lower orbits called "ferrets."

Satellite electronic surveillance is supplemented by over two thousand American ground-based listening posts in places such as Turkey, Norway, China, Alaska, Cypress and Thailand. The U.S. also has ground-based radars to track missiles in flight, such as the huge *Cobra Dane* radar in the Alaskan Aleutian Islands. The *Cobra Dane* radar is reported to have the capability to track one hundred objects the size of basketballs simultaneously at a distance of three thousand kilometres. Finally, additional visual and electronic information is gathered for verification purposes from a variety of intelligence aircraft and ships operating near the Soviet Union. The Soviets mistook Korean Air Line 007 for one of these aircraft when they attacked and destroyed it in the early morning of September 1, 1983, just as it was approaching Soviet airspace.

Another type of national technical means is the seismograph, which measures the movement of the earth to detect earthquakes and underground nuclear explosions. Because these instruments can detect events as far as ten thousand kilometres away, seismographs in many parts of the world are useful for monitoring Soviet nuclear tests.

The ability of national technical means to gather intelligence data for verification is assisted or supplemented by what are known as "co-operative measures." These are procedures both sides agree on to make it easier to verify compliance. Existing co-operative measures include data exchanges, counting rules, prior notification of tests or other activities, a ban on deliberate concealment and non-interference with the other side's national technical means.

The best known and probably least understood co-operative measure is on-site verification, which permits monitoring equipment or personnel from one side to have access to the territory of the other. The access can vary from periodic inspections to permanent stationing, and can be in the form of human inspectors or unmanned tamper-proof monitors. Although on-site verification is thought by some to be the ideal form of verification, there are several reasons why this type of monitoring is much less useful and effective than often assumed. First, neither the Soviet Union nor the United States is likely to give the other side unrestricted access to its most sensitive military installations. Second, on-site verification would not be feasible for a wide variety of military activities because it would require an enormous commitment of manpower. Third, on-site inspections would provide very little information about many types of activities. For example, on-site inspectors could not learn much about a Soviet missile test flight. They could do little more than stand there and watch it fly by! National technical means would provide much more information about this type of activity. The U.S. Arms Control & Disarmament Agency recognizes that on-site inspections are no panacea, noting that "their role will remain limited, and they should be regarded primarily as a supplement to national technical means."[7] Still, while the usefulness of on-site verification is very often vastly over-rated, the procedure can be crucial in some specific situations.

Finally, in addition to national technical means and co-operative measures, verification can sometimes be supplemented by human intelligence, known in the jargon of the spy business as "HUMINT." Valuable information can be obtained about the other side's military programs and activities from spies, defectors, emigres, leaks and even the open literature. Because these sources of information are fortuitous and unpredictable, they are not usually included in assessments of verification capabilities. Nevertheless, a potential cheater must risk the possibility of hidden activities being uncovered by such methods.

The Tools in Use

We shall now examine how verification tools can be used to verify some selected arms control proposals — deep reductions in strategic nuclear arsenals, such as the 50 per cent cut in arsenals agreed to in principle by both the United States and the Soviet Union; a comprehensive nuclear test ban; and a strengthened anti-ballistic missile treaty.

With respect to cuts in strategic weapons, the three major types of strategic delivery vehicles — land-based intercontinental ballistic missiles (ICBMs), ballistic missile submarines, and intercontinental bombers — are large and easy to detect by photo-reconnaissance satellites. ICBM silos take more than a year to build, and require easily identifiable excavation and construction. Ballistic missile submarines are longer than a football field, and their construction and launching occurs at only two shipyards in the Soviet Union. Strategic bombers are also large and difficult to hide, and are deployed at a limited number of airfields that are closely monitored.

The United States and Soviet Union have precise estimates of the numbers of each type of strategic delivery vehicle deployed by the other side. But the deep reductions in strategic weapons now being negotiated in Geneva would involve limits on warheads as well as delivery vehicles. Counting warheads is a more indirect process. The first step is to identify the missile type in each silo and submarine. There are slight differences in the appearance and sizes of silos and launching tubes for different missiles, and they are also accompanied by different command, control and support equipment. The missile may be observed while being loaded into the silo or launch tube, facilitating its identification.

Even though the missile type can usually be determined with a high degree of confidence, missiles of the same type may carry different numbers of warheads. The warheads on every deployed missile cannot be observed or counted directly. But a missile would not be deployed with a particular number of warheads without testing. Radar monitoring of a missile flight test can reveal the number of warheads it is capable of carrying. Therefore, a mutually accepted counting rule is applied whereby all missiles of a given type are assumed to be carrying the maximum number of warheads for which it has been tested.

Using this indirect approach, each superpower can estimate the number of strategic warheads deployed by the other side. The actual number of warheads deployed may be more or less than estimated, but the margin of error is militarily insignificant relative to the current strategic arsenals of over ten thousand warheads on each side. With a 50 per cent cut in strategic warheads, potential discrepancies would probably still be militarily insignificant. Further reductions would, however, eventually reach levels at which potential errors in the estimates would become significant militarily.

The major problems that would be encountered in verifying deep reductions in strategic arsenals would result from two relatively new developments in the arms race: mobile ICBMs and cruise missiles. Until recently, ICBMs were easy to detect and count because they were stationary in large silos. But intercontinental missiles which can be carried and launched from specially designed trains or trailers are being deployed in the Soviet Union and are under development in the United States. Mobile missiles are more difficult to count than those based in silos, since you are never sure whether the missile you see in one place is not the same one you observed fifty miles away the previous day. Some of the missiles might be overlooked altogether.

Fortunately, there are factors that reduce the difficulty of counting at least the first generation of mobile missiles. According to James A. Shear, a verification specialist at Harvard University's Center for Science and International Affairs, the United States "has a pretty good idea how to track mobile ICBMs. They have a long logistics trail."[8] They require support facilities and may have pre-surveyed launch sites which make them easier to find. Mobile missiles rely more heavily on radio communication to ensure their mobility, rather than on land lines which are less susceptible to electronic eavesdropping. Finally, they will usually be stationed in groups at known military installations and scatter only during crises or military exercises.

A variety of co-operative measures could be used to enhance the verifiability of mobile missiles. "Designated deployment areas" could be used to permit each side to focus their national technical means on smaller areas, thus making it easier to count the other's missile force. Within these areas, buildings and other potential hiding places for launchers would be restricted.[9] Even a single observation of a mobile missile outside these areas would signal a violation. U.S. government researchers are also investigating techniques to "tag" mobile missiles for identification while, at the same time, not increasing the vulnerability of the missiles to attack.

Cruise missiles present a more serious problem for verification. These missiles are deployed on land, air and sea. They are small, mobile and easily concealed. Some cruise missiles carry nuclear warheads while others are conventionally armed. The manner in which a particular missile is armed, however, cannot be determined by existing national technical means. So even if cruise missiles can be seen and counted, there is still uncertainty about which ones should be counted against the limits of a nuclear arms control agreement.

Sea-launched cruise missiles, in particular, present difficult problems for verification. Conventional and nuclear-armed missiles are being widely deployed on surface ships and submarines. The U.S.

Tomahawk cruise missile appears almost identical to a torpedo, and can be launched from unmodified submarine torpedo tubes. Verification proposals combining national technical means with co-operative measures including tagging of missiles, on-ship installation of nuclear warhead detectors and on-site inspections have been suggested. Agreement upon such intrusive measures, however, will be difficult to negotiate.

An agreement to reduce strategic arsenals might be negotiated either to permit or restrict modernization. Of the two options, an agreement permitting modernization would be the most difficult to verify. Careful supervision would be required to monitor new missiles being deployed as well as destruction of the older ones being replaced. The current negotiations in Geneva are focusing on a treaty which would allow ongoing replacement of older missiles with newer models, provided the total number of warheads did not increase above an agreed ceiling.

The second specific proposal that requires attention is a comprehensive test ban prohibiting all underground nuclear tests. The first indications of an impending nuclear test in the Soviet Union are usually detected by photo-reconnaissance satellites. Satellite images reveal preparations such as excavation of the hole in which the nuclear device will be implanted. After this initial advance warning, information about Soviet nuclear tests is gathered mostly by seismographs.

Seismographs measure seismic waves produced by earthquakes and explosions, producing information about the time, location and size of the event. The U.S. collects data about suspicious seismic events from a world-wide network of seismic stations. The key challenge in verifying a test ban is to distinguish nuclear explosions from more than ten thousand earthquakes of significant size that occur each year. The first step is to determine the location and depth of the epicentre of the seismic event. This can be done relatively accurately and simply by triangulating the data from three or more seismic stations in different locations. Most events can be identified as earthquakes by their location. Only 1 per cent of all earthquakes are focused at depths of less than fifty kilometres and in areas of potential nuclear explosions. Those seismic events which cannot be classified as earthquakes must be identified by their seismic wave pattern. Relative to earthquakes, nuclear explosions produce more waves which travel deep through the body of the earth. The ratio of body to surface waves is a reliable measure for distinguishing earthquakes from explosions.

Nevertheless, there would be several problems in verifying a comprehensive test ban. It is quite difficult to identify small Soviet tests using instruments placed outside Soviet territory. The seismic signal will dissipate as it moves outward from the test site. If it was small to begin with, the signal may not be detectable by the time it arrives outside the Soviet Union. Even if the seismic signal is detected, small earthquakes and small explosions appear very similar from long distances away. Small nuclear explosions can also be confused with routine mining explosions.

There is an additional problem: the Soviets may attempt to hide some smaller tests by conducting them in large underground caverns. Usually, an underground explosion converts about 1 per cent of its energy into seismic waves. However, if the warhead is suspended in a cavity, not in close contact with the surrounding rock, then much less of its energy is transformed into seismic waves. This technique, called decoupling, is only feasible with relatively small explosions; larger tests would require impossibly large caverns. The seismic waves from a small, fully decoupled explosion can be reduced by a factor of up to one hundred, making small tests even more difficult to detect.

These problems mean that it is probably not possible to verify nuclear tests below 5 kilotons using only seismic data collected from outside the Soviet Union. Of the American tests conducted at the Nevada Test Site from 1980 to 1984, most were above 5 kilotons with a large percentage of the tests having yields between 10 and 15 kilotons. The yields of Soviet tests show a similar pattern with most tests being around 10 kilotons or in the 25 to 75 kiloton range.[10]

The difficulties in verifying small explosions can be alleviated in two important ways. The first is to place U.S. seismographs inside the Soviet Union, since it is easier to discriminate the seismic wave patterns of small earthquakes from small explosions at shorter distances. The U.S. has already developed tamper-proof seismic "black boxes" that can be stationed on foreign soil to record and transmit seismic information via satellite. The Soviet Union has recently indicated that it would be prepared to accept the stationing of these devices on its territory as part of a comprehensive test ban. This type of on-site verification is politically ideal, since it is relatively unintrusive, and yet provides essential information that cannot be obtained by other means.

Another development that is improving the ability to monitor a test ban is the recent finding that nuclear explosions are more easily detected and distinguished from earthquakes at higher monitoring frequencies. Normally, seismographs are tuned to a frequency of about one Hertz, the usual frequency for detecting earthquakes. It is now apparent that frequencies of twenty Hertz or higher are more useful for monitoring nuclear tests, for several reasons. First, there is less background "noise" at higher frequencies so the signals from explosions are clearer. Second, underground explosions produce a greater proportion of high frequency waves than do earthquakes. This is particularly true for smaller yields explosions. Finally, high frequency waves are influenced much less by decoupling, making it less feasible to muffle nuclear tests by conducting them in large cavities. Although high frequency seismic monitoring is new and has not been fully proven, there is strong evidence to suggest that this new technique represents an important breakthrough for verifying a comprehensive test ban.

A recent analysis concluded that by using high frequency seismic monitoring, fifteen monitoring stations outside the Soviet Union along with a network of twenty-five automatic seismic stations within Soviet territory could detect with high confidence a fully decoupled test as small as one kiloton.[11] At present, it is unlikely that any strategically significant tests would be carried out at yields smaller than this. The new high frequency monitoring technique, combined with new Soviet openness to on-site verification, have removed the major technical obstacles to a comprehensive test ban. As leading U.S. seismologists have emphasized, the major remaining obstacle is one of political will.

Finally, there are the verification issues related to strengthening the Anti-Ballistic Missile (ABM) Treaty. The 1972 ABM Treaty restricts the development, testing and deployment of systems for countering strategic ballistic missiles. Historically, such systems have consisted of ground-based launchers, interceptors and radars which are easily detected and monitored by existing national technical means. Following President Reagan's "Star Wars" speech on March 23, 1983, however, a new effort has been launched to develop space-based, rather than ground-based, ABM systems.

Technologies currently exist, or are being developed, which are capable of monitoring military activities in space. The U.S. has an advanced space-tracking capability consisting of a world-wide system of ground-based telescopes and radars to monitor objects and activities in orbit. The U.S. Air Force is developing a space-based system to monitor Soviet satellites, with a deployment goal in the early 1990s. The feasibility of a space-based surveillance satellite to investigate objects in orbit was demonstrated during the first space shuttle flight when a KH-11 was apparently used to examine tiles damaged during the launch.

The largest problem with the new emphasis on space-based systems lies not so much in detecting what activities take place, but rather in defining which activities and devices are permitted under the treaty. Space-based ABM systems may involve lasers and other "exotic technologies" as weapons or sensors. These do not neatly correspond to the definitions of launchers, interceptors and radars used in the treaty text. As a result, there are different interpretations of how the treaty should be applied to these new systems. There is also disagreement over where to draw the line between research (which is permitted by the treaty) and development (which is not). Finally there is no agreed-upon definition for critical terms in the treaty such as "component" and "tested in an ABM mode."

A proposal that has received serious consideration in both Washington and Moscow for removing some of the current ambiguities is known as the "capability-based approach."[12] Under this proposal, the two sides would agree upon "threshold values" for the technical parameters of each type of technology which may be used in a space-based ABM system. No testing of devices that exceed the threshold values would be permitted under the strengthened treaty. For example, the capability of a laser to destroy missiles depends upon a key parameter known as "brightness." The brightness required for weapons in a functional ABM system would be greater than would be required for communications or research. A threshold value for brightness could be established to distinguish between lasers to be permitted by the treaty and those to be banned.

Verification would be crucial to the capability-based approach. Deployment of space-to-space surveillance satellites, provisions for advance notification of tests, and exchanges of data for devices being tested would be necessary to verify the threshold values.

While the capability-based approach may be useful to deal with the treatment of new technologies under the ABM Treaty, it presumes a genuine interest by all parties to honour the original spirit and intent of the ABM Treaty. This, of course, is true of any arms-control measure.

Problems — and Possible Solutions

This brief survey of the verifiability of three potential arms-control treaties shows that there are two opposing trends currently at play. On one hand, verification technologies are getting more sophisticated and effective. The new KH-12 satellite, high-frequency seismic monitoring and space-to-space surveillance systems will all significantly improve monitoring capabilities. On the other hand, there is also a trend towards smaller and more mobile weaponry. The bomb dropped on Nagasaki was twelve feet long, ten feet in diameter and weighed about 10,000 pounds. Today, a typical strategic warhead at least ten times more powerful than the Nagasaki bomb is only about one-and-a-half feet long, one foot in diameter, and a mere 250 pounds. As warheads become miniaturized, they can be carried by smaller, mobile missiles which are more difficult to monitor. Cruise missiles and mobile ICBMs are examples of weapon systems presenting new challenges for verification. Similarly, assessments of the verifiability of a comprehensive test ban generally assume that militarily significant testing would not involve yields below five kilotons. However, research and development of the X-ray laser and other "third generation" nuclear weapons may change that since they could involve yields in the sub-kiloton range.

The balance between these two opposing trends could determine the verifiability of arms control agreements in the future. Currently, the balance appears to favour verification, as current techniques seem capable of monitoring present weapon systems. Some significant activities, such as laboratory research, cannot be confidently verified using existing techniques. However, most of the important activities that should be included in a nuclear arms agreement can be adequately monitored.

The balance is not static and seems to be shifting toward reduced verifiability as more elusive and dual-capable weapons are deployed. There is a window of opportunity for verifiable arms control agreements at the present time, which may not last too far into the future. Comprehensive treaties to "lock in" weapons technology would slow the trend toward unverifiable weapons, while at the same time permitting verification technologies to continue to improve. Without such agreements, the current balance in favour of verification may not last.

So why is verification often used as an argument for not entering into arms-control agreements? The answer revolves around different perspectives on what the word "verifiable" really means. Up to this point, we have been referring to verification as though it were an all-or-nothing concept. Unfortunately, verification is not such a clear-cut proposition. In fact, there is no such thing as perfect or absolute verification. There will always be uncertainty associated with a verification estimate.

This uncertainty has several sources. One is the imperfect nature of the technical means of verification. Although these systems are often overlapping and complementary, it is still not unusual to get incomplete observations. Clouds may obscure the view of a photo-reconnaissance satellite on several successive passes over a suspicious event, or electronic intelligence equipment may malfunction on the day of a missile test.

Another source of uncertainty is from errors in measurement. For example, the Reagan administration has accused the Soviet Union of "likely violating" the 1974 Threshold Test Ban Treaty by conducting tests in excess of the 150 kiloton limit set by the agreement. However, experts felt that the procedures to derive the yield of Soviet tests were overstating the estimates by as much as 20 per cent. In question was a "correction factor" introduced to compensate for geological differences between the Soviet and American test sites. The procedures have, in fact, since been changed by the Central Intelligence Agency. Even without systematic errors such as this one, however, there will always be some degree of uncertainty — thanks to limitations of the instruments, differences in test conditions, human error and many other factors. As a general rule, any quantitative measurement used in verification will automatically introduce a margin of error.

A third source of uncertainty is the processing of intelligence information. National technical means produce mountains of raw data, which must be interpreted, organized, integrated and assessed. Even if something is recorded by monitoring equipment, there is no guarantee that it will be noticed during the analysis of the raw data. An example of how important observations can be missed is the case of the Soviet combat brigade suddenly discovered in Cuba during 1979 by the Carter administration. This discovery caused a major furore in the United States, but the fact is that U.S. intelligence information had been clearly recording the presence of the Soviet troops for over a decade. It had simply never been noticed previously. For every verification task relying upon intelligence information, there is always a risk that an important feature is being overlooked. The more data there is, the greater the chance that something will be missed.

The fourth source of uncertainty is a little more philosophical, but is nevertheless very important in a real sense for verification. It is the question of "whether monitoring is expected to prove compliance against the presumption of violation or prove violation against the presumption of compliance."[13] Consider an arms-control treaty that bans a certain type of missile. If you observe a forbidden missile, you have proof that the Soviets have cheated. But it is fundamentally impossible to prove that the Soviets have *not* cheated. In this case, not observing a forbidden missile does not constitute definitive proof that such a missile does not exist. The longer you look and still fail to observe a missile, the more *likely* it is that the Soviets have not cheated. But you can never be absolutely sure. Since you can only prove noncompliance and not compliance, verification of compliance can never be absolute.

The final source of uncertainty is ambiguity in the interpretation of detailed provisions in arms-control treaties. Verification not only involves gathering and processing of intelligence information, but also matching of this information against relevant treaty provisions to determine whether violations have occurred. Unfortunately, treaty language can often be vague or ambiguous, especially with respect to unforeseen situations. Conflicting interpretations of the meaning of gray areas in a treaty introduce additional sources of disagreement into verification debates.

For the reasons outlined above, there will always be a margin of uncertainty in verifying arms-control treaties. This margin of uncertainty cuts in both directions. The Soviets may be able to operate slightly above treaty limits without being caught; and sometimes the Soviets may appear to be cheating even if they are actually just below the allowable limits.

Opinion is divided into two main political philosophies, which have been termed the "substantive" and "legalistic" schools,[14] about how we should deal with the margin of uncertainty. The substantive school is willing to accept margins of uncertainty which are militarily insignificant. As long as the United States can identify and respond to Soviet cheating that would affect the strategic balance, it is prepared to tolerate the possibility of smaller, undetected Soviet violations. According to this point of view, the Soviets would be unlikely to commit such insignificant violations anyway, since they have little to gain and much to lose if they are caught. The key word used to describe the substantive position is "adequate." The Nixon, Ford and Carter administrations all officially adopted a policy of "adequate verification." In 1979, Secretary of Defense Harold Brown described the concept as follows:

> No arms limitation agreement can ever be absolutely verifiable. The relevant test is not an abstract ideal, but the practical standard of whether we can determine compliance adequately to safeguard our security — that is, whether we can identify attempted evasion if it occurs on a large enough scale to pose a significant risk, and whether we can do so in time to mount a sufficient response. Meeting this test is what I mean by the term adequate verification.[15]

According to the view of the substantive school, the U.S. currently has the capability to monitor adequately most Soviet defence programs, and therefore verification should not be impeding progress in arms control. For example, former director of the U.S. National Security Agency Admiral Noel Gayler asserted that he was "confident that we can verify, by national technical means, any violation that could affect our position relative to the Soviet Union."[16]

Under the Reagan administration, the substantive viewpoint has been replaced as the official U.S. policy by the legalistic approach. The legalistic school believes that any Soviet violation, no matter how small, is important and unacceptable. Even if such cheating does not confer a military advantage, it demonstrates that the Soviet Union is not an honest and worthy partner for arms control. The legalistic school is not willing to accept a margin of uncertainty and tends to classify all questionable or ambiguous activities as violations. The onus is put on the Soviet Union to demonstrate compliance, rather than the United States to prove non-compliance. The legalistic school is unhappy with the verification provisions of past treaties, and demands more stringent standards. Verification systems must even be able to categorize ambiguous activities to ensure Soviet compliance. These new standards, known as "effective" verification, are often difficult to implement and can be an impediment to reaching arms-control agreements.

The tough standards demanded by the legalistic school have other detrimental consequences. One is the large number of false alarms which inevitably arise from an overly sensitive monitoring system. Consider again the example of the Threshold Test Ban Treaty, which forbids underground nuclear tests with yields over 150 kilotons. A series of legal Soviet tests may generate some yield measurements which appear to be over the limit. The substantive school might consider these measurements to be within an accepted range of uncertainty. They would refrain from accusing the Soviets of cheating provided the estimates did not exceed the allowable margin of error and there were not an excessive number of tests in this range. There is some risk that the Soviets might exploit this caution and deliberately conduct tests slightly larger than 150 kilotons, but such marginal cheating would confer no military advantage.

The legalistic school would be more likely to treat the suspicious measurements as evidence of Soviet cheating. For the reasons detailed earlier, however, there will always be some evidence that could be interpreted as indications of cheating regardless of whether or not the Soviets are actually in violation. The legalistic viewpoint has been compared to a smoke detector which is so sensitive that it goes off whenever you burn your toast.[17]

One of the widely accepted tenets of arms control is that it cannot be based on trust alone. Of course, this is why verification is necessary in the first place. One of the functions often attributed to verification, in addition to detecting and deterring violations, is to build trust and confidence between the contracting parties and in the arms-control process. The high frequency of false alarms expected under the legalistic verification regime demonstrates that arms control cannot be based on distrust alone either. Distrust at the outset will breed more distrust. Activities in the inevitable margin of uncertainty will always be interpreted in such a way as to reinforce existing attitudes and biases. Therefore, verification cannot substitute for trust. Blind faith in the other side's good intentions is neither required nor advised. Some trust is necessary, however, if the two sides are going to deal in a calm, responsible manner with the concerns and ambiguities that are sure to arise.

The verification question boils down to a political choice between the values and assumptions of the two schools of thought. The differences between the two schools are largely based on assumptions about Soviet intentions and differing perspectives on the utility of arms control. For example, many advocates of the legalistic school of verification have opposed every arms-control treaty negotiated between the United States and Soviet Union. Since they do not assign much value to arms control, they are not too concerned about the disruptive effects of false alarms on the arms-control process. In contrast, the substantive school does see merit in arms control, and is concerned about false alarms which undermine confidence in arms-control treaties and between the superpowers. While there is an inherent risk of potential cheating in any arms-control agreement, this risk must be balanced against the often greater risk to international security if there were no treaties at all.

Perspectives on arms control usually determine views on verification rather than vice versa. While the technical data from monitoring systems is objective and factual, the interpretation of what the data means is subjective and political. The Reagan and Carter administrations have used essentially the same technical data to reach opposing conclusions about Soviet compliance with several major treaties. Evaluating the views of the two schools of thought requires sound political judgement as much as it requires technical expertise.

One approach that has been suggested for helping to depoliticize verification and make it less susceptible to manipulation is to establish some form of international verification agency. Such an organization, perhaps working under the auspices of the United Nations, might result in a more objective observation and evaluation of military activities. Although the concept of an international inspection body has been around since the late 1940s, the idea gained more public profile when France put forward a proposal for the creation of an International Satellite Monitoring Agency (ISMA) to the United Nations in 1978.

A subsequent study sponsored by the United Nations[18] found that the concept was technically feasible, but the proposal received a cool response from a number of countries. Some of the concerns expressed included:

- rights of nations being monitored — would they have a right of access to the data or the right of prior consent?
- data interpretation — how would conflicting interpretations of ambiguous data be resolved?
- data dissemination — who would it be given to and in what form? Raw data could not be interpreted by nations without the required analysis capabilities. However, distribution of interpreted data might place the agency in a position of interfering in the internal affairs of states.
- scope — huge amounts of data would have to be processed and stored, and perhaps retrieved and then reprocessed since interpretation of the data might often depend upon changes over time.
- cost — while supporters pointed out that the cost of an ISMA would be less than 1 per cent of the world annual expenditure on armaments, critics re-expressed the cost as "possibly equal to the entire United Nations budget."[19]

Neither the United States nor the Soviet Union expressed support for the concept. A potential underlying reason for their aversion to the proposal, in addition to the concerns outlined above, was the inclusion of a suggestion that the superpowers might supply data from their military photo-reconnaissance satellites to ISMA during the initial period when it would not have its own satellites.

A satellite monitoring agency, as envisaged in the ISMA proposal, is not likely to become a reality in the near future. It is clear that future efforts must be more modest in scope as well as more politically sensitive.

Other alternatives are possible and have, in fact, been suggested. The concept of a "Regional Satellite Monitoring Agency" has been proposed. It was suggested that this might be undertaken in Europe as a joint effort of the European Space Agency and its eastern European counterpart, the Interkosmos Council. There is also growing interest in the concept of a "MEDIASAT" which would be owned and operated by a consortium of news agencies and could supply satellite images detailed enough to detect objects three to five metres across. While there are no plans on the drawing boards yet, many experts from the space industry, news media, academia and government have remarked that it is bound to happen.

Third parties are also becoming involved in developing the means to verify a ban on nuclear testing. One such effort is the offer by the Five Continent Peace Initiative, composed of the leaders of Argentina, Mexico, Sweden, Greece, Tanzania and India, to verify a nuclear testing moratorium between the United States and Soviet Union. At the same time, the reciprocal arrangement between the Soviet Union and the private U.S. National Resources Defence Council to set up jointly operated seismic stations in the two countries has established an important precedent for verification of a comprehensive test ban. The NRDC has installed and is now operating three seismic monitoring stations within one hundred miles of the main Soviet test site near Semipalatinsk.

Canada is also making an important contribution in this field since, as External Affairs Minister Joe Clark told the House of Commons in 1985, "verification is an area where Canadian expertise and diplomacy come together."[20] Canada has considerable expertise in remote sensing in the academic, industrial and government sectors. Our traditional involvement in peace-keeping activities has helped to build an "honest broker" image. To take advantage of this opportunity for Canadians to contribute to the arms-control process, the Government of Canada launched the "Arms Control Verification Research Program" in 1983. It is now funded at about one million dollars per year.[21]

The Program focuses on arms control issues within a multilateral context, including:

- the achievement of a comprehensive convention to ban chemical weapons,
- the negotiation of a comprehensive nuclear test ban treaty,
- the development of a treaty to ban weapons for use in outer space,
- the pursuit of arms control and military confidence-building in Europe, and
- the conduct of generic research into verification.

As part of the Verification Research Program, a study focusing on the operational procedures for investigating alleged chemical weapons abuses was prepared and submitted to the United Nations Secretary General. The PAXSAT program is examining the feasibility of using available satellite technology to support arms-control measures related to deployment of space-based weapons and conventional force levels in Europe. Seismic monitoring equipment at Yellowknife is undergoing a $3.2 million upgrade to improve its capabilities for monitoring a comprehensive nuclear test ban as part of an international seismic data network. Research at the University of Toronto, financed through grants from the program, is examining the use of high frequency, regional seismic data for identifying underground nuclear explosions, including those which have been decoupled.

In 1985 Canada successfully promoted a resolution at the UN General Assembly calling upon states "to increase their efforts towards achieving agreements on balanced, mutually acceptable, verifiable and effective arms limitation and disarmament measures" and "to communicate...their views and suggestions on verification principles, procedures and techniques...and on the role of the United Nations in the field of verification."[22] In fulfilling its contribution to the resolution, the Canadian Government submitted a study providing a survey of verification efforts, outlining some of the principles, procedures and techniques and looking at the verification requirements related to a comprehensive test ban, a prohibition of chemical weapons and the prevention of an arms race in outer space.[23]

Canada's verification research is an important and positive contribution. These efforts, however, can be made irrelevant by the policies and actions of other governments, particularly those of the two superpowers. Research to improve verification techniques must also be accompanied by determined efforts to promote constructive attitudes toward arms control and restraint in the development of weapons technologies which would threaten the viability of arms-control agreements. Improved verification capabilities, by themselves, cannot bring about the required political will to make arms-control agreements possible.

At times, the Reagan administration has adopted arms-control policies contrary to long-standing Canadian positions on issues such as adherence to the SALT II agreement, interpretation of the ABM Treaty and a comprehensive nuclear test ban. While the Reagan administration has often demanded more stringent verification standards than previous administrations, it has reduced funding for verification research and increased funding for weapons such as sea-launched cruise missiles which pose difficult verification problems.

Perhaps more than any other country, Canada is closely integrated with the United States in military, political and economic terms. This can present Canada with the dilemma of how to vigorously advocate positions favouring arms control without jeopardizing our close relationship and credibility with the United States. Yet, whatever influence Canada has in bilateral defence and arms-control matters between the superpowers primarily arises from that close relationship and alliance with the United States.

Expressing Canada's concerns and views regarding various arms-control and defence policies, including those of the United States and Soviet Union, is ultimately vital to the value of our efforts to develop verification techniques. In the final analysis, verification without arms control is not much better than *no* verification without arms control.

5

Canada's Arms Control and Disarmament Policy: Redefining the Achievable

John Barrett

The past ten years have demonstrated how changes in weapons technology, strategic doctrine and East-West relations in general keep shifting the ground under arms control and disarmament. In the decade stretching from Prime Minister Pierre Trudeau's "strategy of suffocation" speech at the first United Nations Special Session on Disarmament (UNSSOD I) in 1978 to the present, Canadian governments have wrestled with such issues as cruise-missile testing, participation in the Reagan Administration's Strategic Defense and Air Defense Initiatives, the implications of Mikhail Gorbachev's accession to power in the Kremlin, and, most recently, the removal of intermediate-range nuclear forces (INF) from Europe. Added to this have been pressures arising from constituencies in the Canadian public that have pushed for increased Canadian involvement in disarmament issues. The intractabilities and resistance of the international political environment, however, impose their own imperatives. The issue of arms control and disarmament, particularly nuclear arms control, still remains the handmaiden of Soviet-American relations.

The approach of the government during the Trudeau years was marked by an acknowledgement that control of the application of new technology to weapons development must be part and parcel of any process aimed at securing actual nuclear disarmament. Prime Minister

Trudeau used both UN Special Sessions on Disarmament, in 1978 and 1982, as occasions for important statements on this problem.[1] But there were crucial differences between the two meetings, not only in the prevailing international political and security context but also in the substance and thrust of Trudeau's remarks. In the first meeting, with the unveiling of the "suffocation strategy," the approach had a strong technical or functional dimension. The second speech, in 1982, put a greater emphasis on the restoration of political confidence — presaging the concerns of the peace initiative which Trudeau would embark upon the following year.

The change in emphasis probably reflected what was politically achievable at that time in superpower arms control. The climate of East-West relations had soured markedly after the invasion of Afghanistan and the dawning realization that the SALT II accords, although signed by President Jimmy Carter and General Secretary Leonid Brezhnev, would not gain the requisite support for ratification by the U.S. Senate. The proposals outlined by Trudeau at UNSSOD I were thus far more advanced than the atmosphere of Soviet-American relations could sustain. Since then, Canadian policy has appeared to retreat from the essential aim of the suffocation strategy. Now, as the third UN Special Session on Disarmament (UNSSOD III) is about to take place, the importance of capping or regulating nuclear weapons technology is no longer found on the stated agenda of Canadian arms control and disarmament policy.

What brought about this change? From the government's perspective, the credibility of Canadian policy lies in correctly assessing the present status of the superpower relationship. To remain influential on matters of strategic arms control, middle powers like Canada must govern their actions by closely identifying what is achievable. To those impatient with the inherent restraint such an approach demands, this answer seems more a rationalization for saying little than an explanation. They would suggest that the growing reticence Canadian officials have shown over the past decade to pronounce publicly on nuclear weapons development and modernization stems from an absence of political will on Canada's part; it cannot be ascribed entirely to the imperatives of superpower political relations. Answering this question requires a description of the broad contours of Canadian policy over the last decade in arms control and disarmament, with the main focus on the nuclear arms race and strategic stability. Official statements should be examined against a backdrop of international developments and other factors that may be pertinent to an explanation of the reluctance to keep the objectives of the suffocation strategy at the forefront of Canadian policy.

UNSSOD I (1978) and UNSSOD II (1982)

At UNSSOD I, the "strategy of suffocation" put forward by Trudeau consisted of four main principles: a comprehensive test ban to impede the further development of nuclear explosive devices; an agreement to stop the flight-testing of all new strategic delivery vehicles; an agreement to prohibit all production of fissionable material for nuclear weapons purposes; and a agreement to limit, and then progressively to reduce, military spending on new strategic nuclear weapons systems.[2] The strategy of suffocation was, in effect,a purely technical kind of arms-control approach. If everyone simultaneously turned the screws a notch tighter on restricting weapons development, the effect on halting the arms race would be dramatic and immediate. But was it possible, both technically and politically, given contemporary developments in nuclear arms control?

For years, of course, a comprehensive nuclear test ban (CTB) has been regarded by proponents to be the single most effective means of ending the nuclear arms race. Canadian policy regarded the negotiation of a CTB to be a "fundamental and abiding objective." As Britain, the U.S. and the U.S.S.R. had embarked in 1977 on a round of trilateral negotiations on a CTB (only to be broken off in 1980), this aspect of the suffocation strategy was very much in keeping with the view at the time that an agreement on nuclear testing was within reach. Meanwhile, the strategy's second principle — stopping the flight-testing of "all new strategic delivery vehicles" — was closely aligned to the language and agenda of the Soviet-American Strategic Arms Limitation Talks (SALT). SALT I, signed in 1972, had sought to limit the numbers of delivery vehicles for strategic nuclear weapons (SNDVs), although it did not, significantly, attempt to cap or reduce the number of actual nuclear warheads carried by the SNDVs. But SALT II, which was still under negotiation at the time of UNSSOD I, attempted to tackle this problem by imposing an upper limit to the number of warheads certain categories of missiles would be permitted to carry. The number would depend on how many warheads had already been flight-tested on the missile. In discussing this type of limitation, both superpowers were expressing confidence that restricting flight-tests of ballistic missiles was both possible and verifiable by existing national technical means, even to the level of counting the missiles' warheads.

The prohibition on the production of fissionable material for nuclear weapons purposes, the third point of the Trudeau strategy of suffocation, was an idea that would have had its greatest impact in the realm of nuclear non-proliferation by stopping the horizontal spread of nuclear weapons through strict control of fissile material. In terms of the nuclear weapons states (NWS), such a cut-off would be difficult to verify because the Nuclear Non-Proliferation Treaty (NPT) of 1968 gave the NWS permission to exclude their military reactors and enrichment facilities from the safeguards required by the International Atomic Energy Agency (IAEA). This exemption would have likely had to have been abolished if the cut-off proposal was not to be rejected as discriminatory and one-sided in the obligations it sought to impose. The final point of the strategy, the agreement to limit and reduce military spending on "new strategic nuclear weapons systems," would have run into the extraordinary difficulties not only of obtaining accurate data on the level of spending, but also of reaching any sort of comparability of budgets. While this idea has never entirely left the international disarmament agenda as a possible means of halting the arms race, there has been no discernible progress to date towards its implementation.

Still, the sentiment expressed by the suffocation strategy was not out of step with the times. Although the Committee on the Present Danger had just been formed in the United States, and congressional unhappiness at the direction of the SALT II process was starting to rear its head, detente had not yet died. The possibility of an incremental, across-the-board suffocation, applied through technical means, could be seen by arms-control advocates as plausibly joining forces with the bilateral SALT process to slowly cut off the air to new weapons development, which in turn provided the fuel for a never-ending nuclear arms race.

Yet many events occurred between 1978 and the coming to power in Washington of the new Reagan administration in January 1981 that would make the suffocation strategy, with all its flaws, less politically palatable only a couple of years after it was proposed. To list just a few items that sounded the death-knell for superpower detente in that period:

- in 1979, SALT II was signed, but, lacking support in Congress, was never submitted for ratification
- in December 1979, NATO reached its so-called two-track decision on the modernization of theatre nuclear weapons in Europe, with deployment of cruise and Pershing missiles to begin in 1983
- shortly thereafter, the U.S.S.R. invaded Afghanistan
- the Second NPT Review Conference in 1980 failed to produce a consensus document, since the trilateral negotiations on a CTB had by then been virtually disbanded, and this was seen as an abandonment by the NWS of any effort to end the "vertical" expansion of their own nuclear arsenals
- the first Review Conference of the Biological and Toxin Weapons Convention (BWC) was also torn at that time by charges that Soviet biological weapons research was being clandestinely carried out at Sverdlovsk
- allegations had arisen in U.S. official circles that chemical agents, supplied by the U.S.S.R., had been used in Southeast Asia
- the Mutual and Balanced Force Reduction (MBFR) talks in Vienna regarding NATO and Warsaw Pact conventional weapons had bogged down under a general torpor brought on by the inability to achieve agreement, even on basic data questions

Meanwhile, the Reagan administration came to office with the view that SALT II was "fatally flawed" and promised to rectify the perceived decline in America's nuclear deterrent forces and global power with a massive, across-the-board military build-up. Arms control would not be permitted to get in the way by allowing the Soviets to "codify" the advantages they had wrought, both from the SALT process and from their own build-up in land-based nuclear forces, (such as the long-range SS-18 and SS-19 and the intermediate-range

SS-20 missiles). And in Geneva, the Committee on Disarmament appeared to be dealing with intangibles by focusing on four areas that promised to yield little in the way of concrete results: chemical weapons; negative security assurances (commitments by the nuclear powers not to use nuclear weapons against non-nuclear-weapons states); radiological weapons (such as enhanced radiation, or neutron, bombs); and a comprehensive program for disarmament.

Amid these events, and overshadowed by the worsening East-West climate, the suffocation strategy for nuclear arms control could not be expected to have been reiterated at the second UNSSOD meeting in 1982 as though its four principles were carved in stone and immutable. That would have meant ignoring the limits on what middle-power countries like Canada can hope to achieve when the atmosphere between the superpowers turns icy. In April 1981, external affairs minister Mark MacGuigan, wrote to the UN Secretary-General expressing his hope that the forthcoming UNSSOD II meeting would give the highest priority to continuation of the SALT process, conclusion of a multilateral Comprehensive Test Ban treaty, and of an agreement on the prohibition of chemical weapons, evolution of an effective non-proliferation regime based on the Non-Proliferation Treaty, and promotion of concrete measures to limit and reduce conventional forces.[3] MacGuigan's letter seemed to reflect a realization that the suffocation strategy could not have any effect unless there was an ongoing SALT process. In other words, the strategy had presupposed an extant level of political understanding, a dialogue between the superpowers, which hitherto had not been clearly spelled out as an essential assumption or precondition of the strategy.

As UNSSOD II approached there were two developments indicating a change of perspective vis-à-vis the proper emphasis of Canadian arms control and disarmament policy.

In April 1982, the House of Commons Standing Committee on External Affairs and National Defence (SCEAND) tabled its report on Security and Disarmament.[4] Possibly because of awareness of the urgent need to re-establish political dialogue between the superpowers, the report recommended that the Canadian government adopt a "Twin Pillars" approach to disarmament in UNSSOD II and other disarmament talks. The first "pillar" would include a "strong call for urgent negotiations on strategic armaments limitation and reduction as soon as possible, and for early progress in the U.S.-Soviet negotiations on the limitation of intermediate-range nuclear forces in Europe." The second "pillar" addressed more specifically the need to improve confidence-building measures along a generally multilateral route. In particular, this pillar would stress:

> ...the pursuit in UNSSOD II and elsewhere of rapid progress towards improvement in world political conditions; the establishment of confidence-building measures and crisis-management systems; and the negotiation of effective and verifiable measures of arms control and disarmament including a comprehensive test ban, prohibitions on chemical weapons, the prohibition of weapons for outer space, *a verifiable ban on new weapons based on new scientific principles or new technologies*, and regional force reductions under an MBFR agreement and similar accords. [author's emphasis].[5]

Six members of the committee issued a dissenting minority report, urging Canada to press for a strategy of suffocation at UNSSOD II as a continuation of the policy put forward by Trudeau in 1978.[6] SCEAND's second "pillar" did, however, contain part of the strategy, especially in the reference to "a verifiable ban on new weapons based on new scientific principles or new technologies." Still, both the majority and minority reports were likely inspired by the same source: the growing alarm at the Reagan administration's approach to nuclear weapons and strategic modernization, particularly the MX missile, amid a virtually complete absence of serious arms control negotiation between the superpowers and a new round of missile deployments on both sides in Europe. The minority report's advocacy of continued adherence to the four principles of the suffocation strategy was further inspired by the growing groundswell of support among various constituencies in the United States for the "freeze" movement and for the no-first-use pledge in NATO's nuclear planning.

The second development was the announcement of cruise-missile testing by Trudeau in a speech delivered a month later, in May 1982, at the University of Notre Dame. Trudeau spoke of the response to the suffocation strategy: "In the absence of a positive response from any quarter, the Canadian Government subsequently endorsed NATO's two-track approach — seeking to improve our defensive position by preparing to introduce new intermediate range weapons in Europe, while at the same time pursuing arms reductions negotiations."[7] Consequently, the Canadian government would allow the testing of the cruise missile (a decision duly formalized in February 1983 through an exchange of notes). Was there an inconsistency between Trudeau's earlier nuclear suffocation strategy and the proposal of a framework agreement under which cruise missile testing in Canada would be authorized? It seemed to some that Canadian arms-control policy was now being defined to complement NATO diplomatic requirements, with particular attention to the call for alliance unity in the face of forthcoming deployments of new missile systems in western Europe.

It was clear that, in light of these and other developments, the Canadian approach at UNSSOD II in 1982 would have to be different from that at UNSSOD I. This was indeed borne out in June, when Trudeau repeated his earlier argument for a strategy of suffocation. Now, however, he suggested that it be "enfolded into a more general policy of stabilization" which would have two complementary components: "the current approach aimed at achieving a stable nuclear balance at lower levels; and the strategy of suffocation aimed at inhibiting the development of new nuclear weapons systems."[8] But "stabilization" can have two possible interpretations in the arms-control context. It could mean, for example, stabilizing, through political confidence-building measures, the U.S.-U.S.S.R. relationship, which appeared to be rapidly descending into a nadir of mutual accusation and mistrust. Canadian ambassador Arthur Menzies was quoted shortly before the UNSSOD II meeting as saying that Canada can work only behind the scenes to "try and influence the two superpowers to get back to the bargaining table and to have confidence in each other."[9] But stabilization could also mean identifying pragmatically those weapons systems which, from a pure arms-control technical perspective, threaten to unbalance the superpowers' nuclear-deterrent relationship. Here, Trudeau proposed that an early start be made on a treaty banning all weapons from outer space, a theme he would develop further in his peace initiative in late 1983 and early 1984.

Trudeau's UNSSOD II speech in June 1982 included the suggestion that "the international community should address itself to verification as one of the most significant factors in disarmament negotiations in the 1980s." Canada, Trudeau said, would allocate more funds for arms control and disarmament initiatives, particularly in the field of verification. A few weeks later, on July 7, external affairs minister Mac-Guigan stated that the new initiatives were "directly related to two specific Canadian priorities: to promote the realization of a comprehensive nuclear test ban treaty; and to assist in the preparation of a chemical weapons convention."[10] The thrust of the initiatives was further elaborated by MacGuigan at a Pugwash meeting ("Pugwash" refers to a movement of scientists from East and West dedicated to the prevention of nuclear war), on July 16:

> We will also institutionalize an expanding Canadian role in verification issues, in order to utilize effectively expertise in several government departments and in the private sector in the negotiation of agreements on nuclear, chemical and conventional weapons systems. I'm referring in particular to expertise in seismology, nuclear safeguards, remote sensing, toxicology and protective measures against chemical weapons, and communication satellites.[11]

To this end, a "substantial" increase would be made in the Disarmament Fund of the Department of External Affairs. But on the whole, UNSSOD II did not achieve as much as the Canadian government and many non-governmental observers had originally hoped, with the exception of agreement on establishing the World Disarmament Campaign, a UN program of disarmament education.

Aftermath of UNSSOD II

After the conclusion of UNSSOD II, the Canadian ambassador to the UN Committee on Disarmament in Geneva presented Canada's position to the committee at the outset of its summer session in August 1982. In Canada's view, the committee should focus its main attention on three substantive areas — chemical weapons, a comprehensive test ban and outer space.[12] These priorities were agreed to by other nations.

In lieu of any move from the superpowers, Canada's position seemed to be a pragmatic and achievable narrowing-down of the avenues where it could make a contribution to the arms control and disarmament process generally. The intermediate-range nuclear forces (INF) talks had resumed in November 1981 and START (President Reagan's designation of the Geneva negotiations as the Strategic Arms Reduction Talks) discussions had got underway at the beginning of 1982. Although no progress was reported in either of these negotiations, at least the talks were continuing. In addition, while SALT II had never been formally ratified, both sides had agreed informally to abide by the main provisions of the SALT agreements. At the Committee on Disarmament in Geneva, external affairs minister Allan MacEachen singled out "particular issues on which Canada believes progress should be made in 1983."[13] These issues were: a comprehensive test ban; a strengthening of the non-proliferation treaty; the negotiation of a chemical weapons convention; and the development of a legal regime and verification techniques for a treaty preventing an arms race in outer space.

In the same speech, MacEachen also spelled out in detail Canada's position on the issue of intermediate-range nuclear missiles in Europe and the NATO two-track policy. It was clear that the decision to allow cruise-missile testing in Canada had caused the government considerable concern, and it was felt that greater public explanation and justification was required. Shortly after MacEachen's speech, Trudeau himself issued an "Open Letter" on May 9, 1983 on "Canada's Position on Testing Cruise Missiles and on Disarmament," in which he said: "Having declared our support for the two-track strategy, Canada should bear its fair share of the burden which that policy imposes upon the NATO alliance." Further:

> I hope that my explanation of our policy will have established that, were we to agree to collaborate in testing the guidance system of the cruise missile, it would be because of our solidarity with the other Western democracies, in a world which has turned a deaf ear to our suggested strategy of suffocation.[14]

This sort of explanation has, of course, given rise to all types of arguments and disputes over whether Canadian cruise-missile testing was thereby exclusively linked to INF missile deployments or whether it reflected a commitment to alliance solidarity, and as such was a contribution to nuclear deterrence. But there is absolutely no doubt that the decision to allow cruise testing was connected to the NATO two-track philosophy, which integrates weapons deployments and arms control into a perspective on deterrence. Enhancing deterrence through weapons testing cannot be considered independently from the relationship of the weapons system to the arms-control process and the seeking of stability through it.

This justification of cruise-missile testing in terms of the two-track philosophy was to colour Canada's approach to arms control and disarmament considerably but, at the time, it had not sunk completely into Trudeau's own approach. As the autumn approached and the time drew near for the INF deployment decision — and as NATO began preparing the way psychologically and militarily with the Montebello decision in late October 1983 to reduce the NATO nuclear arsenal in Europe by 1,400 warheads on nuclear artillery shells, nuclear-capable aircraft and short-range missiles over the next five to six years — Trudeau addressed a Conference on "Strategies for Peace and Security in the Nuclear Age" at Guelph on October 27.[15] In his speech, he said he would add a "third rail" to the existing two-track NATO policy. This would be a third rail "of high-level political energy to speed the course of agreement — a third rail through which might run the current of our broader political purposes, including our determination not to be intimidated."

Trudeau also referred to a "strategy of political confidence-building," which would invoke "steps that reduce tensions caused by uncertainty about objectives, or caused by fear of the consequences of failure; steps that mitigate hostility and promote a modicum of mutual respect; steps that build an authentic confidence in man's ability to survive on this planet." He revealed that what he had in mind was regular high-level dialogue based on openness regarding intentions, mutual respect, reciprocal acknowledgement of legitimate security needs, a determined approach to crisis management, and incentives for flexibility.

In some ways, the speech was a testimony to the state of East-West relations at that time. The reasons for needing "confidence-building measures of a political nature" were not hard to find in the autumn of 1983. The INF talks were at a standstill and the deployment date of

December 1983 for cruise and Pershing missiles was looming. All summer there had been unrest in Europe over the forthcoming deployment, and the Soviet Union, under a succession of ageing and dying leaders, was unable to do anything bold or imaginative to break the impasse. They insisted on retaining a clear numerical advantage in INF systems while at the same time seeking to block the NATO deployments and to this end, the Soviets tried to play on the clearly visible disgruntlement and political difficulties some NATO governments in Europe were experiencing. Tensions had further heightened that September with the downing of the Korean Airlines passenger jetliner by the Soviets. And in October the U.S.S.R. announced planned additional deployments of shorter-range INF missiles in the German Democratic Republic and Czechoslovakia.

The only sign of optimism in East-West arms-control relations was the upcoming Conference on Confidence- and Security-Building Measures and Disarmament in Europe (CCSBMDE), established at the Madrid Follow-up meeting of the Conference on Security and Cooperation in Europe (CSCE) and slated to open the following January in Stockholm. On November 1, 1983, Michael Pitfield, in a speech to the First Committee of the UN, referred to these upcoming talks and, with respect to the committee's own agenda, stated:

> In this forum, our objective is surely to reinforce the mul-
> tilateral approach to arms control and disarmament. What
> we do must contribute to multilateralism and not detract
> from it. Our efforts, essentially, must be directed to estab-
> lishing consensus and to working out practical frameworks
> for negotiations which will result in tangible arms control
> and disarmament measures. We must continue with the
> necessary preliminary work for the time when an improved
> atmosphere permits the successful conclusion of these
> negotiations.[16]

Pitfield then outlined the priorities of the Canadian government in the arms control and disarmament process. Canadian priorities, he said, are:

> (1) to support strongly negotiations to limit and reduce
> nuclear arms; (2) to promote early progress towards the

> realization of a multilateral comprehensive test ban treaty; (3) to assist in preparing a convention which would completely prohibit chemical weapons; (4) to promote the evolution of an effective non-proliferation regime based on the Non-Proliferation Treaty; (5) to work towards the objective of prohibiting the development, testing and deployment of all weapons for use in outer space; and (6) to participate actively in negotiations to limit and reduce conventional forces.

He then went on to refer specifically to nuclear weapons:

> On the urgent nuclear issues, our objective is twofold: the inhibition of the development of new weapons systems and the reduction of nuclear arsenals designed to achieve a stable balance at lower levels. We are also considering making proposals for other international agreements which could help to restrict destabilizing qualitative developments in strategic technology.

It is this specific reference to inhibiting the development of new nuclear weapon systems and restricting destabilizing strategic technology that merits attention. The Trudeau peace initiative, launched only days earlier with the Guelph speech, was able to flesh out this concern about qualitative improvements in nuclear arms and their implications for strategic stability.

The Trudeau Peace Initiative

It is not the intention to recount here the story of the Trudeau Peace Initiative, which has been described in detail elsewhere.[17] Briefly, after his speech in Guelph, Trudeau visited NATO capitals in Western Europe. Upon returning, he outlined in Montreal on November 13 the proposals for world disarmament that he had put forward during the discussions with NATO leaders. The proposals included: a five-powers conference of nuclear states within the next year; a strengthening of the nuclear non-proliferation treaty to include nations other than the present signatories; the need for new initiatives to advance the MBFR talks; a ban on the testing and deployment of high altitude anti-satellite weapons systems; and an agreement to restrict the "excessive mobility" of intercontinental ballistic missiles.[18]

After his travels abroad to publicize the initiative in various capitals, Trudeau summed up his efforts for peace and security in a statement in the House of Commons on February 9, 1984.[19] Canadian insistence that the opening of the Stockholm Conference be held at the foreign minister level, he said, was an important factor in re-establishing "broad political contact" between the countries of East and West after the "acrimonious" conclusion of the Madrid CSCE Conference in September 1983. He also stated: "From a confrontational deadlock where INF deployment must continue, and negotiations must be restored, only the 'third rail' of political confidence and communication can ensure an early and constructive outcome." With respect once again to the original strategy of suffocation, Trudeau said that Canada would circulate at the current session of the Conference on Disarmament three proposals designed "to gear down the momentum of new technology". These proposals would be: "a ban on high-altitude anti-satellite systems; restrictions on the mobility of ICBMs; improvements in the verifiability of future strategic weapons." This decision was reached by Canadian officials after "further consultations" with the NATO allies.

The proposal for a five-powers conference did not materialize. However, the NPT-strengthening proposal may have had some effect in bringing about a tacit understanding between the U.S. and the Soviet Union not to jeopardize the chances of the Third Review Conference of the NPT (scheduled for 1985) reaching an agreement on a final document. There have been suggestions that Trudeau's peace initiative led to a NATO high-level review of East-West relations and a later commitment from NATO to try and break the logjam at the MBFR talks on conventional force reduction in Europe.[20] In any event, the MBFR talks did proceed to the next round in March 1984 and the Stockholm Conference opened on schedule in spite of the Soviet walk-out from the bilateral superpower arms-control talks in Geneva in December 1983.

The Trudeau approach, despite its lack of success in generating substantive responses from the five powers, particularly the two superpowers, did contain a level of detail which suggested a far greater

Canadian involvement in the nuclear weapons and arms-control debate than had occurred since Howard Green's tenure in the early 1960s as secretary of state for external affairs.[21] Implicit in this approach is the suggestion that Canada felt it both important and necessary for NATO allies to pronounce independently on current trends in strategic weapons technology. The call for a ban on high-altitude anti-satellite (ASAT) systems flew directly in the face of U.S. Air Force preferences and the U.S. Department of Defense's own effort to push continued ASAT research and development funding through Congress. Similarly, the call for restrictions on the mobility of ICBMs was obviously a comment on the debate in U.S. strategic circles that started with the controversy over the many proposed basing modes for the MX missile — some of which were mobile — and expanded into questions regarding the stability-enhancing potential of mobile, single-warhead ICBMs such as the proposed "Midgetman" missile.[22]

The Mulroney Era

In the aftermath of the peace initiative, and with Trudeau's resignation from the leadership of the Liberal Party shortly thereafter, a brief interregnum under John Turner ensued before the Conservative Party was elected to office in September 1984. None of the initiatives, rhetoric, or jolt of political energy survived the transition to Brian Mulroney's government. In fact, the main impression given in the Mulroney government's early speeches is that of a concentration mainly on the multilateral arms control and disarmament process. In September 1984, in a speech to St. Francis Xavier University, the new prime minister stressed Canada's commitment to increasing Canada's "positive and constructive" influence in the multilateral process.[23] He added: "It is in these forums that Canada can work most effectively to reduce tensions, to alleviate conflict, and to create the conditions for a lasting peace."

The new political masters in Ottawa took a cautious approach to arms control and disarmament at the United Nations as well. When external affairs minister Joe Clark addressed the 39th Session of the UN General Assembly on September 25, he said: "Multilateral efforts, led and encouraged by the medium and smaller-sized countries, can help improve the atmosphere, and can put specific, workable ideas on the agenda."[24] Generally, the Conservative government seemed content, in the first year or so at least, to have its newly appointed ambassador for disarmament, Douglas Roche, act as its chief representative and spokesman on these issues. In a speech before the UN's First Committee on October 30, 1984, Roche remarked: "The message I bring is this: the determination of the Canadian government to take practical measures, at home and abroad, to make inch-by-inch progress in meeting the threat of war, particularly nuclear war. We believe in sure-footed steps towards collective security and mutuality of interests in equitable development."[25] It was not long, however, before the new ambassador was faced with three resolutions at the UN on the desirability of a comprehensive "freeze" in the development and deployment of nuclear weapons, an approach the Canadian government and its allies rejected in the subsequent voting.[26]

Towards the end of 1984, there was news that the superpowers were about to consider re-establishing some form of talks on arms-control issues. In January 1985, Secretary of State George Shultz and Foreign Minister Andrei Gromyko met to finalize the format for the new "Nuclear and Space Arms Talks" (NST), a tripartite set of negotiations that would involve separate groups dealing with strategic offensive weapons, intermediate-range weapons and "space and defence" issues. In the House of Commons on January 21, 1985, Clark welcomed the talks — scheduled to begin in Geneva on March 15 — as well as the announcement that a principal theme would involve discussions on the relationship between offensive and defensive systems.[27] He said: "It is appropriate that the defensive systems of each side, both actual and potential, figure in these negotiations." He then went on to say:

> However, actual development and deployment of space-based ballistic missile defence systems by either side would transgress the limits of the ABM Treaty as currently constituted. That could have serious implications for arms control and would therefore warrant close and careful attention by all concerned. We welcome in this regard President Reagan's affirmation that the U.S.A. would not proceed beyond research without discussion and negotiation.

This was essentially the first comment on the emerging issue of strategic defences based on advanced or "exotic" technologies. The issue elicited comment about the restriction on development and deployment imposed by the ABM Treaty on ballistic missile defence systems. However, the reference to the ABM Treaty "as currently constituted" suggested that , in principle, the Treaty might at some time be modified by mutual agreement of the superpowers to loosen existing constraints. Despite the fact that the debate between the "broad" versus the "narrow" interpretation of the ABM Treaty was not to emerge full-blown until October 1985, there were certainly hints that Canadian officials were reluctant to close the door entirely on the future introduction of such systems under certain conditions. What those conditions might be, however, has never been made exceptionally clear.

The first Reagan-Mulroney summit (now known as the Shamrock summit) was to take place in the middle of March 1985. Since the Mulroney government was pledged to the improvement of U.S.-Canada bilateral relations, and since a Green Paper on foreign policy was in preparation and a White Paper on defence promised for the near future, there was little incentive for the new government to "interfere" at this time in the new arms-control talks between the superpowers. Given this perception and political environment, the multilateral route seemed to be the most propitious way of developing an approach to arms control and disarmament. But the issue of strategic defence, whether space-based, as conjured up by the White House visionaries, or ground-based, as thought more realistic by those who recalled the largely futile ABM efforts of the 1960s, was not going to disappear.

Between March and October 1985, three developments of relevance to arms control and disarmament policy began to force the government from its somewhat quiescent position. First, only a fortnight after the great success of the Shamrock summit, Defense Secretary Caspar Weinberger issued his invitation for U.S. allies to join in the Strategic Defense Initiative (SDI) and compete for research and development contracts. This put the Canadian government on the spot. Hitherto, the president's vision had remained confined to military and defence circles in the United States, and Canada had not been forced to evaluate it publicly, except to suggest, as Clark did earlier in the year, that Canada assumed that everything concerning strategic defence research would be discussed between the superpowers in the context of the Geneva negotiations and would be fully consistent with the provisions of the Outer Space Treaty (1967) and the Anti-Ballistic Missile (ABM) Treaty (1972).

The government's response was twofold: first, to commission the Special Joint Parliamentary Committee on Canada's International Relations, chaired by Tom Hockin and Jean-Maurice Simard, to consider the Weinberger invitation and issue an interim recommendation by August 23, 1985, and second to instruct career civil servant Arthur Kroeger to conduct his own evaluation of the SDI program and the role Canada should or could play in this regard. A declassified version of the Kroeger report gives the impression, despite the deletions, of being rather well-disposed to the ambitions of the SDI and the desirability of Canadian involvement.[28] The interim report of the parliamentary committee was rather more circumspect, laying out the pros and cons of the main options facing the government. Still, it did seem to emphasize, if only in length of treatment alone, the option calling for no direct government-to-government participation while allowing private firms to compete for SDI-related contracts from the U.S. Department of Defense.[29] The result, of course, was Prime Minister Mulroney's announcement on September 7 that: "After careful and detailed consideration the Government of Canada has concluded that Canada's own policies and priorities do not warrant a government-to-government effort in support of SDI research." However, "private companies and institutions interested in participating in the program will continue to be free to do so."[30]

The second development came in mid-October with the Reagan administration's "discovery" that the ABM Treaty did not in fact preclude the development and testing of ABM systems and their components. Whether present-day or future, "exotic" technologies were used or contemplated made no difference. Only deployment of the fully tested systems would be banned; even then, some thought that this new, "broad" interpretation of the ABM Treaty allowed the deployment to go ahead as long as the technologies were exotic and a promise to discuss the deployment with the Soviet Union was fulfilled. This view had the arms-control community in the United States in a turmoil, and it reverberated throughout many NATO capitals. The effect would be to force allied governments to take sides in the debate and pronounce publicly on the role of the ABM Treaty in restricting strategic defences.

The third development was Prime Minister Mulroney's first speech on arms control and disarmament issues, given before the Consultative Group on Disarmament and Arms Control Affairs in October 1985.[31] In this speech, Mulroney reiterated the six specific objectives of his government within the field of arms control and disarmament. They were essentially identical to those listed by Senator Pitfield in his speech to the First Committee on November 1, 1983. The biggest difference lay in what was left out. Pitfield's speech had made reference to "the inhibition of the development of new weapons systems" and indicated that the government was hoping to establish "international agreements which could restrict destabilizing qualitative developments in strategic technology." This nuclear arms control dimension was entirely missing from the Mulroney speech before the Consultative Group two years later; the final vestiges of the suffocation strategy were gone.

To be fair, however, the Mulroney government had a different set of preoccupations within a very different political environment surrounding superpower dialogue over arms control. Yearly reports were issuing from the White House alleging Soviet non-compliance with existing arms-control and disarmament treaties.[32] Some of these allegations seemed based more on political concerns than hard evidence, especially the charge that the Soviet Union had supplied chemical warfare agents and weapons to its Southeast Asian allies.[33] Charges that the large radar built near the Soviet town of Krasnoyarsk constituted a violation of the ABM Treaty were rather better-founded and extended beyond the Reagan administration to various arms control commentators.[34] The Mulroney government also had the difficulty of being presented with the Weinberger invitation just when it was trying to re-establish a favoured position within the inner councils of the White House. The Conservatives had come to power with promises to "undo" the damage they thought the Trudeau years had wrought in Canada-U.S. relations. Free trade with the United States was something they were considering seriously as a way of putting the relationship on a newer, more cordial footing. As a result, U.S. insistence on continuing nuclear testing despite the Soviet moratorium imposed in August 1985 elicited little in the way of comment during the quarterly bilateral exchanges between external affairs minister Joe Clark and secretary of state George Shultz, which had been established at the Quebec summit in March 1985.[35] And, after parliamentary hearings before the Standing Committee on External Affairs and National Defence on the subject of the North American Aerospace Defence (NORAD) agreement, the two heads of state signed a five-year renewal of the agreement with little fanfare at the second Shamrock summit meeting in March 1986, despite the concerns of some witnesses that Canadian involvement in a U.S. strategic defence system through NORAD was by no means remote.[36]

Partly because of the recriminatory environment and partly not wanting to clash head-on with the United States over strategic arms control issues, the main effort of Canadian policy was geared towards emphasizing compliance with existing treaties, stressing the need for improved and effective verification of arms control, and pursuing these objectives through multilateral diplomacy.[37] Canada concentrated its diplomatic activities and consensus-building skills on preserving existing multilateral treaties such as the Nuclear Non-Proliferation Treaty and the Biological (and Toxin) Weapons Convention, both of which were subject to pressures generated from charges that obligations undertaken by some of the parties to the treaties were not being fully observed. Rebuilding political consensus at the periodic review conferences to affirm the treaties' original design was a central Canadian arms control preoccupation. Another was the building of political confidence between East and West at the Stockholm Conference, which produced an agreement on European confidence- and security-building measures on September 19, 1986.

Bilaterally, the main preoccupation of the Mulroney government throughout 1986 and into 1987 on issues of superpower arms-control was to comment in as even-handed a way as possible on the need for both the U.S. and the Soviet Union to comply with the SALT accords and the ABM Treaty, restrictively understood. In the House of Commons in early 1986, external affairs minister Joe Clark described the state of Soviet-American nuclear arms control negotiations, outlining the avenues for "practical contributions" by Canada to this process:

> Canada firmly supports the regime created by the ABM
> treaty and the existing SALT agreements on limiting

strategic forces. Our stance towards SDI research is rooted in the need to conform strictly with the provisions of the ABM Treaty. We will continue to urge the parties to these treaties to do nothing to undermine their integrity, but rather work to reinforce their status and authority.[38]

Statements such as these on treaty compliance were clearly aimed at both superpowers equally. Clark's concern over the fate of the ABM Treaty was certainly legitimate. The unresolved issue of the Soviet radar at Krasnoyarsk had given White House SDI enthusiasts the lever of Soviet non-compliance with which to begin prying apart the Treaty's constraints in areas such as development, testing and eventually deployment of ABM systems based on "other physical principles." Meanwhile, the SALT accords were also coming under fire in the United States. Again, the lever was ostensibly provided by allegations of Soviet non-compliance, particularly over Soviet insistence that their soon-to-be-deployed land-based missile, designated the SS-25, was a modernization of an existing missile already limited by the SALT II agreement, not a new one, and therefore permitted.

This and other SALT-related allegations culminated in Washington's announcement on May 27, 1986 that the U.S. administration would no longer consider itself bound by the numerical limits on strategic systems imposed by SALT II. Joe Clark's response to this announcement emphasized that Canada took "very seriously the U.S.A. charges of Soviet non-compliance with arms control agreements."[39] He expressed the hope, however, that, before the president's decision would take effect late in 1986, the two superpowers would "reach an understanding on means to ensure continued respect for the limits of the SALT II accord," until such time as a new agreement on strategic weapons replaced it. Further, just as Canada had raised the issue of alleged non-compliance with the Soviet Union, so too had the government conveyed to the Americans "our views on the importance of the U.S.A. abiding by the provisions of the SALT II agreement." Six months later, on November 28, the U.S. took action to exceed one of the limits specified in the agreement. On this occasion, Clark issued a statement regretting the administration's decision.[40] Until the Geneva negotiations put a new accord in place, he said, "we consider the interests of nuclear arms control and strategic stability are best served by both the U.S.A. and the U.S.S.R. continuing to abide by the provisions of the SALT II agreement."

But if much of the Mulroney government's public position was caught up in the cross-fire of non-compliance allegations, the Reykjavik summit between the superpowers on October 12 and 13, 1986, produced a different headache. One of the central ideas put forward at the summit was to scrap all strategic ballistic missiles, leaving only bombers as nuclear-weapon delivery vehicles (SNDVs) with loadings of short-range attack missiles (SRAMs), gravity bombs and long-range air-launched cruise missiles. The reaction from the NATO allies upon learning of this proposal was fast and furious: to them, such whimsical tinkering with the fundamentals of nuclear deterrence constituted an example of superpower irresponsibility and high-handedness. Had the superpowers gone through with their plan, its consequence would have been a world filled with cruise missiles. For countries like Canada, whose territory falls in the main flight paths of strategic bombers and their warheads, the threat posed from this source would increase dramatically in the absence of ballistic missiles. Countering this threat through enhanced air defences would entail vast expenditures without any certainty of success, particularly if the radar-evading "stealth" technology is used in more advanced versions of cruise missiles.

After being briefed by U.S. officials at NATO headquarters in Brussels immediately after the summit, Clark commented on the "considerable progress" made at Reykjavik, while pointing out the continuing impasse between the superpowers over the ABM Treaty that brought about the failure of the two sides to reach any agreement.[41] Nevertheless: "We welcome the U.S.A.'s proposal for non-withdrawal from the ABM Treaty for ten years, in parallel with a progressive reduction of strategic offensive forces." Not mentioned in Clark's statement, however, was that this proposal, originally suggested by the Americans some months before the summit, involved cutting strategic and nuclear missiles by 50 per cent in the first five years of the ten-year program and then reducing ballistic missiles to zero by the end of the ten years.[42] A subsequent statement by Clark on October 21 did in fact mention that the two sides had tentatively agreed at Reykjavik to eliminate ballistic missiles completely, only to have differences over ABM Treaty obligations and SDI scuttle the deal.[43] But no further comment on the potential implications for Canadian security was made, apart from the statement that "what happens at the negotiating table between the U.S.S.R. and the U.S.A. has a direct bearing on our own security."

The ramifications of the Reykjavik proposals for Canada were finally elaborated in Clark's remarks before the Standing Committee on External Affairs and International Trade on January 21, 1987:

> A world with fewer ballistic missiles could increase the relative importance of bombers and of cruise missiles. We are studying the implications of that for our air defences. All of this requires us to sustain our full involvement in the consultative process, regardless of the final outcome.[44]

In response to a question concerning sea-launched cruise missiles, a strategic nuclear system currently outside the framework of the START talks, Clark admitted that Canada had not made the suggestion, privately or publicly, that these missiles be included on the agenda of the Geneva negotiations.[45] Later, before the Standing Committee on National Defence on April 28, Clark responded to a similar kind of question regarding Canada's interest in having sea-launched cruise missiles banned or constrained under arms control limits:

> Frankly our view has been that there is not much utility, that it does not work for countries not at the table to try and insert items that are not on the table if the people who make the decisions are going to regard that as being another agenda or potentially counter-productive to the agenda they are pursuing.[46]

The tenor of these remarks suggests a strong reticence to press a Canadian view of nuclear arms control beyond the acknowledged need for continued compliance by the superpowers with existing treaties. The Reykjavik episode demonstrated both the unpreparedness of the government to react to the zero ballistic missile proposal and the lack of consultation preceding it. It also demonstrated the need for Canada to appraise the options for weapons deployment afforded both superpowers through their strategic modernization programs. Reykjavik showed that the course of nuclear arms control can be drastically altered by these options, with results that do not necessarily contribute to the enhancement of strategic stability or to the security interests of Canada.

Another area of concern arising out of this summit involved the relationship between the START negotiations on offensive weapons and the discussion concerning the restrictions imposed on strategic defence by the ABM Treaty. Quite rightly, the governing principle of this relationship should be "stability." Although the Canadian government had largely been preoccupied with the preservation of existing treaties, it had not articulated in detail what Canada would like to see achieved at the nuclear and space talks in Geneva. Nor had it provided an analysis of the much-heralded "transition to defence" advocated by the United States arms control advisors as a central objective at the talks.[47] The only view expressed was the report of the parliamentary secretary to the Secretary of State for External Affairs which told the House of Commons two months later in December that "both super-powers should indeed consider the possibility of jointly and progressively abandoning a deterrent system based on guaranteed mutual destruction through offensive nuclear weapons and opt instead for defensive systems combined with reduced arsenals of offensive weapons."[48] Despite this endorsement, there was still a missing ingredient, an acknowledgement that any move towards less offence combined with more defence could potentially be destabilizing. The prospect of destabilizing the East-West strategic relationship is something that is diametrically opposed to Canadian security interests.

Given the scarcity of comments by senior political officials on this issue, the speech by Prime Minister Brian Mulroney before the North Atlantic Assembly meeting in Quebec City in May 1987 is noteworthy.[49] In this speech, Mulroney noted that "we cannot provide for the needs of the coming decades with the equipment and strategies of past decades." But then he added the following qualification:

> First, extreme care must be taken to ensure that defences are not integrated with existing forces in such a way as to create fears of a first strike. And second, we cannot allow strategic defences to undermine the arms control process and existing agreements: the transition should be mutually agreed upon. Without such mutuality, chaos would follow and stability could crumble.

To these points he added the criteria of cost-effectiveness, survivability and affordability. Together they form the basis on which decisions concerning strategic defence should be assessed. The key is to prevent the erosion of strategic stability through the unilateral deployment of defensive systems. Indeed, a further endorsement of this view came in Mulroney's statement of December 10, 1987 at the conclusion of the Reagan-Gorbachev summit held in Washington. The goal in all areas of Canadian arms control and disarmament policy, he said, is stability — "stability at lower levels of arms, and stability in the relationship between offence and defence."[50]

But details over what constitutes stable deterrence are still elusive. Little else can be found issuing from the government apart from these very occasional statements by the prime minister. For example, on the question of strategic ballistic missile defence, the government's recent White Paper on defence, presented on June 5, 1987, states non-committally: "future decisions on Canada's role, if any, in ballistic missile defence...will have to be considered in light of the impact ballistic missile defence could have on strategic stability and on Canadian security."[51] Yet throughout the section of the White Paper discussing strategic defence, there is no mention of the ABM Treaty or its importance to Canadian security, or, for that matter, the impact of ballistic missile defence deployment on existing arms control treaties. Instead: "Stable deterrence at the strategic level is essential. The Government will continue to contribute to the maintenance of an effective Allied deterrent according to our own independent analysis of the strategic environment."[52] The constituent elements of that stable deterrence are not discussed in any detail, nor is any independent analysis, especially on strategic modernization, offered.

Accordingly, there is reason to suspect that, under Mulroney, Canada has inadvertently undermined its ability to set out useful markers defining the general shape of superpower relations in a way that addresses specific Canadian security interests. The tardiness of the Mulroney government's remarks concerning strategic defence cannot be attributed to any one source. Perhaps it has resulted from the decline in influence of the arms-control voices vis-à-vis those of the defence planners who have been beguiled by the promise of ballistic missile defence and have bought its doctrinal trappings directly from Pentagon and White House SDI enthusiasts. Perhaps the Ottawa policy-makers do believe that there is a need for the transition to a defence-oriented form of nuclear deterrence. It could, however, be attributable simply to a belief at the Prime Minister's Office level that more cautious and prudent language in pronouncing on strategic affairs would be beneficial to other Canadian interests when dealing with the U.S. on a range of non-defence issues. As well, the push for high-tech research into new military uses of space has a constituency in Canada, and this constituency feels that it will not get or keep its foot in the door unless the country is disencumbered of traditional beliefs concerning the nature of mutual assured deterrence. Granted, some of these reasons may be speculative. But it still remains that the government's willingness to elaborate on the problem of nuclear weapons modernization and its impact on Canadian security, arms control and East-West relations has, since the days of the suffocation strategy, been greatly lacking.

Conclusion

With one year remaining in the Mulroney government's term of office, any assessment of what this government is seeking in strategic arms control, or thinks to be achievable, must remain partial and preliminary. That said, there have definitely been changes over the last few years in the shape of Canadian arms control and disarmament policy. Silence on the details of strategic stability seems to have arisen from a reluctance at the higher political levels in Canada to articulate a framework of guiding principles concerning potentially destabilizing weapons systems and technologies. Instead, senior political figures appear to have been guided by the view that it was not Canada's place to tell the superpowers what or what not to discuss and negotiate. Whatever the legitimacy of this view, it would be interesting to speculate how Trudeau might have applied his criteria of suffocation to, for example, the Weinberger invitation on SDI, the U.S. administration's insistence on the "legally correct interpretation" of the ABM treaty, the far-reaching and potentially destabilizing proposals bandied about at the Reykjavik summit meeting in October 1986, and so on.

The role of Canadian territory in U.S.-Soviet strategic considerations has changed since Trudeau's original suffocation speech in 1978.

The most obvious difference has been the revival of interest in anti-ballistic missile technologies, coupled with the possibility that Canadian territory might at some point in the future be required by a U.S.-deployed strategic defence system. But another important difference can be found in the current U.S.-Soviet START negotiations. Unlike the SALT II accord, which imposed some limitations pertaining specifically to the modernization of long-range ballistic missiles, the START proposals would permit every current and future U.S. and Soviet nuclear weapon system.[53] Some of these could have profound implications for strategic stability. Unconstrained development by the superpowers of cruise missile and bomber technology would have a greater impact on specific Canadian security interests than ever before in the past decade because of the requirement for enhanced continental air defences.

Whatever the reasons, new weapons systems and technologies are not being assessed for their impact on arms control. Since all weapons systems can be seen as "shoring up deterrence," in a transition-to-defence era we are no longer able to judge what is stabilizing and destabilizing. A technological optimism often disguised as "prudence" has kept the door open to new technological advances as a hedge against Soviet advances in strategic defence. But this has not been conjoined with arms-control efforts in any meaningful way to produce a policy statement along the lines of that represented by Trudeau's suffocation strategy. The current government's cautious approach may produce artificial limits on the vision of what might be possible in arms control and disarmament. It may also have an impact on Canada's security by not setting out in advance the conditions on which Canada bases its defence needs and priorities and its understanding of what is desirable in strategic nuclear arms control and defence developments.

In summary, the present government has set the limits of its objectives at a lower level than Trudeau attempted with his suffocation speech, especially on the right of third parties to pronounce on the stability impact of new strategic weapons technology. The question is, has this reluctance come from an accurate reading or a misreading of the present political limits of what Canada can achieve in nuclear arms control? Identifying these limits is largely an act of political judgement, which in turn is based on assessments of technical feasibility, doctrinal consistency, alliance solidarity and, perhaps at the end of it all, specific

Canadian security interests. If Canada's arms control and disarmament policies — on the nuclear and strategic level at least — are to be more than a reaction to decisions reached elsewhere, then the government will have to develop more clearly defined objectives in the area of nuclear weapons development and modernization.

6

New Approaches to Security

Ernie Regehr

Military responses to political conflict remain strangely compelling to human beings. More than five million soldiers from more then forty countries are currently fighting in about thirty-five wars.[1] Some of these are low-level military conflicts — on and off again affairs that have gone on for up to four decades — while others are brand new. In fact, except for the periods of the two "Great" European wars, the 1980s are stacking up to be the bloodiest decade, so far, of the twentieth century.[2] While the Iraq-Iran war now, by conservative estimate, passes the one million mark in combat deaths, the industrialized world rallies round to provide both sides with all the firepower they need to continue flirting with oblivion.[3] Before the Soviets and Americans had put their signatures to an agreement to eliminate all intermediate and short-range, land-based nuclear missiles, the military planners of their respective military blocs were making plans to step up deployments of similar missiles at sea or to retarget some of their surplus of long-range missiles to targets formerly covered by those missiles slated for elimination.[4] In southern Africa, where the international comunity is rendered impotent by South African intransigence, the solution offered to the problem of apartheid — at least by weapons suppliers such as Britain — is the arming of the frontline states. And then there is the Canadian North — our sovereignty is challenged, so what do we do if we really want to do something? We propose to arm ourselves with attack-submarines. That these submarines would attack neither friend nor foe, should they find such (of course, they would most likely encounter friends), arouses no concern. Somehow submarines show resolve — finally we are going to do something real.

The Insecurity System

Of course, it is not something real at all — it is an approach to security that is firmly grounded in unreality. The appeal of military "solutions" to political conflict defies rationality. The objective is ostensibly security, but the result is overwhelmingly and unmistakably insecurity. Despite the ever-present potential for nuclear annihilation, the personal insecurity (political represssion and human rights violations) that is the inevitable fruit of militarization,[5] and the devastation caused by the world's endless wars, military responses are habitually sought and touted as solutions. It is a phenomenon that seems to call most strongly for the attentions of psychologists and theologians.

While original sin ought not to be discounted as an explanation for our collective fatal attraction to military prowess, some important explanations are nearer the surface, and thus are also more amenable to political influence.

Not the least of the possible explanations for the enduring habit of turning to military responses to settle political conflict is to be found in vested interests — a lot of people make a lot of money producing military hardware and are in positions to shore up the continuing demand for weapons. No less important is our frequent and utter failure to come up with credible alternatives — South Africa being the pre-eminent example of the bankruptcy of an international community that, apparently devoid of constructive influence, abandons generations of people to the travesty of apartheid.

But it may also be that our collective infatuation with military responses is, after all, not so much an innate obsession as it is an inevitable product of the way in which we arrange or *organize* for our security. A more routine pursuit of non-military solutions to political conflict may not require a reshaping of human nature as much as a rethinking and reorganization of our security institutions. The American researcher Daniel Deudney put it this way: "Fortunately for human survival, the control of nuclear armament requires neither a transformation of human nature, an abolition of the nation-state nor an outburst of universal goodwill."[6] It requires, in particular, an examination of current assumptions about national responsibilities and prerogatives in security arrangements. A look at these assumptions within our own communities can provide an instructive analogy.

If we think of our own community as the world, and of our home as one of the many states in that community, the absurdity of the present international security regime comes into focus. In our own homes we accept certain basic security responsibilities — like locking our doors and windows. These are not only acts of self protection, they are also acts of respect toward our neighbours. Each of us has the responsibility to maintain our home in such a way that it not become a threat to others. If we were in the habit of leaving our windows and doors wide open when we left our homes, we might soon attract burglars and vandals to our community, diminishing not only our own security but also that of our neighbours. Similarly, each household has a responsibility to clean up its garbage, so that it does not become a fire-trap and thus overtax the resources of the fire department or threaten the neighbouring house. These are sensible responsibilities that members of a community must meet, not only for their own immediate benefit, but also for the benefit of the entire community (and thus also for their own long-term benefit).

But when a burglar has come through the door, whether because it was unlocked or through forced entry, security is no longer our individual responsibility. It is then a community responsibility. It is not required of our families that we stock arsenals of weapons and arrange for daily family shooting practice, just to be prepared for whatever may present itself. If the worst happens, our responsibility is to appeal to the community and its police force, which we support with our taxes.

Things obviously work a little differently in the world community. There it is insisted that every house on the block be armed to the teeth to meet all possible threats. Each household stocks an arsenal, trains its inhabitants in the finer points of street fighting, and makes regular trips to the local weapons dealer for new equipment (and to the bank for new credit). It is a formula for chaos and the brutalization of social and political relationships. What would happen to the social relations in our homes if we had to stock weapons to meet all comers? It would not only be the hapless burglars that would be brutalized — the main victims would be our own households. The normal arguments and quarrels, the exercise of parental prerogative and authority, the normal and healthy rebellion of teenagers, all of these social interactions and developments would be radically altered. They would become perverted and destructive as a result of the home's militarization.

That, of course, is precisely what is meant by militarization in the international community. An international-security regime that requires every country to maintain an arsenal to meet all potential threats to its security is a security regime that inevitably, and sometimes it seems irretrievably, brutalizes societies. The militarization of national societies brutalizes them. Heavily militarized societies, without exception, concentrate decision-making in elite circles and deny popular participation in that process. Ruth Sivard's documentation has shown that militarized societies, as surely as the night follows the day, engage in officially sanctioned violence against their citizens.[7] Human rights are violated, civil rights are abrogated — and the weekly grocery money is spent to buy and maintain the weapons.

It is not a system in which disarmament is likely to have much currency. If you are on your own, without the help of police, you must arm yourself — and your neighbours, seeing your arsenal, begin to think that they had better develop their own arsenal just in case you get ideas about them. And then there is no stopping it; one block gets together to form a pact (in the international community we drop the k and call them blocs) against a neighbouring block. The powerful and well-armed swagger out onto the street and sell protection to the weaker neighbours in exchange for loyalty and other privileges. These are not the possible consequences of militarization, they are the inevitable consequences.

It is a reality we ought to have in mind when, for example, we consider the matter of military aid to southern Africa's frontline states. To give Mozambique the volume of military equipment and training which it would need to develop an effective military capacity to counter South African interventions would condemn Mozambique to a level of militarization from which it would take generations to recover. To give Mozambique that level of arms would *not* be sharing her security burden because a critical element of the burden is the burden of militarization. For the donors, military aid is just one more public quarrel about which region of the country should receive the dubious benefits of yet another inefficient, publicly-funded job-creation programme. For Mozambique it is the burden of perverted political and social processes, human rights violations and all the other consequences of militarization.

Obviously, the answer is not to abandon Mozambique; on the contrary, our responsibility is to share its burden. But there are not now effective international means of making Mozambique's security a collective burden. Mozambique is a threatened home in a community without a fire department or a police department.

The existing system is not properly called a security system — it is "the insecurity system," and around the world there is a serious search underway for alternatives to this armed anarchy. If there is one fundamental lesson to be learned from the world's repeated descent into warfare and the preparation for it, it is that nation states acting unilaterally are counterproductive to the pursuit of security. The unilateral pursuit of national security spells insecurity on a global scale. The very idea of security must become attached to a multinational or common perspective, because security is collaborative and must be jointly pursued. It is possible to reorganize the global community in ways to reduce the prejudice toward arming so that we may move concretely toward the goal, as articulated by the Canadian government, of increasing "the security of all countries at progressively lower levels of armaments and forces, both nuclear and conventional."[8]

A fundamental element of lowering levels of armaments is a redefinition of security. Arms were, after all, not simply developed out of cynicism and malice; they were for the most part built out of a desire for security. The build-up of the means of self-destruction is an obviously misguided pursuit of security, but if we do not come to new understandings about the nature of security and about the kind of human behaviour and institutions that are most likely to yield genuine security, it will not be very long — as Leonard Johnson points out in chapter two — before those same arsenals will be rebuilt.

A term most often used to characterize this search for alternative approaches to security is "common security."

Towards a Common Security System

Common security is not a technical term; it has acquired a variety of complementary but differing meanings, almost all of which represent a variation on the theme that "we're all in it together." It is a compelling sentiment — our security really does depend on co-operation rather than competition — but sentiment is not a compelling foundation on which to base alternatives to the insecurity system. Proposals for security alternatives need to be partly attitudinal and conceptual, and partly political and technical. Thinking about, or imagining, new approaches to the pursuit of security is not by definition the abandonment of realism or an escape into utopian realms. Indeed, the search for alternatives is a hard-headed realism that recognizes the unreal expectations of security that are attached to the current "insecurity system." Even so, it is not grand, global blueprints that are called for. Robert Johansen, an American writer and academic who has made a point of envisioning security alternatives, cautions that "our search should be for policies to initiate a process leading toward a new international security order — one which matures as it is gradually demilitarized — rather than for an immediately workable, detailed, alternative system itself."[9]

The word "common," as it is used in the phrase "common security," points to three elements of a more rational and effective global security system. These are characterized here as Whole Earth Security,[10] Mutual Security and Collective Security.

Whole Earth Security

It is an inescapable truth (though not, by virtue of that, necessarily obvious) that our security is common to, and depends on, all areas of human activity and environment. Our security, as individuals and as communities, cannot be separated from our physical environment, from our social and economic order, or from our psychological well-being. Human security requires a "holistic" approach. It is a sentiment that found urgent expression in the report of the World Commission on Environment and Development (better known as "the Bruntland Report," after the Commission head, Gro Harlem Bruntland of Norway)[11]. The Bruntland Report suggests that the chief threat to human security — even survival — is the way in which humans live: uncontrolled population growth, unrestrained energy consumption, pollution, economic inequities, uncontrolled military spending, weapons of mass and environmental destruction, and the list goes on. From this perspective, it is realistic to conclude that current levels of military preparedness are more likely to contribute to human insecurity than they are to a solution to security problems. The $1 trillion and more that the world spends annually on military preparedness is not only a misuse of material resources, it is also a denial of the resources of the spirit and the imagination. It denies the possibility of alternatives, consuming extraordinary human resources in the struggle to sustain funding for military programmes, as well as in the even more consuming effort to devise the weapons systems on which those great sums are spent. The point is made by Canadian Inuit, who have joined others in the Inuit Circumpolar Conference (ICC) to explore northern security alternatives. In addition to Arctic demilitarization and the call for concrete action on arms control and disarmament, the ICC says a peace policy for the Arctic means honouring "the right to peace, the right to development, and the right to a safe and healthy environment,"[12] none of which will be notably elevated by the acquisition of a fleet of nuclear-powered attack-submarines.

This idea of whole earth security is a challenge to engage our imaginations and understanding in the pursuit of new approaches to global security. It is no less than an invitation to explore new visions of a global society. But greater human security need not await the final fulfillment of these visions. In the meantime there is a need for transitional or bridging strategies for the pursuit of security — mutual and collective security arrangements that will not themselves establish the world of our visions, but that offer a plan for working toward the vision of wholeness that the concept of whole earth security involves.

Mutual Security

A first step toward the development of transitional security institutions is the acknowledgement that security is mutual rather than competitive. One's own security is enhanced by the security of others; our security cannot be purchased with the insecurity of others. Mutual

security is the opposite of what might be called "fortress security" —
the attempt, within a hostile environment, to build a fortress to insu-
late oneself from external threats. Indeed, it is the mutuality of security
that renders the pursuit of insular fortress security both futile and
destructive. The economic drain of the militarization that attends the
attempt to build fortress security, as the Bruntland Report suggested,
is itself destructive of human, social and economic security.

The most obvious insecurity in the present international order
derives from the fact that the drive to build weapons of autonomous
national defence makes us all permanent hostages to the threat of mass
destruction, and even annihilation. At the base of this drive rests the
assumption that security, far from being mutual, is exclusive and competitive, that one nation's security can be enhanced by threatening
others. Nuclear weapons, representing the ultimate threat, are relied
upon for ultimate security — they are the final recourse. That is hardly the product of rational realism. Realism cannot but recognize the
fact of the mutuality of security, not to mention the fact that nuclear
and other weapons of mass destruction are inimical to mutual security
and thus can have no rational place in national or international defence
policies.

The principle of mutuality also counsels against the pursuit of national security in isolation. It is ultimately not possible to isolate and
cushion one's self from a hostile environment. Instead, national
security is assured in common with others through measures to trans-
form the environment itself. Reliable peace is the fruit of a just and
reliable international order, and Canada knows this better than most.
Canadian security, as successive Canadian governments have told us,
relies, not on Canada's ability to defend itself militarily, but on an international order that recognizes and respects Canadian sovereignty
and territorial integrity. It follows, therefore, that Canada contributes
to its own defence when it takes measures to bolster a just international order.

Many of the measures that individual states take to support a just
world order, in which peace can flourish and in which people thus find
security, are non-military in nature: equitable trade and investment
policies, sound environmental regulations, development assistance
and so on. This point is central to the report of another world commission, the Independent Commission on Disarmament and Security Is-

sues (better known as the Palme Commission, after its head, the late Olof Palme of Sweden)[13]. The Palme Commisssion's report emphasizes that military preparedness cannot be the sole basis of enduring security, that security cannot be attained through military superiority, and that, indeed, security requires quantitative and qualitative limitations on armaments. The commission affirms the legitimate right of states to security but rejects unilateral military force as a legitimate means of resolving conflicts between states.

Collective Security

The Palme Commission, then, does recognize the legitimacy of limited state force. But inasmuch as it denies the legitimacy of the pursuit of military superiority by individual states or alliances, it suggests a third way in which the word "common" is used in the concept of common security. Specifically, it argues that responsibility for implementing the military elements of effective security measures is a common or shared responsibility. The need to make military-security measures a collective responsibility is consistent with the idea of mutual security. In collective security arrangements, the security of individual states is the business of all states. Far from being evidence of the weakness of individual states, this is evidence of our common humanity and interdependence. In its most visionary form, of course, common security looks forward to the progressive removal of force as an instrument of security. But the idea of collective security speaks to a world that currently falls well short of our visions and thus counsels a transitional strategy designed to minimize and organize the common use of force to deter aggression. The international order on which the security of Canadians (and others) depends is threatened militarily beyond our own borders, and we have a responsibility to respond constructively and collectively to such threats.

"Collective security" is to be distinguished from the "collective defence" policies that animate military alliances such as NATO and the Warsaw Pact. Military alliances in the present international system are really the equivalent, as we have said, of groups of households in our local community banding together to form neighbourhood vigilante groups to take over the role of the police department. Conversely, and staying with the analogy of the local community, the effort to make security a mutual and collective affair implies two basic obligations on states: first, states, rather than acting as vigilantes, must act collectively to arrange for appropriate community police and fire protection; second, individual states must exercise internal responsibilities to prevent themselves from becoming fire-traps. These obligations, by extension, need to be reflected in the external disarmament and security policies of Canada, and in its internal domestic, or national, defence policies.

Canadian Policies for International Security

Canadian policies for common security should reject isolationism and acknowledge Canada's obligation to contribute to the stability of the international order — the order on which Canadian security depends. They should acknowledge the real threats to that order and provide for Canadian participation in the collective responsibility of states to meet those threats. Canada has traditionally, and properly, viewed the threat of nuclear war as the chief military threat to the international order. And it has gone on to identify two regions in which there is a serious threat that political conflict could escalate to war and eventually to nuclear war — namely, Europe and the Third World, (Europe, of course, being where the most destructive arsenals in human history face each other across a curtain, not of iron, but of political ignorance, chauvinism and competition). In the Third World, the many simmering and active disputes threaten not only the people of those regions, but ultimately, through the potential involvement of nuclear-armed states, the entire world.

For these threats to international order to be dealt with collectively by the international community, the principles of common security need to be reflected in new national and international security arrangements. Four external-policy areas which should be the subject of intensive Canadian diplomacy are: disarmament; confining national military forces to limited defence roles; the dissolution of military alliances; and the development of international peacemaking and peacekeeping institutions.

Disarmament — Saying No to Nuclear Insecurity

The nuclear threat is a pre-eminent threat to our common security, and it follows that nuclear and other weapons of mass destruction have no proper place in national or international defence policies. Nuclear weapons promise mutual destruction, not mutual security. The ideas of "whole earth" and mutual security cannot contain within them the rational use of nuclear weapons. And if it is not rational to use nuclear weapons, it is irrational to threaten to use them. It is true that the nuclear genie cannot be put back in the bottle, but it does not follow that nuclear technology must therefore inevitably be deployed as nuclear weapons.

Disarmament, thanks to the superpowers' response to worldwide outrage at the nuclear arms spiral, has recently received an overdue and welcome boost. Even so, the moves towards abolishing inter-mediate-range nuclear weapons, and towards cutting strategic nuclear arsenals by up to 50 per cent, still leave nuclear arsenals of incom-prehensible destructive capacity. The prevailing "realist" view of nuclear weapons will not be easily dislodged. Self-styled "realists," (a more apt designation would be "fantasists"), continue to insist that nuclear weapons are here to stay and are in fact a long-term means of preventing conventional war between major powers. The extreme of this view was presented in 1973 by Fred Ikle, a U.S. security advisor to successive U.S. administrations, including that of Ronald Reagan: "This [international] order is so constructed that it cannot move toward abolition of nuclear weapons. It demands, as the necessary condition for avoiding war, the very preservation of these arms, always ready to destroy entire nations."[14] In the face of irrational attitudes such as this — with security founded in the persistent readiness, and willingness, to destroy nations — disarmament will proceed only if states develop the persistent courage and insight to make the search for rational alter-natives to nuclear security through suicide an even more urgent priority.

While Canada's current and potential contributions to the task of eliminating nuclear weapons are discussed in greater detail in other chapters, it is useful to explore briefly the framework for disarmament policies in the context of common security.

Total nuclear disarmament is the obvious way to deal with the threat that nuclear war will destroy the international order on which the security of states such as Canada depends, but that goal is not likely to be achieved in one fell swoop. Thus, all nations have an obligation, while pursuing disarmament, to promote conditions in which there is the least likelihood of existing nuclear arsenals being detonated. For Canada to effectively promote disarmament and help prevent war, it will require a clear understanding of the conditions that are most likely to prevent nuclear war, or those conditions that make such a war more likely — in other words, Canada needs what it so far seems to have successfully avoided, a strategic doctrine.

The heart of strategic doctrine is an understanding of the nature of deterrence — the conditions that are most likely to deter the use of nuclear weapons. Deterrence, for those interested in getting rid of all nuclear weapons, is not a synonym for "military balance" or "strategic equivalence" or "symmetry" or any other term implying power balances or stalemate. Neither is nuclear deterrence a synonym for "nuclear intimidation," as in the case of "extended deterrence." Nuclear deterrence refers exclusively to the role of nuclear weapons in discouraging the use of nuclear weapons. That which deters is that which creates a disincentive to use nuclear weapons. It is, of course, a deadly irony that, in the context of confronting nuclear arsenals, a pre-eminent disincentive to use nuclear weapons is the very threat to use them. To say the very least, it is a primitive and morally vexed means of regulating state behaviour; and it bears repeating, over and over again, that nuclear deterrence cannot form the basis for a long-term and stable (civilized) peace. The abolition of nuclear weapons is a prerequisite to genuine security, but while nuclear weapons remain, their use must be deterred.

Unfortunately, while there is a trend toward the abolition of nuclear deterrence, nuclear disarmament is not the chosen means. Instead, deterrence is currently being abandoned in favour of nuclear war-fighting strategies (see chapters one and two). Hence, an immediate objective must be to preserve or restore deterrence as a limited and controlled strategy to keep before military adversaries disincentives to use nuclear weapons. The reason is not that nuclear deterrence can ever be the basis of a just peace, but because it is necessary to preserve what the American Catholic bishops called "a peace of a sort"[15] that provides the opportunity to pursue the real peace of international detente and harmony and the elimination of the nuclear threat.

Currently, a serious threat to nuclear deterrence is strategic defence, whose most immediate and only forseeable impact will be to increase incentives to use nuclear weapons. The great danger, as Prime Minister Mulroney warned the Atlantic Assembly,[16] is that, when deployed in conjunction with counterforce weapons, strategic defence will produce first-strike options. Strategic defence, whether used against ballistic missiles, airborne or sea-based weapons, is a destabilizing force. It threatens the retaliatory capacity, on which deterrence depends, of nuclear arsenals without offering even the remotest possibility of national protection from nuclear attack. Strategic defence — and Bill Robinson makes this point in chapter seven — promises to be most effective against anticipated and reduced retaliatory strikes (notably when a pre-emptive strike has already reduced the size of retaliatory forces to, perhaps, more manageable proportions). Since strategic defence forces will have a better chance of succeeding if they have been preceded by a first strike, strategic defence, in a crisis environment, performs the remarkable dual function of making first strikes both theoretically possible and necessary. In short, the combination of strategic counterforce and defence leads to instability, creates incentives to use nuclear weapons and expands nuclear options.

Canadian security policy must aim to reduce, not increase, the nuclear options of the nuclear powers. To this end an urgent objective ought to be the preservation of the 1972 Anti-Ballistic Missile (ABM) Treaty. This treaty has for a decade-and-a-half restrained strategic defence rivalry between the United States and the Soviet Union, but is now threatened by U.S. efforts to re-interpret it to permit testing and development of space-based "exotic" defensive systems.[17] In support of the ABM Treaty, Canada should not only declare its insistence on a restrictive interpretation, but should go beyond that to give the details of the limits to research and testing which it understands the Treaty to impose on the signatories.

Even without strategic defence forces, nuclear strategists have been trying to develop weapons that will make the other side's nuclear forces vulnerable to pre-emptive attack. These counterforce strategies are epitomized by highly accurate MIRV systems (multiple, independently targetted, re-entry vehicles) — resulting as they do in radically fewer launch vehicles targetted by the other side's radically increased numbers of independently targetted warheads. Another disarmament requirement, therefore, is the elimination of MIRV systems, with the deep cuts in land-based ICBMs now contemplated by the superpowers being an important start. The elimination of MIRV systems would reduce incentives to use nuclear weapons by eliminating the temptation to use one's own relatively few launch vehicles, which are targetted by the other side's many warheads, to shoot first and use one's own multiple warheads to destroy the other side's relatively few launch vehicles. A committee of Soviet scientists, coming to the same conclusion, has recently published a study arguing that, in the absence of complete abolition of nuclear weapons, the most stable strategic environment would be achieved by the arsenals of each side being reduced to about six hundred light, mobile single-warhead ICBMs.[18]

It is an unwelcome irony that current strategic-arms-control discussions, though they hold unprecedented promise, could produce additional security problems for Canada. The focus on the control of ballistic missiles could not only fail to control cruise missiles (at the 1987 Washington Summit the Americans and the Soviets for the first time agreed to look more closely at cruise-missile controls), but could actually produce incentives for the Soviet Union to increase dramatically its cruise-missile force (air and sea). A significant number of these missiles would make use of Canadian airspace to reach their North American targets.[19] This danger makes cruise-missile disarmament doubly important for Canada.

In the meantime, a clear Canadian strategic doctrine will be needed to guide Canada's response to the Soviet cruise-missile threat. What deterrence requires in this context is not comprehensive interception capabilities, but rather assured early-warning coupled to an assured U.S. retaliatory capacity. In the longer term, of course, the objective must be the elimination of strategic cruise missiles, and to this end Canada should support Soviet-American talks aimed at banning the production and deployment of all such missiles.[20] Indeed, Canada should now also reconsider its permission to test cruise missiles in Canada. Political support for cruise-missile testing has always been related to the European ground-launched cruise missiles covered by the 1979 NATO "two track" decision (the one track being to deploy them, the other track being to negotiate their removal). With the elimination of these weapons, as the result of the intermediate-range nuclear forces (INF) agreement, now imminent, the main rationale for Canadian testing of the cruise missile, according to the government's arguments, will also be eliminated.

A serious commitment to security would focus political, diplomatic and technical resources on the elimination of those weapons that most urgently threaten our security — not only the security of particular states, but the security of all states which, by virtue of a common humanity, depend upon a just world order for their security.

Controlling Conventional Weapons and Defence

The elimination of nuclear weapons is an urgent requirement, but for people in countries now torn by warfare and perverted by militarism, a no-less urgent requirement is to control conventional weapons and to confine military forces to limited defence roles.

The need to explore alternative, non-military security arrangements partly derives from the recognition that the security of smaller states in particular relies, not on their ability to defend themselves militarily, but on an international order that acknowledges and respects their sovereignty and territorial integrity. This is not merely the abstract principle of what we are calling mutual and common security; rather it is a description of a fact of international life.

The international community's respect for smaller states is perhaps best measured by the effectiveness with which it constrains the global bullies — the militarily obese that are tempted to throw their weight around the neighbourhood. Respect for national integrity and self-determination mean rejecting the assumed right or legitimacy of national or alliance uses of force in violation of the integrity of smaller states. Afghanistan, Nicaragua, Grenada, Vietnam and Czechoslovakia are names that witness to the failure of the world order to protect the less powerful from the bullies.

A commonly proposed instrument for changing this state of affairs, for increasing the international community's respect for the sovereignty and territorial integrity of individual states, is a multinational convention through which states agree to forego military intervention in other countries. Such a convention would also support a strategy to restrict and reduce the role of national military forces, thus promoting conventional disarmament as well. Robert Johansen makes the point when he says that "the establishment by Moscow and

Washington of a nonintervention regime would yield progress in both depolarization and demilitarization....A nonintervention regime would reflect converging interests among the East, West and South. The United States and Soviet Union each have an interest in keeping the other out of nonaligned countries, and the Third World supports the exclusion of both superpowers."[21]

An initial focus would most certainly be on the Third World, where military force is almost routinely used by foreign powers to influence the course of political and economic events within sovereign states. Military intervention can take several forms. The most overt is obviously direct invasion, but it is also becoming the least usable, according to U.S. analyst Randall Forsberg: "The utility of force as a tool of power — a means to wealth, resources, territory, or control — has been declining throughout the 20th century. The United States is militarily capable of intervening on a large scale in Central America or the Persian Gulf but is extremely unlikely to do so for political reasons."[22] Less overt forms of military intervention include the long-term presence of foreign military bases, extensive military training programs, military exercises and arms exports — all of which can be means of violating the sovereignty and territorial integrity of states. What is needed is a diplomatic offensive to restrict national military forces to limited defence roles. The limited utility of direct intervention may be creating the genuine possibility of a non-intervention pact as part of a policy of respect for the integrity, independence and self-determination of smaller states. And the move to constrain the legitimate roles of military forces has direct implications for the manufacture and sale of weapons. Within the principles of collective security, military commodities can legitimately be produced for only two purposes: the first is to equip the multinational peacemaking and peacekeeping forces under the control of the collective security arrangements; the second is to equip national forces for their limited roles — to revive the analogy of the local community — of locking the windows and doors. This makes the control of the international arms trade central to the pursuit of common security.

Actions of this kind, to reduce the role of military force in relations within and between states, is urgent, and something to which Canada can make a contribution. It is primarily a question of political legitimacy, and while Canada is not in a position to make decisions about military interventions or most international arms transfers, it is in a position to influence the environment in which such decisions are made by others. Military invasions rely on political support as surely as they rely on military capability. Even superpowers cannot throw their military weight around indefinitely if they do not have the support of their allies. Canada has the choice of providing that support or withholding it. Energetic support for an international convention against military intervention would signal Canada's intention not to offer political legitimacy to military adventurism — whether it takes place in Afghanistan, Nicaragua, Angola, or anywhere else.

Alliances: Canada and Europe

If a non-intervention agreement is intended to restrain the neighbourhood bullies, the more fundamental requirement is to disarm and disband the bullies — particularly those that run in gangs. These gangs currently have a stranglehold on Europe. The security of the international order, and thus Canada's security, is directly threatened by the continuing military confrontation on that continent. Although NATO has clearly failed as an instrument (as originally intended) through which detente and harmony are restored, Canada persists in the claim that competing alliances are the most reliable means of preventing war in Europe. Indeed, official statements in Canada characterize this policy as a means of collective security. But NATO is not, in the analogy of the neighbourhood, the community police or fire department. Instead, it is one block's attempt to be sufficiently threatening to the gang of a rival block to keep it at bay. Competing military alliances, particularly alliances that rely on offensive conventional and nuclear weapons, take as their premise the notion that one's own security can be purchased with the insecurity of others. They may be an example of a collective threat, but they are not an example of collective security.

Military alliances, which thrive on military entrenchment and on images of enemies, require transformation and transarmament[23] into security arrangements that do not derive their credibility from the size of the threat that they pose to others. While chapter eight explores the situation and options in greater detail, one thing can be said in this context with clarity — it is in the interests of Canada and the international community to dismantle heavily-armed and dangerous arsenals, along with the military alliances that sustain them. In the interests of global security, NATO and the Warsaw Pact need to be simultaneously dismantled. The question that remains for Canada is whether its contribution to this process is best made from within or without the current structures. This is a question of political strategy, not of principle, and ought to be examined on that level. Since alliances are most likely to dissolve when they are no longer perceived to be functional, the best approach may very well be to advocate the policies and approaches that are necessary for peace with justice. If the alliance supports these policies its own constructive dissolution will soon follow. If the alliance does not support those necessary policies, it should be revealed as an impediment to peace and abandoned. Continued Canadian membership in NATO should at the very least be conditional on progress being made for the transformation of European security arrangements from those dominated by competing vigilantes to ones of true collective security within the pursuit of common security. Interim measures of transformation should include:

- adoption of a nuclear no-first-use policy
- movement toward the elimination of all nuclear weapons from European soil
- conventional disarmament and transarmament to non-provocative (defensive without being a threat to the other side) force structures
- pursuit of ways of preparing for the eventual dissolution of NATO and the WTO

Peacekeeping, Peacemaking and Common Security

An obligation of states under a mutual, collective security regime is to develop institutions that are capable of protecting individual states when they are threatened, and disciplining states that threaten others or undertake aggression. The world needs a police department; the disarming of individual households is unlikely to proceed without it. National security should not be the sole responsibility of each nation state. To the extent that the exercise of force is present and necessary, the authority or monopoly of force needs to be vested in the community and not in the individual household or in vigilante groups. This calls for multinational policing functions under the authority of the world community, through the United Nations.

Such an authority requires a peace-restoring, as well as a peacekeeping function, to restrain the use of force by individual states. Part of this obligation is obviously to prevent the outbreak of war. This applies notably to the Third World, where war has been frequent and persistent. Third World wars make a mockery of the idea of security for those people directly affected, and they hold the potential for spilling over into general regional conflicts and into conflicts involving nuclear powers and nuclear weapons.

But the most effective means of preventing war is obviously an effective capacity for the just settlement of disputes, without resorting to violence. Beyond that is the requirement, in those instances where nonviolent settlement of disputes has failed and hostilities have broken out, to persuade warring parties to cease hostilities and then to keep the peace while they pursue alternative means of resolving their conflict. An international police force, in Johansen's formulation, would differ from UN peacekeeping operations in two important ways: such a police force would be permanent, and would consist of individually recruited persons (instead of contingents from various national military forces). "Because," says Johansen, "it would be more efficiently integrated, more readily available, less subject to charges of unreliability due to allegedly divided loyalties, and better able to build useful precedents over time, a permanent global police force would be a further small step in the process of domesticating the international system."[24] It is an idea strongly deserving of Canada's support.

Canadian Policies for National Security

Canada's internal policy obligations are no less important to the international community than to itself. Internal events and conditions have implications for the world, and individual nations have a responsibility to maintain their affairs in such a way that they will not become a "firetrap". In the case of Canada, there is little danger that it will become a fire-trap by virtue of internal disorder. But Canada has special responsibilities by virtue of Canadian territory being strategically situated between the two superpowers. This strategic territory can be a means of either stabilizing or threatening the international order. The principle of common security requires that Canadian territory not be made available to any other country for the purpose of attacking or threatening to attack a third country.

In our continuing analogy of the local community, Canada is a small bungalow nestled between the enormous gothic mansions that are the U.S. and the U.S.S.R. What is more, these two mansions are so strewn with flammable and incendiary materials that even the most innocent flame in the bungalow could set the whole neighbourhood alight. In the circumstances, both the United States and the Soviet Union can make legitimate requests of their common neighbour, Canada, that it not permit activity within its territory that could be detrimental to their legitimate security interests. Canada, in turn, most surely has the right to challenge its two neighbours to redefine their view of legitimate security interests and to clean up the flammable debris in their sprawling mansions.

Current Canadian defence policy concludes that the way to use Canadian territory to stabilize the international order is to use it to enhance the military capacity of the United States. It is a policy that denies common security and is inimical to disarmament. It is especially shortsighted at a time when U.S. development of nuclear arsenals, as well as strategic defence initiatives, is perceived by the Soviets as a threat that necessitates counter-deployments.

Of particular concern is the Arctic.[25] Contrary to the requirements for reducing the risk of nuclear war, the Arctic — one of the world's "commons," the others being the ocean depths, the atmospere and orbital space — has become a focus of efforts to expand nuclear options. It is also in the Arctic that the U.S. maritime strategy envisions confrontations with the Soviet Union's northern submarine fleet. Canada now faces the prospect of concentrated efforts to enlist Canadian territory in support of this destabilizing trend. This, in turn, suggests a responsibility, not only to advocate arms control and disarmament measures for the entire region, but also to govern the use of Canadian Arctic territory in such a way as to reduce the incentives to use nuclear weapons and to create greater confidence between the nuclear belligerents.

We have already referred to the urgent need to prevent deployment of strategic defence and to dismantle counterforce weapons. It is not clear, however, that this is recognized by the government. While characterizing the research of Reagan's Strategic Defense Initiative as "prudent," wholehearted support for strategic defence deployments has been wisely withheld. Still, while continuing support for the ABM Treaty and speeches by Prime Minister Mulroney[26] have established some welcome Canadian distance from strategic defence, the Defence White Paper (DWP) seems intent on closing the gap.[27] The DWP refers to destabilizing Soviet military developments, but offers no criticism of American efforts to undermine mutual deterrence by threatening Soviet strategic forces. And by indicating the government's plan to participate in the Air Defense Initiative (essentially an airborne version of Star Wars), the DWP in effect declares the government to be amenable to opening Canadian territory to airborne strategic defence or interception forces.

In spite of this, however, the White Paper hints at an important principle regarding Canadian territory and international security: "We [Canada] enhance deterrence to the extent that we are able to deny any potential aggressor the use of Canadian airspace, territory or territorial waters for an attack on NATO's strategic nuclear forces"(p. 17). If removed from its context of Western chauvinism — a chauvinism which implies that the West, through the United States, should retain an invincible and invulnerable nuclear arsenal, but that the Soviet arsenal should be threatened and made vulnerable — it becomes a welcome principle. As a statement of general principle it should substitute for the reference to "NATO's forces" a reference to "an adversary's forces". This would acknowledge that deterrence would also be enhanced by denying a potential aggressor the use of Canadian territory for an attack on the Soviet Union's strategic forces. What is good for the goose ought to be good for the gander. If deterrence is to be the guide, it is clear that *both* sides must be deterred.[28] To threaten the deterrent of either side undermines the stability of the strategic environment, increases the likelihood that a crisis will lead to nuclear war, and thus increases what the DWP calls "the principle direct threat to Canada," namely, "a nuclear attack on North America by the Soviet Union"(p.10).

This brings us back to the more fundamental principle identified earlier: Canadian territory should not be made available to any other country for the purpose of attacking or threatening a third country.

Canada certainly does have the responsibility to ensure that the Soviet Union does not use Canadian territory for the purpose of threatening or undermining the security interests of the United States. By the same token, Canadian territory should not be made available to the United States for the purpose of threatening or undermining the security interests of the Soviet Union.

To assure the superpowers that Canadian territory is not being used contrary to global-security interests, Canada must meet two basic obligations. First, there is the requirement for surveillance and patrol of Canadian territory in order to know as far as possible what is going on in Canadian territory. Second, Canada has a minimal obligation not to host military installations or activities that are part of strategic defence or counterforce capabilities. Fulfilling this obligation would represent a unilateral disarmament initiative that, far from destabilizing the strategic environment, would support multilateral efforts to prevent strategic-defence deployments and to reduce and eliminate counterforce weapons.

The current Canadian policy on early warning is entirely consistent with this principle. The upgraded early-warning system is intended to maintain a capacity for early detection of an airborne attack, supplemented with sufficient interception capability to identify intruders into Canadian air-patrol areas. The upgraded system specifically does not include, or currently plan, a capability to repel or even substantially reduce an all-out Soviet attack. Deterrence in the sense in which we have been using the term requires no more.

The same point has been made by the U.S. chief of the defense staff, General Paul Manson, in reference to the size of the Canadian fighter/interceptor fleet: "...in the sense that the airplane does not have the task of shooting down every bomber of a mass raid that might invade Canada, then the numbers we have are not bad. Their purpose — and this is a very important point — is not primarily to shoot down bombers [but to] identify a raid....The primary role, and I emphasize this, is detecting and classifying a potential raid."[29] Early warning alone provides the disincentive for a Soviet atack.

It has been suggested that what is required is an all-party House of Commons resolution acknowledging the need for peacetime surveillance of Canadian airspace and Canada's responsibility for early warning, and declaring that "the political leadership in Canada cannot envision ever participating in active air-defence plans for North America that would be intended to provide a comprehensive, and therefore provocative and destabilizing, 'shield' around the continent."[30] Such a resolution would signal to both of Canada's neighbours that Canadian territory is out of bounds for strategic defence operations — that neither has something to fear from Canadian territory. It would also make it clear that Canada would not see increased cruise-missile deployments by the Soviets as a reason to upgrade strategic-air-defence capabilities to comprehensive levels (capable of intercepting a full-scale attack), and that Canada would also not permit the use of Canadian territory for elements of space strategic defence operations — thus providing the U.S. with incentives to rethink its Star Wars preoccupations.

The same principles apply to the government's interest in nuclear submarines, which would be assigned to operations in the Arctic as well as in Canada's two other oceans. The question, again, is whether the prevention of nuclear war and the promotion of disarmament in the Arctic would be aided or undermined by the deployment of Canadian nuclear-powered subs. While long-range nuclear-powered submarines in the numbers proposed by the Department of National Defence (DND) should not be construed as highly destabilizing, at the very least they are unnecessary. It is impossible to imagine that Canada would take military action against either an American or Soviet submarine should one enter Canadian territory. If, as has been argued above, nuclear-war prevention and arms control in the Arctic depend upon surveillance and detection, not on strategic-defence operations, the "fixed sonar systems" for detecting foreign intrusions into Canadian waters, referred to by the DWP,[31] offer the greater promise.

The danger that nuclear-powered attack-submarines could participate in a dangerous maritime strategy designed to threaten the Soviet submarine-based second-strike deterrent should not be dismissed out of hand.[32] The strategy of making the Soviet deterrent vulnerable, as we have already argued in the context of counterforce weapons, is dangerous and destabilizing. Even if not intended for that purpose, Canadian nuclear-powered submarines operating in the Arctic would inevitably and understandably be seen by the Soviets as being available to American anti-submarine forces, and thus as adding a new threat to Soviet subs. The DWP, in fact, describes the characteristic of the planned Canadian submarines that could make them a destabilizing addition to the Arctic: the nuclear-powered submarine "can maintain high speed for long periods. It can, therefore, reach its operational patrol area faster and stay there longer. The [nuclear-powered attack-submarine] can also shift more rapidly from one area to another to meet changing circumstances."

The fear that Canadian nuclear-powered submarines could become involved in a destablizing maritime strategy with the U.S. is given additional force by Defence Minister Perrin Beatty's comment that the Canadian government is considering entering into a continental naval defence pact with the United States in order to counter the Soviet submarine "threat" in the Arctic.[33]

If Canadian attack-submarines in the Arctic are not an aid to the prevention of nuclear war or the promotion of disarmament, neither are the attack submarines of other states. Indeed, a disarmament measure that Canada should pursue is turning the Arctic in general into a zone from which attack-submarines are permanently banned. This would, in effect, make such a zone a sanctuary for Soviet ballistic-missile submarines. Canadian researcher Ron Purver notes that "if the entire Arctic Ocean could be made such a sanctuary...it would have the effect of greatly reducing the incentives for increased militarization of the Arctic and attendant likely pressures on Canadian resources and defence budgets, as well as contributing to the broader aim of enhancing strategic stability more generally."[34] Such a measure would also ultimately encourage significant reductions in sea-based ballistic missiles and contribute to the gradual demilitarization of the region. If its sea-based ballistic missiles were not threatened by direct attack, the Soviet Union would have fewer incentives to increase their number, and the U.S. would be more secure inasmuch as there would be no circumstances in which the Soviets would have incentives to launch them for fear of losing them. Such Arctic demilitarization was recommended by the June 1986 report of the Special Joint Committee On Canada's International Relations, *Independence and Internationalism*: "Canada, in co-operation with other arctic and nordic nations, seek the demilitarization of the arctic region through pressure on the United States and the Soviet Union, as well as through a general approach to arms control and disarmament".[35]

This call for co-operative international measures supports a common security approach that can be extended broadly to disarmament and verification policies. Indeed, the point is reinforced by the statement of the ambassador for disarmament, Douglas Roche, that "Canada favours moving steadily towards the eventual creation of a general IVO (International Verification Organization), once the international community agrees on the desirability of establishing such an institution."[36] Hence a long-term goal ought to be the negotiation of international agreements for the multilateral monitoring of Canadian territory (to the extent that this is beyond Canadian national capabilities) and certainly for the multilateral monitoring of the Arctic as a whole.

It is true that states have rather strong inclinations to opt for military responses to political conflicts, but it is not ordained that they always exercise that option. If we spent as much time, money and ingenuity on the pursuit of non-military alternatives as we do on refining our military responses to conflict, the world would be, not the new Jerusalem, but most assuredly more humane and more reflective of what human civilization should be.

War in the Heavens: "Star Wars" and the Military Use of Space

Bill Robinson

The first satellite, *Sputnik 1*, was launched by the Soviet Union on 4 October, 1957. The military use of space was quick to follow this event: the first military-related satellite was launched a little over a year after *Sputnik*, and the first anti-satellite weapon test, Bold Orion, was conducted by the United States in October 1959, just two years after *Sputnik* opened the space age. But although the military use of satellites (the "militarization" of space) grew rapidly and continues to this day, the development and deployment of space weapons (the "weaponization" of space) remained embryonic. Only since 1983, with U.S. President Ronald Reagan's famous "Star Wars" speech, has the prospect of the weaponization of space become imminent.

The Star Wars program has been billed as an alternative to disarmament for ending the nuclear arms race, as a protective shield in case of nuclear attack, and as a prudent response to threatening Soviet space-weapons developments. But what is the reality behind these claims? Does Star Wars make arms control and disarmament irrelevant or unnecessary? Will a "Peace Shield" over our heads mean an end to the nuclear confrontation between the superpowers? Is there a high-tech solution to the danger of nuclear war?

The answer to these questions, unfortunately, is no. The militarization of space has carried with it both good and bad consequences for global security, but the weaponization of space promises only to open up a whole new arena of nuclear-arms competition, increasing the dangers posed by nuclear war-fighting technologies and doctrines, promoting an accelerated war-fighting arms race on earth, undermining existing arms-control agreements and increasing the chances of nuclear war.

Canadians have a special responsibility to be concerned about the future military use of space for at least two reasons: first, Canada's location between the superpowers ensures that Canadian territory almost certainly will play a role in any future Star Wars defence (and in future advanced air defences, which would be an essential part of any strategic defence against nuclear weapons); and, second, Canada has the potential, as one of the limited number of nations with advanced space technology, to make a significant contribution to the common security uses of space.

This chapter will look at developments in the militarization and weaponization of space, examine some of the possible common security approaches to the use of space, and outline the role that Canada could play in these developments. It will look in particular at the probable consequences of the weaponization of space through the Star Wars program and at the reasons why this program promises to increase, not decrease, the chances of nuclear war.

The "Militarization" of Space

The military use of space has existed for nearly the entire history of outer space exploration. Since 1958, some 2,500 military-oriented satellites have been put into orbit, comprising about 75 per cent of all satellites launched. Military activities in space have consisted primarily of five non-weapon roles (most of which also have direct civilian counterparts): intelligence-gathering; communications; navigation; weather monitoring; and geophysics, the study of the shape and characteristics of the earth and near space. It is useful to review these roles to understand the part that military satellites play in the overall military balance.

Intelligence-gathering satellites are the most common military satellites. These include observation and electronic monitoring satellites — often called spy satellites — and missile attack early-warning satellites. Observation and electronic monitoring satellites locate and identify military targets and gather much of the information necessary to verify compliance with arms-control agreements. Observation satellites use cameras or other sensors, such as radar, to spy on military activities and to identify objects on the earth's surface as small as a few inches across. Electronic monitoring satellites eavesdrop on military communications, radar signals and other radio emissions. Other spy satellites use radar or electronic monitoring to detect and track the other side's naval movements around the world. Early-warning satellites detect and warn of nuclear missile attack. These satellites use infrared (heat) sensors to detect the flame produced by the missiles as they are boosted into space by their rocket engines.

Military communications satellites transmit information and orders around the world. They also facilitate superpower consultations: the famous "hotline" between Moscow and Washington travels over military communications satellites. These satellites play a vital role in the command and control of the military forces of the larger powers, carrying some 80 per cent of their long-distance military communications.

Navigation satellites enable ships, submarines, aircraft and missiles with the proper equipment to determine their position and velocity at any time with great accuracy. The newer satellite navigation systems, such as the U.S. NAVSTAR system, create the potential for amazing precision in navigation and in weapons delivery. These satellites could play an important part in the operation of first-strike weapons that require pinpoint accuracy.

Military weather satellites monitor weather conditions around the world. This information is used to plan naval and land operations, airborne bombing and reconnaissance missions — including satellite reconnaissance — and other wartime and peacetime military missions. Up-to-date weather information would be used during a nuclear war to predict radioactive fall-out from nuclear attacks.

Finally, geophysical satellites measure the shape and size of the earth and its gravitational field with great precision, enabling the production of detailed maps of the locations of cities and military targets. Precision mapping is crucial to the accuracy of ballistic missiles and cruise missiles, which are designed to strike within metres of their targets from launch points thousands of kilometres away. Other satellites study the physical characteristics of the upper atmosphere and near space, to determine, among other things, how these characteristics would affect equipment operations during a nuclear war.

Existing military satellites do not contribute to the weaponization of space, but they are not entirely peaceful either. Although in many cases they share or duplicate services performed by civilian satellites, such as weather forecasting and communications, each of them also plays a role in the preparations to fight nuclear or conventional wars on earth.

Many military satellites contribute both to peaceful uses of space and to war-fighting preparations. For example, a radar satellite might be able to count mobile missiles in order to verify an arms-control agreement, but it might also be able to target those missiles so that they would be vulnerable to a first-strike attack. A single communications satellite might carry both educational TV programs to remote areas and nuclear attack orders to distant military commanders. Thus, the militarization of space to date has had both positive and negative consequences for global security. The role played by these satellites frequently is determined as much by the circumstances of their use as by their capabilities.

Daniel Deudney has argued that military satellite technologies are part of a larger, planet-wide "transparency revolution," which has served to sharpen the senses of the war-fighting machines of the superpowers but which has also planted the seeds for a future global security system:

> Transparency technologies (such as satellites that can monitor activities on earth) make possible both the coordinated, highly accurate targeting of weapons and the comprehensive verification of arms limits. Planetary-scale information systems bring the strategic competition between the superpowers to its least stable and most dangerous state. At the same time these systems make planetary-scale security possible for the first time in human history. Within the planetary war machine at its most advanced, unstable state may lie the embryo of a new security order.[1]

How can the existing militarization of space be controlled to limit its contribution to war-fighting missions? An attempt to ban research, communications and surveillance satellites is not the answer. Too many valuable civilian, defensive military or common security purposes are served by these satellites to expect (or to want) their elimination. Yet it seems inevitable that as long as these satellites exist their technologies will also be used to support developments in the arms race which threaten the future of humanity. This support role in the arms race is in many ways as important as the weapons and forces themselves:

> Scientific research, information gathering, and early-warning surveillance are part of a qualitative arms race. The superior ability to detect and target the enemy's forces, to hide and communicate with one's own, and to control military operations, have become more important than the weapons themselves. The means to chart the battlefields of nuclear war and the peacetime military operations to prepare for it...are integral parts of the military forces of the nuclear era.[2]

The impulse to use satellite technologies in support of war-fighting comes from the war-fighting competition on earth. As long as that competition continues, it seems certain that satellites will play a role in it. The key to the peaceful use of space, or to the use of space for common security, therefore, must be to bring a halt to the drive for war-fighting capabilities both in space and on earth. It is this drive which is leading also to the next great step in the militarization of space, the weaponization of space.

The Weaponization of Space: Star Wars

Although the military use of space has existed for thirty years, the weaponization of space has not yet taken place. Both the United States and the Soviet Union developed and deployed small numbers of ground-based anti-satellite (ASAT) rockets and anti-ballistic missile (ABM) interceptors in the 1960s and 1970s, but none of these ground-based weapons was very effective (the U.S. systems have since been retired), and no space-based weapons were produced at all.[3] The deployment of space weapons designed to cause "mass destruction," such as orbiting nuclear weapons, was banned by the Outer Space Treaty in 1967, and ABM development and deployment were sharply limited by the U.S.-Soviet Anti-Ballistic Missile Treaty in 1972.

Then came Star Wars (officially called the Strategic Defense Initiative, or SDI) — the leading edge of the current drive to weaponize space. When President Reagan proposed the Star Wars program on 23 March, 1983, he cast it in terms of a defence that would replace the global balance of nuclear terror by rendering nuclear weapons "impotent and obsolete."[4] In Reagan's vision, American (and Soviet) high-technology defences would eliminate the nuclear threat while avoiding the dangers of relying on "flawed" arms-control agreements. Strategic defences would keep the peace in a world made safe by the wonders of modern science.

Eliminating the nuclear threat remains the stated ultimate goal of SDI. However, even SDI director Lieutenant-General James Abrahamson has admitted that "a perfect astrodome defense is not a realistic thing."[5] SDI officials prefer instead to speak of a "defence-dominated" world — a world in which defensive systems are not 100 per cent effective but in which they are effective enough to dominate the strategic equation. Nuclear weapons would continue to play a role in this world, but the balance would be ensured by the defensive systems of both sides. A Star Wars system with this capability is technologically distant, however, and there are serious political and strategic problems with the whole concept.

In recent years, less ambitious goals for Star Wars have also been outlined. These interim goals are being used to argue that early deployment of some simpler Star Wars weapons in the 1990s is both feasible and useful for limited purposes. The primary interim goal is the protection of U.S. missile silos and command centres from Soviet missile attack (such a system would also have a limited capability to protect populations). This system, its supporters feel, would prevent a Soviet first-strike that could disarm the United States.

The reality is that such an attack is not going to happen. President Reagan's own Commission on Strategic Forces concluded in 1983 that a strategic defence of U.S. silos is unnecessary — the Soviet Union is not capable of conducting a "disarming" first-strike against the total

U.S. nuclear force. Furthermore, the goal of protecting U.S. missiles and command centres from attack does not justify a space weapon research program like SDI. As the Union of Concerned Scientists has argued, this goal "is really an argument for terminal, hard-point defense of U.S. missile silos, not for layered, area defenses proposed by the president. The administration's initiative is not only vastly more expensive and complex than is necessary for the protection of retaliatory forces, but it is provocative to the Soviet Union in a way that would reduce, not enhance, deterrence stability."[6]

A final common justification for the Star Wars program is that the Soviets are conducting similar research, which the U.S. must be prepared to match with its own program of research. The spectre of a Soviet Star Wars system is relatively new: it did not appear at all in President Reagan's Star Wars speech. Nevertheless, the United States has attempted in recent years to justify its drive to develop space weapons by pointing to Soviet work in this field. The implication of this argument, which has been picked up by the Canadian government and others, is that SDI research is being pursued purely out of "prudence," in order to hedge against potential Soviet developments in ballistic missile defence.

The major weakness of this argument is that it is wrong. SDI was never necessary as a hedge against Soviet developments: both the United States and the Soviet Union were already pursuing limited programs of strategic defence research — primarily to hedge against the other's developments — years before the birth of SDI. In any case, SDI goes far beyond the requirements of that kind of program. SDI is a crash program to *develop* ballistic missile defences for later, probable, deployment. (Indeed, President Reagan has stated that "we will research it; we will develop it; and when it is ready, we will deploy it."[7])

Furthermore, despite the inflated rhetoric about the Soviet Star Wars program, it is the United States, not the Soviet Union, that has enjoyed the lead in developing the technologies necessary for a space-based defence system. As the U.S. Congress' Office of Technology Assessment (OTA) has confirmed:

> *...in terms of basic technological capabilities, the United States clearly remains ahead of the Soviet Union in key*

> *areas required for advanced BMD [ballistic missile
> defense] systems,* including sensors, signal processing, op-
> tics, microelectronics, computers and software. The United
> States is roughly equivalent to the Soviets in other relevant
> areas such as directed energy and power sources. The
> Soviet Union does not surpass the United States in any of
> the 20 "basic technologies that have the greatest potential
> for significantly improving military capabilities in the next
> 10 to 20 years" which were surveyed by the Under
> Secretary of Defense for Research and Engineering.[8]

The Soviet strategic defence program does not justify the SDI
program. It is the SDI program, not the Soviet program, that currently
poses the frightening prospect of a deployed Star Wars system and of
an arms race in space.

How a Star Wars System Might Operate

A Star Wars defence would work by intercepting ballistic missiles or
their nuclear warheads as they travel through space on the way to their
targets half a world away.

The trajectory of an attacking ballistic missile can be divided into
four phases: boost, post-boost, mid-course and re-entry. The boost
phase, lasting from about three to seven minutes, occurs while the
missile's booster is still burning, propelling it out of the earth's atmosphere and towards its target. The post-boost (or busing) phase, lasting
another few minutes, is the period during which the missile is releas-
ing its nuclear warheads (if it has more than one) and any decoys or
penetration aids it carries to confuse or impede the defences. After the
post-boost phase all of the nuclear warheads fly on an unpowered ballistic trajectory, like the path of a fly-ball in baseball. This ballistic
phase, the mid-course phase, ends about twenty minutes later as the
warheads re-enter the earth's atmosphere. The final phase, the re-entry
phase, lasts about one minute, terminating when the warheads —
travelling at ten to twenty thousand kilometres per hour — arrive at
their targets and explode.

Most proposed Star Wars "architectures" consist of a number of
layers of different defences (three or four layers are often suggested),

each attempting to intercept the incoming missiles as they pass through one or more of the different phases of flight. These defence systems might include "kinetic-kill" interceptors (destroying warheads by direct collision with them); futuristic "directed-energy" weapons, such as laser battle stations and high-energy particle-beam weapons; passive and active surveillance and tracking satellites to monitor continuously the "threat cloud" (which could consist of thousands of nuclear warheads and hundreds of thousands of pieces of missile debris, decoys and penetration aids); and high-speed jam-proof communications equipment and extremely complex battle management computing systems to sort out the targets and co-ordinate all the defences.

At least one layer of the defence would be dedicated to intercepting the attacking missiles in the boost and post-boost phases (this is usually called "boost-phase defence") before they have released their warheads. This is the most efficient time to destroy the missiles because few or no decoys have been released and every missile destroyed eliminates up to ten or more warheads, each of which would otherwise have to have been separately tracked and destroyed. However, it is also one of the most difficult times to destroy the missiles because the boost and post-boost phases can be reduced potentially to as little as two or three minutes in total. Even at up to ten minutes duration for the two phases, the boost-phase defence would have to work very rapidly to assess the attack, select targets, and perform the interceptions before the warheads were safely deployed. Laser or other directed-energy systems based in space would probably be necessary in order to intercept the missiles in the time available during these phases.

Mid-course defence layers could consist of both directed-energy and kinetic-kill interceptors. The "threat cloud" during the mid-course phase might consist of hundreds of thousands of objects, so mid-course defences would require highly effective sensors capable of discriminating the warheads in the "cloud" from the objects they were hiding among. Mid-course defences would probably be based in space in order to have the shortest possible reaction time; however, in this case (and in the case of boost-phase defences) only a small fraction of the orbiting defences would be in range of the attacking warheads at any time. To avoid this problem, some mid-course interceptors might be based on the ground in northern areas, such as the Canadian Arctic, and launched only when an attack begins. Some mid-course sensors might also be ground- or air-based in the Canadian North.

Following the mid-course phase, terminal defences would attempt to intercept incoming nuclear warheads during their final moments of flight, after the force of re-entry into the atmosphere had stripped away the decoys and debris surrounding the warheads. Some of these defences might be nuclear-armed, in order to ensure the destruction of the warheads they were fired at; others might be non-nuclear. If the incoming warheads made evasive manoeuvres as they re-entered the atmosphere, non-nuclear interception could prove to be extremely difficult.

The feasibility of terminal defence varies according to the target to be defended. Missile silos and other heavily fortified targets could be defended at very close ranges — a silo could survive even if the attacking warhead exploded only a few hundred metres away from it. "Soft" targets like cities, on the other hand, would have to be defended at much longer ranges — city defences would have to stop incoming warheads tens of kilometres away. This means that a terminal defence for cities is much more difficult than it is for "hard" targets such as missile silos.

A Star Wars "roof" would also require a vast and elaborate air-defence system in order to close the "doors and windows" of the United States — and Canada — against bombers and cruise missiles. (An "Air Defense Initiative" is already underway with Canadian participation to develop the air-defence technologies necessary to support the Star Wars system.) This air-defence system would probably operate under the control of NORAD, the joint U.S.-Canada continental air-defence command. Finally, the complete defence system would still face the intractable problem of nuclear weapons smuggled in on commercial airliners or transport ships, or otherwise delivered in a way that circumvented the defences against more traditional forms of attack.

Can Star Wars Bring Peace?

The prospect of a technological solution to the nuclear threat is attractive to many people. But there are numerous reasons why a Star Wars defence such as the one described would fail to provide an effective defence against nuclear weapons. The potentially huge number of attacking warheads could simply overwhelm the defences. Penetration aids, such as decoys or chaff, could prevent the defences from reacting effectively to the attack. Technical weaknesses of the defences, such as unreliable computer software, could cause the defences to fail during the critical minutes of an attack.

But more important than these technological reasons is the simple fact, admitted by SDI officials, that a 100 per cent effective defence is just not possible. A Star Wars defence could stop *some* missiles, but almost certainly it could not stop all of them.

This is a crucial point, because a less than perfect defence holds little prospect for making nuclear weapons "impotent and obsolete." Even if a Star Wars defence were 90 to 95 per cent effective, 45 to 95 million Americans would die "prompt" deaths in a major nuclear war (more would die "delayed" deaths).[9] In addition, many millions in other countries, including Canada, would also be killed in direct attacks. Subsequently, the disastrous effects of the war — possibly including "nuclear winter" — would be suffered worldwide. Some of these effects would persist for generations.

Consequently, despite the serious technological feasibility questions about Star Wars, the key question is not "would Star Wars work?" It would not: if nuclear war ever occurred, Star Wars weapons would stop some attacking missiles, but they would not stop nuclear Armageddon. The key question has to do with what effect a partially effective Star Wars defence would have on the chances of nuclear war — would the deployment of Star Wars defences make a nuclear war more likely, or less?

Tipping the Nuclear Balance

Given that Star Wars defences could not eliminate all nuclear weapons, the most likely outcome of building strategic defences would be a new nuclear balance composed of both offensive and defensive weapons. SDI supporters think that this new balance would create a defence-dominated world, which they believe would be safer than our existing world.

But replacing the current strategic nuclear balance with a defence-dominated nuclear balance might be no improvement at all. As a number of analysts have pointed out, the deployment of even a limited strategic defence could create a highly unstable situation in which one superpower, or each superpower, might be able to disarm the other in a first-strike attack. Such a situation is extremely unlikely with the existing offence-dominated nuclear balance, because a first-strike attack would destroy most, but not all, of the other side's strategic nuclear weapons: hundreds or thousands of weapons would survive to be launched at the attacker in retaliation. However, if the side that launched the first strike had even a partial strategic defence system (such as that proposed for early deployment by some SDI supporters), the other side's retaliatory strike might be reduced to hundreds or even tens of nuclear weapons. The retaliatory strike would inflict terrible losses on the attacker, but the disparity between the destruction inflicted on the two countries would be enormous. In the calculations of the war planners, the side which struck first under such circumstances would "win" the nuclear war while the other side would "lose."

The danger that would be created by this unstable situation would be greater than just the possibility that it could tempt one side to launch an aggressive nuclear attack against the other. It could also lead to a nuclear war starting in the name of simple self-defence. As the OTA has argued, "both sides could arrive at a highly unstable situation in which each might perceive a chance of assuring its own survival by striking first, *and only by striking first*"[10]

What does all this mean? It means that unless the new balance created by strategic defences could somehow be made stable, *and kept stable over time* (in the face of what would probably be a continuing and accelerated arms race), the deployment of the defences would increase, not decrease, the chances of confrontation and nuclear war.

Shootout at the OK Corral?

Can a defensive system be made to survive and function in the face of hostile counter-measures aimed at disabling it? This question is crucial to the future stability of any Star Wars deployment.

Obviously, if one side could disable the defence of the other, then that defence would be no defence at all. But the survivability problem is worse than that: vulnerable defences would greatly decrease the stability of the nuclear balance, since the side which struck first could destroy the other side's defence while still remaining defended itself. As President Reagan's arms-control advisor, Paul Nitze, has stated:

"The [SDI] technologies must produce defensive systems that are survivable. If not, the defences would themselves be tempting targets for a first-strike. This would decrease, rather than enhance, stability."[11]

This problem would be even greater if both sides' defences were vulnerable. One SDI official has speculated that "the re-enactment of the Shootout at the OK Corral" might result if both U.S. and Soviet defences were vulnerable to destruction by the other side's defences.[12] Under these conditions, even the smallest indication of attack might be enough to start the two defence systems blasting away at each other in "self-defence."

It is evident that the survivability problem would have to be solved if strategic defences were to help bring about a more stable and secure strategic environment. Unfortunately, survivability is not a problem for which there can ever be a simple or enduring technological solution. Technological advances could be used to protect Star Wars defences, but they could also be used to attack them. If technologies can be developed that will destroy a nuclear warhead no matter how well protected it is, then technologies can probably also be developed that will destroy space defences no matter how well protected those defences are.

The "two-edged sword" of technology promises a continuing survivability problem for Star Wars defences, resulting in a continuous and unpredictable defensive arms race, and a less stable nuclear balance than currently exists. As Kosta Tsipis has argued: "...spaceborne weapons systems are subject to technological instability, i.e., they will be faced with frequent crises of vulnerability that would have to be remedied promptly. The counter-measures and counter-counter-measures cycle promises to be rapid and endless."[13]

What is the current overall outlook on the survivability of Star Wars defences? A 1986 report by several U.S. Senate staff members concluded that:

> ...at this point it appears bleak. Scientists at the [U.S. government's] Sandia Laboratory who have been intensely studying this question have come to the conclusion that space-based, boost-phase defences can *never* be made survivable unless by treaty — that is, unless the United States

and the Soviet Union agree to certain rules of the road and deployment restrictions through arms control.[14]

Arms Control in Orbit

It seems evident that some form of superpower co-operation and space arms control would be essential if an endless arms race, or worse, were to be avoided following the deployment of space defences. The OTA has noted that, if the Soviets were willing to accept the transition to a defensive strategy (currently they are not), "it would probably be necessary to negotiate adequately verifiable arms control agreements on reducing present and restricting future offensive forces and on the manner, effectiveness and timing of defensive deployments."[15]

But can a verifiable and enduring arms-control regime to control and stabilize space weaponry be realistically envisaged? These are the conditions the OTA has outlined for an agreement covering the transition to strategic defences:

> An arms control agreement for phasing in BMD [ballistic missile defence] would have to establish acceptable levels and types of offensive and defensive capabilities for each side and means for verifying them adequately. It would have to specify offensive system limitations that prevented either side from obtaining a superior capability to penetrate the other's defenses. It would have to specify the BMD system designs for each side that would not exceed the BMD capabilities agreed to. *It is important to note, however, that no one has as yet specified in any detail just how such an arms control agreement could be formulated.*[16]

It is difficult to imagine such an extensive and unprecedented agreement ever being negotiated, and even more difficult to imagine it enduring the stresses of continued technological competition and being able to account for the continuous evolution of each side's defensive systems as they were repaired, upgraded or modernized.

An effective and enduring agreement that would maintain balance and stability in the face of space-weapon deployments would require a consensus of analysis about strategic doctrine and the capabilities of weapons that has never been achieved in the past. It would require either a level of verification that seems impossible or a level of trust that seems highly improbable. And it would require a willingness not to be distracted by minor asymmetries in the forces of the two sides — even though the history of the arms race is dotted with meaningless or non-existent "gaps" used to justify new weapon deployments and to condemn arms-control agreements. In comparison to these problems, the technological challenges in developing Star Wars defences appear minor.

Offensive Uses of "Defensive" Weapons

One further factor that would have to be controlled somehow for a stable future of strategic defence involves the possible offensive capabilities of nominally defensive weapons. "The same characteristics of BMD technologies which enable them to intercept and destroy ballistic missile attacks," OTA has noted, "will also provide the capability to accomplish other military missions, including offensive ones."[17] Such offensive attacks could be made using the "defensive" weapons themselves, or by applying the "defensive" technologies developed by SDI and similar research in new offensive weapons.

A 1986 study for R & D Associates, a major SDI contractor, concluded that laser weapons might prove to be powerful enough to pose a destructive threat to towns and cities as great as that posed by nuclear weapons. "In a matter of hours a laser defense system powerful enough to cope with the ballistic missile threat can also destroy the enemy's major cities by fire. The attack would proceed city by city...[taking] only a matter of minutes. Not nuclear destruction but Armageddon all the same." Albert Latter and Ernest Martinelli, the authors of the study, concluded that: "After spending hundreds of billions of dollars, we would be back where we started from: deterrence by retaliation. Our cities would be hostage to lasers instead of nuclear weapons."[18] Other analysts have reached similar conclusions about the offensive potential of some Star Wars weapons.

Direct offensive uses of space-based weapons could include ASAT attack, anti-aircraft attack, precision ground attack and large-scale ground destruction. Space-based lasers capable of penetrating the atmosphere have obvious potential as offensive weapons, but kinetic-kill vehicles might also have offensive applications, and virtually any space weapon could be used offensively against satellites, space weapons themselves or other orbital facilities.

Some "defensive" weapons might also prove helpful in conducting a first-strike. As already discussed, defences would aid a first-strike by mopping up surviving nuclear forces launched by the victim, preventing him from carrying out his retaliation. But space weapons might also have an *offensive* role in the strike, attacking weapons, command centres and communications. For example, Peter Zimmerman, an analyst for the Carnegie Endowment for International Peace, has pointed out that: "These weapons could destroy the bomber 'leg' of our strategic triad while it's on the ground during the opening seconds of war."[19]

Star Wars: Not the Answer

For all of the reasons mentioned (and many not), Star Wars weapons hold no promise as the road to a safer world. Star Wars weapons would not replace nuclear weapons, but would be deployed alongside them in a complex mix of offensive and defensive forces. This mix would create pressures for a greatly accelerated arms race and might lead to a much less stable nuclear balance that could tip rapidly into all-out war. Unless the defences were unable to destroy opposing defences, the new nuclear balance would be disastrously unstable, favouring the attacker in any conflict. (And if the defences *were* unable to destroy opposing defences, how could they be very effective against similarly protected and more numerous nuclear warheads?) Some of these problems might be removed if an extensive arms-control regime could be devised to regulate the offensive/defensive balance, but there is little reason to believe that such an agreement is even remotely feasible. Further, any agreement would also have to control the offensive potential of Star Wars weapons, which might be impossible to defend against.

This last factor points towards the *fundamental* flaw in the Star Wars vision. Even if all of the problems associated with Star Wars could be solved, high-tech defences simply could not protect the United States if the Soviet Union or some other "adversary" were really intent on doing it harm. How could a Star Wars defence be built against environmental warfare, for example? How could a Star Wars defence be built against genetically engineered biological weapons? The reality of the technological world is that one side's security relies ultimately not on defences, but on the restraint and the self-interest of the other side. That is the situation now with nuclear weapons and that is the way it will remain until a global common security system — one that does not rely on force and the threat of force — is created to replace security based on military might. In short, it is a political solution — common security — that is the ultimate answer to the nuclear threat. Certain space technologies can assist in the creation of a global common security system, but there will never be a technological solution that bypasses the political problem of nations learning to live together in peace on this planet.

Common Security and Space

Can the weaponization of space be avoided? The existing legal regime governing the military use of outer space consists of the Outer Space Treaty, a handful of other agreements, and a number of arms-control agreements with provisions relating to outer space, the most prominent of which is the U.S.-Soviet Anti-Ballistic Missile (ABM) Treaty. (See Table.) These existing treaties have established some precedents for the non-militarization and common use of space, but they present few obstacles to the weaponization of space.

The Outer Space Treaty (a multilateral treaty signed by the United States, the Soviet Union, Canada and nearly one hundred other countries) is considered to be the cornerstone of international law in space. The treaty takes as its mandate the free exploration and use of space by all nations, and calls for co-operation and mutual assistance in these activities. In addition, it establishes several rules for the peaceful use of outer space.

The treaty prohibits the placing of nuclear weapons or other "weapons of mass destruction" in orbit around the earth, on celestial bodies, or elsewhere in space. Star Wars weapons which require a nuclear explosion to power them, such as X-ray lasers, would violate this provision if they were placed in orbit. (A nuclear explosion in space would also violate the Partial Test Ban Treaty.) The Outer Space Treaty

Treaties with major provisions relating to military activities in space

Partial Test Ban Treaty (1963, multilateral)
Art. I bans nuclear test explosions in outer space, among other environments.

Outer Space Treaty (1967, multilateral)
Art. IV para. 1 prohibits the placing of nuclear weapons or other "weapons of mass destruction" in orbit around the earth, on celestial bodies, or otherwise stationed in space. Art. IV para. 2 mandates that the moon and other celestial bodies shall be used "exclusively for peaceful purposes."

Anti-Ballistic Missile (ABM) Treaty (1972, U.S.-U.S.S.R.)
Art. V.1. prohibits development, testing or deployment (but not research on) ABM systems or components which are sea-based, air-based, space-based, or mobile ground-based. ABM systems are defined by the treaty as "currently consisting" of ABM interceptor missiles, ABM launchers, and ABM radars. In contrast to previous understanding, a new "broad interpretation" by the Reagan administration claims that the development and testing of ABM systems based on new physical principles, such as lasers, is permitted by the treaty.
Under a 1974 protocol, each country is permitted to deploy one site of up to one hundred ground-based ABM missiles.

SALT I Treaty (1972, U.S.-U.S.S.R.: expired, but currently observed)
Art. V.2. commits each party not to interfere with "national technical means of verification" (e.g. spy satellites).

Environmental Modification Convention (1978, multilateral)
Art. II bans the changing — through deliberate manipulation of natural processes — of the "dynamics, composition or structure" of outer space (or of the earth) to produce widespread, long-lasting or severe effects.

SALT II Treaty (1979, U.S.-U.S.S.R.: U.S. considers treaty "dead")
Art. VII.2. (c) prohibits the conversion of space vehicle launchers into intercontinental ballistic missile launchers.
Art. IX.1 (c) bans the development, testing or deployment of systems for placing into earth orbit nuclear weapons or any other kind of weapons of mass destruction, including fractional orbital missiles.

Moon Treaty (1979, multilateral)
Art 3.2 prohibits the threat or use of force (and other hostile acts) on the moon, or from the moon, in relation to the earth, man-made space oblects or spacecraft personnel.
Art 3.3 prohibits the placing of nuclear weapons or weapons of mass destruction in orbit around or on the moon.
Art. 3.4 forbids the establishment of military bases, weapons testing, or military manoeuvres on the moon.

stipulates, as well, that the moon and other celestial bodies shall be used "exclusively for peaceful purposes." This provision bans military bases, weapons testing and military manoeuvres on the moon and other celestial bodies; however, it permits the use of military personnel for scientific research and other "peaceful purposes" on these bodies. Except for these provisions, the treaty does not limit the military use of space.

The ABM Treaty is a bilateral treaty between the United States and the Soviet Union. As modified in 1974, the treaty permits each side to maintain one site with up to one hundred fixed, ground-based anti-ballistic missiles, launchers and associated radars. All development, testing and deployment of sea-based, air-based, space-based, mobile land-based or rapidly-reloadable anti-ballistic missile systems is prohibited. Basic research on such systems, such as current SDI research, is not prohibited by the treaty, but the testing of weapon prototypes or their components is prohibited.

Since 1985, the Reagan administration has attempted to promote a revised view of the ABM Treaty (the so-called "legally-correct interpretation" or "broad interpretation") that would permit the development and testing of futuristic space-based or other anti-ballistic missile systems based on "other physical principles," such as lasers and particle beams. This interpretation of the treaty has been rejected both by its original U.S. negotiators and by the Soviet Union; however, the Reagan administration continues to argue that its interpretation is the "legally correct" one. The effect of the change would be to permit Star Wars research to proceed to actual development and testing of futuristic weapons before a decision to scrap the ABM Treaty entirely would have to be made.

The existing legal regime in space contains only the seeds of effective space-arms control. The deployment in space of nuclear weapons and other weapons of mass destruction is prohibited, but ballistic missiles, which would carry nuclear weapons through space on their way to targets, are not constrained. The development, testing and deployment of anti-ballistic missile systems in space is prohibited (under the normal interpretation), but current research is pushing hard against those limitations. Both countries have conducted activities which the other considers to be in violation of the ABM Treaty (in fact, the ABM Treaty may be entirely abandoned by the U.S. before 1990).

The deployment of other kinds of conventional weapons is prohibited on the moon and other celestial bodies (including orbit around the moon), but it is permitted in outer space in general (including orbit around the earth). Interference with satellites used to verify arms-control agreements is prohibited, but attacks against other satellites are not, except by the general principles of international law and the free use of space. There are no limitations on the development, testing and deployment of the ASAT weapons that would be used for such attacks, and as noted both the United States and the Soviet Union are conducting research on ASAT systems.

Clearly, other, more comprehensive, measures will be necessary (in addition to compliance with existing agreements) in order to close off the prospective arms race in space. The following are some of the routes that could be taken to ensure the peaceful use of space. Also included are suggestions on the ways in which Canada might contribute to the development of a common-security approach to space activities.

Space Weapons Ban

A ban on space weapons would be the most important step towards foreclosing the weaponization of space. Ideally, such an agreement would ban the testing and deployment of all weapons based in space, used against objects in space or from space against objects on earth. This could be accomplished through a treaty banning ASAT and other space weapons, an enlarged and strengthened ABM Treaty, or simply a set of agreed limitations on permissible space-weapons testing. Currently, the United States government refuses to enter negotiations on any of these possible agreements for fear of hindering the progress of the SDI program. Nevertheless, there is considerable U.S. interest outside of the Reagan administration in negotiating a space-weapons ban of some sort in conjunction with deep reductions in U.S. and Soviet strategic nuclear weapons. Progress in this direction will probably depend on the policies of the next U.S. president. Canada could help matters by withdrawing its political support for the SDI program and by encouraging the U.S. and the Soviet Union to negotiate a comprehensive space-weapons ban.

One important question surrounding any proposal to ban space weapons is verification — can U.S. and Soviet compliance with such a ban be verified? The answer is yes. Such a ban would be relatively easy to verify because no effective space weapon system could be developed without extensive testing of its components. This testing would be detectable by the other side. It is important for this reason, however, that the ban be in place before extensive space weapon tests have taken place. Once such weapons are tested and proven it would be much harder to guarantee that neither side was secretly preparing to deploy them at some time in the future. Canada has a unique contribution to make on the question of verification: Canadian research on a verification satellite, the PAXSAT A study, has established that the verification of a space-weapons deployment ban is practical with existing technology. Other surveillance technologies would be capable of monitoring space-weapon tests. Canada could assist in the verification of a space weapons ban by moving ahead with the development of PAXSAT A and by working actively to promote a moratorium on all ASAT, Star Wars, and other space weapon testing until such a ban is in place.

Co-operation in Space

Efforts to build co-operative, international space projects would also be an important part of any common security regime in space. One extremely valuable project would be the establishment of an International Satellite Monitoring Agency (ISMA). The ISMA proposal, originally made by France in 1978, calls for the creation of an international agency to operate surveillance satellites for arms-control verification and crisis monitoring. An ISMA would break the superpower monopoly on spy satellites and open the way for international monitoring of arms-control compliance and for the identification of suspicious military activities. One important role for ISMA could be to monitor space objects in order to ensure that no weapons were being deployed or weapons tests being carried out. Canada's PAXSAT A satellite and PAXSAT B satellite (PAXSAT B would verify arms control limitations on earth) could make important contributions to ISMA's operations. Canada should continue its development work on these satellites and lend its political and financial support to the ISMA proposal.

Other, non-military, projects would also be important for building common security. These projects could include new or expanded co-operative efforts in global communications, environmental monitoring, weather forecasting, resource management, scientific research, space resource development and many others. (Many of the projects also could be undertaken unilaterally, with the information made available for global use.) All of these uses of space would contribute positively to global common security: for example, by helping nations around the world to understand better and deal with many of the non-military trends, such as hunger and environmental destruction, that threaten human security.

Common Security on Earth

Finally, it is important to recognize that common security in space cannot be divorced from common security on earth. The ultimate role of space activities is determined primarily by the security system prevailing on earth: it seems extremely unlikely that the war-fighting race in space (both weaponization and militarization) can be foreclosed permanently without an end to its impetus, the war-fighting race on earth.

A continuing war-fighting competition on earth would probably lead to the eventual weaponization of space no matter what agreements to ban space weapons had been made in the past. One reason for this is that a successful space-weapons ban might encourage the greater militarization of space, which might then lead to pressures to abandon the ban on space weapons. (A ban on space weapons would protect the monitoring, targeting, and command and control satellites that support war-fighting strategies. This situation might encourage the superpowers to launch even more war-fighting satellites. The increasing significance of those satellites in the war-fighting competition would then create incentives for each side to develop ASAT weapons to destroy them.) In the words of one space analyst, this problem is the basic paradox of ASAT arms control: to the extent that space-weapon development is suppressed, "the superpowers will be more and more tempted to deploy threatening spacecraft. And to the extent they do so, pressures will in turn build to set aside the treaty and deploy ASATs."[20]

The ultimate answer to the problem of controlling war-fighting in space, therefore, has to be to control war-fighting weapons and doctrines on earth. A common security approach to space has to be supported by a common security approach to the entire planet.

This fact has particular significance for Canada because of this country's strategic location between the superpowers. In order to promote an integrated approach to common security, Canada should make it clear that it opposes the continuing nuclear arms race on earth and in space, and that it will not make Canadian territory available to the offensive or defensive nuclear forces of either side for pursuing the competition in war-fighting capabilities. This position would mean that Star Wars weapons or sensor systems and extensive NORAD air-defence systems (such as those being developed under the Air Defense Initiative) could not be based in Canada. Canada would not support Strategic Defense Initiative research and would withdraw from participation in Air Defense Initiative research.

The significance of Canadian territory for strategic defence lends considerable importance to the stance that Canada adopts on this issue — Canada could, in effect, veto some types of Star Wars and Star Wars-related deployments. At the same time, Canadian space technology allows Canada to make important contributions to the future common security uses of space. Canadians have the ability, and the responsibility, to play an important role in determining the future direction of the utilization of space.

8

On the Front Line: Disarmament in Europe

Ernie Regehr and Simon Rosenblum

Not since World War II has there been such disagreement on how best to defend western Europe. It is a security crisis whose source is disarmament — both its failure and its success. The failure of disarmament produced its sharpest public reaction in the early 1980s with the introduction of the Soviet SS-20 missile and NATO's deployment of cruise and Pershing II missiles in Europe. While public pressure has now led to an agreement to eliminate those weapons, and a whole class of similar weapons (intermediate-range) on both sides, critics of a defence policy that relies finally on a capacity for nuclear self-immolation remain well aware that some 15,000 nuclear warheads remain aimed at the European targets of NATO and the Warsaw Pact.[1] For those millions of Europeans who identify with its peace movements, what the U.S.-Soviet INF agreement on intermediate-range nuclear forces (INF) illustrates most clearly is the unconscionable size of the nuclear arsenals that remain. After immense public and diplomatic effort, only 3 or 4 per cent of the world's nuclear stockpile is affected, and NATO's defence strategy remains tied to the unrealistic and suicidal reliance on fighting a European war with nuclear weapons. For those Europeans, the situation is dangerous and intolerable.

For others, the danger is in the success of disarmament. The elimination of intermediate-range nuclear weapons is seen to have both short- and long-term negative implications. In the short-term, say some

West Germans in particular, the elimination of intermediate-range nuclear weapons shifts the focus to short-range nuclear and conventional weapons. With a diminished capacity to strike deep into the territory of the Soviet Union, the danger increases, they say, of protracted war on German territory — not a pleasant prospect with nuclear or modern conventional weapons of mass destruction. The long-term danger, say those who are frightened by the success of disarmament, is that Europe's defence will ultimately be "decoupled" from the American strategic nuclear deterrent, presumed to be the ultimate means of dissuading Soviet adventurism.

Neither group of Europeans finds security in the status quo. Significant changes in European security arrangements are both imminent and inevitable. The real question is whether those changes will bring further disarmament and progress towards East-West political harmony, or whether they will bring rearmament and continuing confrontation.

The agreement by the United States and the Soviet Union to eliminate their land-based intermediate-range nuclear forces and shorter-range nuclear missiles is a welcome confirmation that genuine disarmament is indeed possible. It is a landmark event in the history of arms control — assuming, that is, that the treaty is ratified by the U.S. Senate. Although both sides can reassign strategic (long-range) weapons to cover European targets formerly assigned to INF warheads, it is the first treaty to dismantle existing, state-of-the-art missiles, instead of merely decommissioning obsolete systems or setting limits on future deployments. The elimination of Pershing II ballistic missiles is of special importance due to their extreme accuracy and short flight-time to targets in the western Soviet Union (up to, if not including, Moscow). The Soviets considered the Pershing II a threat to their command-and-control systems, which meant that if war seemed imminent, they would have had considerable incentive to launch a pre-emptive strike to eliminate that threat. That, in turn, would have given the United States an incentive to fire their own missiles before they were destroyed. The elimination of the Pershing missiles is a positive, stabilizing measure which reduces first-strike incentives on both sides.

The agreement is an extension of President Ronald Reagan's 1982 "zero option," which called on the Soviets to destroy all their SS-4,

SS-5, and SS-20 missiles, in return for which the U.S. would not deploy its new Pershing II and cruise missiles — a proposal that former U.S. Secretary of State Alexander Haig deemed too advantageous to the Americans for the Soviets to take seriously. Indeed, the scale of Soviet concessions needs to be appreciated. Besides delinking the INF agreement from their insistence that the Americans abandon the Strategic Defense Initiative, the Soviets dropped the requirement that limits on the independent British and French nuclear arsenals be included in any INF deal. As a result, the Soviets will remove three times as many nuclear warheads (1575 to 436) as the Americans.[2]

Unfortunately, many, including Prime Minister Brian Mulroney, are learning the wrong lesson from this agreement. Mulroney's praise of President Reagan for "staying the course" implied that the Pershing II and cruise missiles were effectively used as a "bargaining chip" in negotiations to remove Soviet SS-20 missiles. But in fact, NATO had begun nuclear "modernization" planning prior to the SS-20 deployments. The deployment of the highly accurate cruise and Pershing missiles was a provocative "response" to the SS-20s[3] and did not bring the Soviets to adopt the zero option. Soviet acceptance of the INF agreement is, first of all, a product of a new Soviet leadership that is more flexible and that sought the INF agreement as a catalyst to strategic arms reductions.[4] Furthermore, the agreement improves the internal political standing of Gorbachev and will help create a stable foreign environment for his domestic reforms. Asked why the Soviets were willing to make such a historic agreement, U.S. Secretary of State George Shultz replied: "They say they're doing it because they want a less threatening, less nuclear world — and maybe we should just take them at face value." Indeed, the striking disarmament proposals put forward by Gorbachev, as well as the ambitious reforms he has initiated, have given new impetus to hopes for an end to the European cold war.[5]

For NATO officials, however, this is not always taken as evidence of hope. Instead, they now warn Europe not to move down "the slippery slope of denuclearization." It seems a premature fear. Even after the INF agreement, NATO retains well over four thousand land-based nuclear warheads and a variety of delivery vehicles — aircraft, short-range missiles, and artillery. Furthermore, four hundred American sea-launched ballistic missiles remain assigned to NATO and the British and French nuclear systems are untouched. It is hardly a matter, as a Canadian diplomat at NATO headquarters said of the INF agreement, of "stripping NATO to its nuclear underpants."[6] Nevertheless, NATO officials are urging the allies to compensate for the withdrawal of ground-launched cruise and Pershing missiles by introducing "compensatory" nuclear weapons. Some thought was given to bringing sea- and air-launched U.S. cruise missiles into the European region but, since that would be such an obvious circumvention of the INF treaty, NATO has for the time being shifted its focus to additional nuclear F-111 bombers and stealth (invisible to radar) fighter bombers in Europe. On top of that are the development of new tactical nuclear weapons (for use within a particular battlefield, say, against approaching tanks) and major additions to both the French and British nuclear forces.[7] Such deployments to "fill in the gap" left by the INF treaty would obviously undermine the "zero-zero" agreement. A modest treaty could quickly become a meaningless one.

The Nuclear Umbrella: Myth and Reality

"Nuclear weapons provide the glue that has held the western alliance together," according to former U.S. Secretary of Defense James Schlesinger. From the first days of the Cold War, when the "nuclear umbrella" was extended to Europe, NATO has looked to the threat of nuclear retaliation to deter conventional and nuclear attack by the Warsaw Pact. NATO thus refuses a nuclear "no first use" pledge on grounds that its inferior conventional forces alone are not sufficiently powerful to deter such an attack.

NATO's policy of "flexible response," adopted in 1967, requires a "spectrum" of nuclear delivery systems — from short-range artillery to long-range bombers — to provide a variety of options short of "massive nuclear retaliation" in the event of war. The policy assumes that, in a war, nuclear weapons could be used selectively, with some held in reserve to be used later in controlled escalation — even escalating to the point of drawing in America's strategic nuclear arsenal.[8]

As nuclear weapons deployed in Europe become more sophisticated, nuclear deterrence relies increasingly on nuclear war-fighting scenarios. Flexible response is itself a nuclear war-fighting strategy inasmuch as controlled escalation envisions a capacity to match each level of attack — conventional or nuclear — and then to escalate the war to a higher level. At each stage, the threat of escalation is used to try to deter the attacker from continuing. There would be roughly three stages of nuclear escalation: in the first, battlefield nuclear weapons would be fired by artillery or from short-range ballistic missiles on the ground or on aircraft at advancing enemy forces; in the second stage, nuclear weapons would be fired behind front-line forces to destroy resupply depots and transportation facilities; and in the third stage, intermediate-range or Euro-strategic weapons would be fired deep into the enemy's homeland to destroy industrial bases, to disrupt the social order and to terrorize the enemy into surrender.

The first question that arises from this strategy is whether escalation to the use of nuclear weapons could be limited or halted at any of these stages. The nearly unanimous conclusion of those who have studied the issue is that a nuclear war could not in practice be controlled in this manner[9] — hence the old joke that "NATO strategy is to fight like hell for three days, then blow up the world." Furthermore, as has been pointed out by four eminent Americans (McGeorge Bundy, George Kennan, Robert McNamara, and Gerard Smith — who have all held major positions in either the Pentagon or State Department), even "controlled" use of nuclear weapons in Europe would be destructive beyond reason: "Every serious analysis and every military exercise, for over 25 years, has demonstrated that even the most restrained battlefield use would be enormously destructive to civilian life and property. There is no way for anyone to have any confidence that such a nuclear action will not lead to further and more devastating exchanges."[10]

The second question, given the likelihood that any use of nuclear weapons would result in uncontrolled escalation to intercontinental nuclear war, was asked by former prime minister Pierre Trudeau in 1984. "Do you think the President of the United States," he asked a symposium in Switzerland, "in answer to an overrunning of Europe by conventional Soviet forces, will want to start World War III, an atomic war?"[11] That the question had to be asked, and by a NATO government leader, was itself the most persuasive evidence that nuclear deterrence, as a European defence strategy, had lost its credibility. By the early 1980s there were widespread public and official doubts that

European security strategies, which seemed to have come down to assembling competing arsenals of mass destruction, achieved anything but insecurity. Before Mr. Trudeau voiced his doubts, mainstream analysts writing in military journals had voiced the same doubts, but more forcefully: "In the event of war, NATO's theatre nuclear weapons are unlikely to achieve their intended purpose. Most will probably be destroyed at the outbreak of war, and NATO is unlikely to decide to launch any that survive."[12]

The practical and logical consequence of these doubts is that Europe needs to find a new, non-nuclear, answer to its security concerns. To persist in nuclear deterrence or nuclear war-fighting strategies when neither enjoys political credibility is a formula for inevitable military escalation. You obviously cannot demonstrate to your adversary your political will to use nuclear weapons (essential for a credible deterrence), so both sides are confined to symbolic gestures to show political resolve. And the most favoured symbolic gesture is to deploy more nuclear weapons. Each new deployment creates new doubts in the opposing camp about the reliability of its deterrent — doubts which in turn are dealt with by new deployments. And so the spiral continues.

While the INF agreement on its own does not mean a reversal of this spiral — modernization of battlefield weapons still seems a priority — it does represent an important opportunity to reassess Europe's security needs. Such reassessment has at least two dimensions. The first is to examine the current force structure of the competing nuclear alliances and to reshape the nuclear strategies of the two sides to strengthen assurances that these nuclear arsenals will not be used. The second is to examine alternative, non-nuclear, means to security.

From the point of view of NATO, the policy in most urgent need of re-examination is its nuclear first-use policy. NATO strategy reserves the right to introduce nuclear weapons into a conflict in order to offset the claimed conventional superiority of the Warsaw Pact. While this policy lacks credibility — would the Americans sacrifice Boston in a futile gesture to save Bonn? — it also lacks sense. If the use of nuclear weapons invites their certain use in response, it is obvious, to the extent that rational thought remains dominant in the process, that the use of nuclear weapons runs directly counter to the security interests of western Europe. At a minimum, NATO must revamp its nuclear policy to include a nuclear no-first-use pledge. Such a pledge would at least confine the threatened use of nuclear weapons to the deterrence of the other side's use of the same weapons. Since British and French nuclear weapons may remain in place for a long time to come, a NATO no-first-use doctrine would at least confine the role of western European nuclear weapons to one of retaliation in the improbable event of a Soviet nuclear attack.[13]

A second critical step to enhance European security would be to withdraw tactical nuclear weapons. Since these battlefield weapons are so integrated with conventional weapons, and the decision to use them can be made at such low levels in the military hierarchy, the risk of escalation from conventional to nuclear conflict would remain unacceptably high as long as those weapons remain. In a conventional battle, they could fall easily into enemy hands, which further increases the pressure to use them before they are seized or destroyed by the opponent. West Germans keenly appreciate these dangers and some have proposed the elimination of tactical nuclear weapons in what is referred to as a "triple zero" agreement. As Volker Ruehe, a foreign policy advisor to Chancellor Helmut Kohl, has recently observed: "The shorter the [missile's] range, the deader the Germans."[14] Kohl, too, has called on President Reagan to go slow on plans to modernize U.S. short-range nuclear weapons in Europe, asking instead that these systems be dealt with in a broad arms-control strategy.[15]

NATO strategy in general, and the nuclear first-use strategy in particular, rest on the following assumptions: Warsaw Pact conventional forces in Europe are superior to those of NATO; and the Warsaw Pact will use that superiority to attack Western Europe unless NATO maintains nuclear weapons to deter such an attack. Hence there is the fear that further denuclearization of the two alliances would make Europe safe for a conventional war.

While it gets more and more difficult to sustain the conviction that the Soviet Union and its allies stand poised for an assault into western Europe just as soon as the West's finger strays too far from the nuclear button, it is their capacity to launch such an attack that understandably preoccupies western military planners. So the question is not, would they attack, but could they rationally launch a *successful* attack. Second, if such a possibility remains, must it be dealt with through

Western conventional rearmament and nuclear weapons, or through reductions?

Calculating the balance of conventional forces between the Warsaw Pact and NATO is a complex exercise and open to misleading "bean counts." Quantitative comparisons are insufficient because they take no account of geographical advantages, military technology, training, morale and so on. Indeed, the assumption that the Warsaw Pact would be able to win a conventional European war is now widely challenged by military analysts. John Mearsheimer, for example, argues that, "the conventional wisdom is wrong; NATO presently has the capacity to thwart a Soviet attack."[16] The non-nuclear threat from the Warsaw Pact is vastly inflated by defence establishments conditioned to cry wolf in order to boost budgets. Now and again, a military official admits that the conventional situation is not precarious. For example, in 1983 the Commander of the U.S. Army in Europe, General Frederick Kroesen, rejected all the talk about overwhelming Soviet conventional military strength: "We can defend the borders of Western Europe with what we have," he said, "I've never asked for a larger force. I do not think that conventional defence is anywhere near hopeless."[17]

But even if the Soviets are granted to have a conventional advantage in Europe in numerical terms, qualitative factors must also enter the equation. Both the quality of its aircraft and the experience of its pilots deliver an air power advantage to NATO, according to Donald Fredericksen, deputy undersecretary of defense for tactical warfare programs. He told the American Defense Preparedness Association in January 1987: "I'm absolutely sure we would take over the air in a week."[18] The frequently cited Warsaw Pact advantage in tanks is another good illustration. Top-of-the-line U.S. tanks — the M-60 and M-1 Abrams — account for a much greater percentage of NATO's tank inventory than do the Soviet Union's newest tanks — the T-64, T-72 and T-80 — in the Warsaw Pact supply.[19] Similarly, NATO's combined naval forces are superior to those of the Warsaw Pact both in numbers of surface combatants and in total naval tonnage (a measure of the size of the ships). More important, NATO vessels have direct access to the open ocean. In contrast, to operate in the European theatre, Soviet and Warsaw Pact ships must pass through bottlenecks controlled by NATO and other U.S. allies.

It is only after distorting the numerical count and making a series of implausible "worst case" assumptions that the Soviet advantage becomes significant. But sober assessments find little evidence that the Soviets could rationally consider a conventional attack on Europe and expect an outcome that could be classified as "winning." For example, in a classified report, leaked to the press in 1987, the U.S. Joint Chiefs of Staff concluded that NATO has sufficient conventional strength to make a Soviet attack highly unlikely.[20] The London-based International Institute for Strategic Studies also concedes that "the conventional military balance is still such as to make general military aggression a highly risky undertaking for either side."[21]

It is not the conventional imbalance that makes full nuclear disarmament in Europe impossible, rather it is the overall high level of conventional weapons that prevents it. The standard argument is that conventional rearmament in the West will facilitate nuclear disarmament — but that deserves another look.

High levels of conventional weapons do not reduce the perceived requirement for nuclear weapons. Indeed, historically, in the industrial world as well as the developing world, the greatest pressure to acquire and expand nuclear arsenals has come from those states that have the largest conventional arsenals. In the European context, the argument is advanced that, with higher conventional forces, NATO would not have to rely on nuclear weapons to deter a Warsaw Pact conventional attack. But conventional parity, at current high levels of arms on both sides, would only engage the "Hiroshima argument." At Hiroshima, the argument was that nuclear weapons were required to save lives — to bring the costly war with Japan to an early conclusion. In Europe, the same rationale would run as follows. With high levels of destructive conventional weapons, nether side could afford a protracted, stalemated conflict in Europe. The destructive power of conventional weapons is so great that any extended war would devastate the continent. Nuclear weapons must be kept available to bring such a war to an early conclusion — to break the stalemate.

The main point of the Hiroshima argument is that high levels of conventional weapons are not a means to nuclear disarmament, rather they become the chief impediment to it. Accordingly, the reduction of conventional arms is an urgency in its own right, and a prerequisite to nuclear disarmament.

While some analysts argue that there are ways to improve the West's defensive capabilities without resorting to increases in its offensive forces — for example, faster mobilization procedures, stronger armored reserves, more and better anti-tank weapons and more effective tank barriers along the West German border[22] — even current levels of conventional forces are much too high and pose the risk of intolerably destructive warfare in Europe. Further, given the power of emerging conventional weapons, a non-nuclear defence of Europe is just as unthinkable as a nuclear one. George Kennan, former American diplomat and arms-control specialist, points out that "a war fought with them [newly developed conventional weapons], particularly a defensive war presumably conducted largely on our territory, promises nothing but a degree of devastation that makes a mockery of the very idea of military victory." The point bears repeating — if a catastrophic war on European soil is to be avoided, the weapons of war on both sides must be reduced.

There is no evidence that any European leader or regime has ambitions to change the borders between western and eastern Europe by the use of armed force. When confronted with various scenarios of the possible course of war in Europe, the famous English military historian, Michael Howard, asked: "What is this war supposed to be about?"[23] Officialdom in the United States increasingly shares the view that there is no compelling evidence that the Soviet Union is actually intent on invading Europe. As Jonathan Dean, former head of the U.S. delegation to the Mutual and Balanced Force Reduction (MBFR) talks, has concluded: "The possibility of deliberate, aggressive Soviet attack for the sake of conquering and holding Western Europe, however large it may have been in the past, has become so small as to be negligible."[24]

The Soviet Union is decidedly better off seeking what it wants from western Europe by trade and diplomacy, and the present task is to dismantle the military confrontation in ways that both promote East-West detente and maintain stability and security in central Europe. As Ambassador Dean has noted, the Soviet Union has become a "status quo" power in Europe and "the NATO-Warsaw Pact military confrontation has passed its peak and is now on the downward slope."[25]

While a deliberate attack, out of the blue, is highly unlikely, the danger of war in Europe remains real. While war could be triggered by a crisis in Europe, such as a political revolt in East Germany or elsewhere, the more likely scenarios involve events outside the continent. Conflicts on the perimeter of Europe or beyond might spill over into the continent. Indeed the increased involvement by NATO countries in "out-of-the area" military operations increase the possibility that Europe could get drawn into a confrontation between the United States and the Soviet Union in the Third World or at sea.[26]

Europe, meanwhile, remains the most heavily militarized continent in the world, with the largest peacetime military concentration in history: 40,000 heavy tanks, 10,000 combat aircraft, over 2,600 naval vessels in the seas bordering Europe and over 10 million troops on active duty — not to mention 10,000 nuclear warheads.[27] These huge forces consume at least two-thirds of the world's total yearly expenditure for all armed forces. It would be a great understatement to say that military force levels in Europe are totally out of proportion to the political tensions of the region. Europe is an armed camp which, in the words of European military critic Mary Kaldor, "is the stage for an imaginary global war which is daily played out in the scenarios of military planners, in military exercises and military intelligence, [and] in the rhetoric of political leaders...."[28]

The primary military task in Europe is obviously the prevention of war — the threat of which derives from the sheer size of the arsenals that have been assembled there. The Soviet Union and the Warsaw Pact are a major contributor to this threat. Their forces are structured on the principle of pre-emptive conventional defence in Europe by means of a blitzkrieg attack into West Germany in the event of war, and their emphasis on mobile war-fighting through "Operational Manoeuvre Groups" constitutes a considerable offensive capability.[29] A Soviet offensive capacity has also been maintained, of course, as part of the apparatus for disciplining its eastern European allies. Traditional Soviet doctrine says that, if the Soviet Union is to avoid ultimate defeat in a conventional war, it must take over NATO Europe and prevent it being used as a bridgehead by the United States. Fortunately, there seems to have been a recent (1982-83) doctrinal change by the Soviets which, according to military analyst Michael McGwire, has changed the nature of Soviet military requirements in Europe and opens up the possibility of much less offensively structured Warsaw Pact forces.[30] Previously, the Warsaw Pact had said that its doctrine was defensive at the "socio-political" level, but offensive on the "military-technical" plane — that is, a European war would be fought on the opponent's territory. Now the Soviets have concluded that a world war is less likely than a regional conflict with the United States, which might well be contained outside Europe. That conclusion has provided the occasion for the Soviets to promote the concept of a "reasonable sufficiency" of forces.

NATO's non-nuclear forces have been largely defensive in structure and orientation. But NATO itself has unfortunately chosen a new, provocative, conventional-weapon strategy. In what is referred to as "Follow-On Force Attack" (FOFA), or "deep strike," the intent is to be able to attack enemy forces beyond those on the frontline in order to delay, disrupt, divert or destroy selected elements of oncoming Warsaw Pact reinforcements (known as second-echelon forces) before they could join the battle.[31] It is a strategy which capitalizes on recent advances in conventional-weapon technology and relies on "smart" conventional weapons — guided munitions and conventionally armed ballistic or cruise missiles — to carry the battle into Warsaw Pact territory.

Rapid military escalation would be hard to avoid in a war between Warsaw Pact forces which are committed to early control of western European territory, and NATO forces which are committed to a deep-strike strategy that emphasizes going on the offensive.[32] In the event of a crisis that could lead to war, each side might feel pressed to pre-empt the other. The Warsaw Pact might consider it necessary to disperse its troops before they were attacked by NATO deep-strike forces; NATO, feeling that it must move before the Soviet troops are dispersed, might feel compelled to strike. To the degree that NATO's deep-strike policy involves the targeting of Warsaw Pact strategic assets, such as command-and-control centers, this would further encourage possible Soviet pre-emption. Conventional first-strike weapons are as destabilizing as nuclear first-strike weapons.

An equally serious problem with the new strategy is that, if NATO launched a deep attack with conventional missiles, how would the Soviets know that the attack was a conventional and not a nuclear one? Given the large numbers of nuclear weapons still in NATO arsenals, and given the destructiveness of new conventional weapons, the firebreak, or line between nuclear and conventional weapons, has become dangerously blurred. It may, for example, be impossible to distinguish conventionally-armed cruise missiles from nuclear ones while in flight, and if a large-scale attack is launched the Soviets may assume the worst. Moreover, powerful non-nuclear weapons could be used to destroy targets on the ground with the effectiveness of small tactical nuclear weapons, further increasing the scope for misunderstanding.

There is now the possibility of a negotiated reduction of Soviet forces in eastern Europe. The Soviet Union tabled a proposal — known as the second Budapest Appeal — in June 1986 calling for reductions of 25 per cent (approximately 500,000) in each side's ground troops and tactical air forces in Europe over a period of ten years, with initial reductions of up to 150,000 troops in the first two years. The entire area of Europe, from the Atlantic to the Urals, would be covered under the proposal, which also incorporates nuclear- and conventional-weapon-free-zones. Even more promising is Mikhail Gorbachev's acknowledgement of "asymmetries" in the forces of the two sides. The Soviet Union, he has said, is "in favour of removing the disparity that arose in some elements, not through their increase by the side that stayed behind, but by reducing their numbers on the side which has a superiority in them."[33]

Easy progress in conventional-arms reductions cannot be expected, given the past difficulty of negotiating European troop reduction and the serious problems of determining who exactly has what. The Soviets have always resisted substantial European troop withdrawals since they could lead to a loosening of their grip on eastern Europe. Yet Gorbachev has now introduced new possibilities. The "zero-zero" nuclear-weapons agreement involves substantially disproportionate reductions by the Soviets and bodes well for conventional-weapons negotiations. Similarly, the successful completion in September 1986 of the Stockholm Accord, a multilateral agreement containing detailed measures to reduce the risk of surprise attack in Europe, is a good omen. The agreement requires the thirty-five signatories to give prior notification of troop exercises above certain defined thresholds (13,000 or more troops or at least 300 tanks) within specific periods of time (forty-two days). Mandatory on-site inspections of military facilities to provide for the verification of compliance with the treaty were also agreed upon.[34]

Towards a Stable Peace

As long as the countries of Europe feel threatened by conventional attack it will be difficult to eliminate nuclear weapons from Europe. And the order of the day for discussions of European security must surely be how to prevent a war rather than how to fight one. To this end, the elimination of nuclear weapons plus radical reductions in conventional weapons are essential but not sufficient. A strategy to prevent war requires more. Conventional military forces can be configured either to maximize the capacity to attack and retaliate, or to maximize the capacity to defend and deny an opponent's access to territory and key assets.[35] Thus a major requirement for creating a truly stable peace is to restructure western and eastern conventional forces so that they provide an adequate territorial defence without posing a threat of attack or intervention.

The past few years have seen the emergence of a new security concept variously termed non-provocative defence, defence without offence or just defence.[36] Non-provocative defence embraces the principle that defence should be based, not on the threat of retaliation, but on effective resistance to attack. A non-provocative defence force is one that is incapable of seizing and holding the territory of an adversary, or of inflicting serious damage on the other state's people or resources, as long as the armies of the adversary remain on their own national territory. A non-provocative defence strategy deters invasion by demonstrating the will to prolonged resistance and by ensuring that an aggressor will have to pay a heavy price. By signalling adversaries that they need not fear attack but that they will not succeed if they act aggressively, a non-provocative strategy removes the incentive for a pre-emptive attack in a crisis.

Weapons for non-provocative defence must be non-threatening to other countries. They must be weapons with limited range and mobility which can be used to fight primarily inside a country's own territory, or close to its borders, and which can be easily protected and widely dispersed so as to avoid attracting large-scale attack.[37] Modern weapons can be judged according to these criteria. Tanks, for example, are provocative — but fixed barriers at strategic locations, while they cannot be used to attack another country, might be helpful in thwarting an attempted tank invasion. Similarly, while anti-aircraft weapons are useful in defending a country, they are not sufficient means to attack another country, even if they are mobile. "Defensive" is not an attribute of weapons per se but of forces in their totality — their size, weapons, logistics, training manoeuvres and so on.

There is a wide range of non-provocative defence proposals. One alternative defence strategy, for instance, would use a multi-layered conventional military defence emphasizing mobility, concealment and dispersal, and would employ a new military technology known as precision-guided munitions (PGMs). PGMs are extremely accurate conventional weapons that possess a high probability of destroying opposing forces, like tanks or planes.[38] Non-provocative defence can also be planned with an emphasis on much simpler technology, using border fortifications, tank traps and mines, maximizing the value of natural barriers and relying on territorial reserves armed with simple missiles and artillery. There is obviously room for considerable debate about the best strategy and technical mix.

Considerable portions of a non-provocative defence could be introduced unilaterally. There is a limit, of course, to how far one side can change the structure of its forces and remain secure without reciprocal change on the other side. A non-provocative defence would be vulnerable to an opponent who attacks the defensive system with offensive arms from within its own territory. For a complete reformation of conventional forces into a non-offensive posture, reciprocity is required.

Gorbachev has signalled what could be a significant change in Soviet military doctrine — from the offensive to the defensive. He has invited NATO to a dialogue on military doctrine to "ensure that the military concepts and doctrines of the military blocs and their members rest on defensive principles"[39] A constructive response to this proposal is a matter of first importance. Opposition (social democratic) parties in Britain, West Germany and Denmark have already embraced the principles of non-provocative defence. Western governments have been slow to respond to the Soviet initiative but must now examine what the Soviets may have in mind, even though they have not developed specific proposals of their own.

A non-provocative defence strategy could enable NATO to trade constraints on the modernization of Western conventional forces for cuts in Soviet main battle tanks and artillery. Western Europe would find reassurance in Eastern reductions of large mobile armored forces and a shifting away from its doctrine of massive conventional retaliation. Eastern Europe, on the other hand, would be reassured by the West's abandoning of its deep-strike strategy. Negotiations in pursuit of this goal could follow on an agreement between the Warsaw Pact and NATO to limit the number of long-range strike aircraft, heavy tanks and long-range conventional missiles on both sides. Ideally, this approach would lead to further reducing and restructuring of military forces in Europe — East and West — so that all nuclear weapons would be removed from the continent and only small, short-range, purely defensive conventional forces remain.

As they stand now, the Warsaw Pact and NATO are agents of collective insecurity. Genuine security requires the present competition to evolve into arrangements for the common security of East and West in Europe. Ultimately, European security requires the removal of American and Soviet troops from European soil and the dismantling of the two alliances.[40]

The idea of "de-alignment" is presently being explored by the European peace movement.[41] It differs from non-alignment in that the goal is not to stand aside from the blocs, but to radically reform the alliances and eventually to end them. De-alignment is, then, not simply a goal but a staged process which recognizes that fundamental restructuring cannot happen overnight. If the denuclearization of Europe were accompanied by new, less provocative conventional weapon deployments, then the conditions might exist for beginning to dissolve the military alliances as they become increasingly unnecessary. As the influential West German Social Democrat Erhard Eppler told the European Nuclear Disarmament (END) convention in Coventry, England: "We cannot just dissolve NATO and the Warsaw Pact, but we can make them obsolete."

The European security crisis is grounded in the failure of disarmament. It is now time to rethink Europe's defenses. The INF agreement, more significant for its political implications than for its military implications, has provided an opportunity for reappraisal by both blocs. If the option of demilitarization is chosen, the logjam can be broken, and a new era of stability in Europe achieved.

9

The Way Out: Canada as a Nuclear-Weapon-Free-Zone

Ernie Regehr, Bill Robinson and Simon Rosenblum

The proposal that Canada become, by formal declaration and by implementation of appropriate policies, a nuclear-weapon-free-zone is a prominent plank in the platform of the Canadian disarmament movement. National or local nuclear-weapon-free-zones have the support of two major federal political parties (the the New Democratic Party and a national convention of the Liberal Party have endorsed the idea), three provincial and territorial legislatures (Manitoba, Ontario, the Northwest Territories), major national church organizations (including the Canadian Conference of Catholic Bishops and the United Church of Canada), labour organizations (including the Canadian Labour Congress and provincial federations of labour), and more than 150 Canadian municipal councils (including Toronto, Vancouver, Montreal and Edmonton). Well over half of Canada's population now lives within jurisdictions or is related to organizations that have expressed support for Canada becoming a nuclear-weapon-free-zone.

This chapter explains the basic features of a nuclear weapon-free zone, the form it should take in Canada and the policy changes necessary to make it a reality.

Limiting Nuclear Options

Within the context of the nuclear confrontation between the United States and the Soviet Union, Canada occupies a critical piece of territory. Events in Canada can have an important impact on the relationship between its two superpower neighbours. Current Canadian defence policy recognizes the importance of Canadian territory for stabilizing or destabilizing the strategic environment in which the nuclear arsenals of the world confront each other. Yet, while acknowledging the importance of Canadian territory, Canadian defence policy unfortunately draws the wrong conclusions. The government's line of argument is that, since nuclear war is prevented by nuclear deterrence, Canadian territory should be given over to the "strengthening" of the nuclear forces of one of the superpowers, the United States.

This is a wrong conclusion because it is no longer possible, if it ever was, to assume that additions to the U.S. nuclear arsenal are a contribution to deterrence and stability. Even within the framework of nuclear deterrence, developments in American and Soviet nuclear arsenals are designed not so much to enhance nuclear deterrence as they are to enhance nuclear flexibility and to create new nuclear "options." First-strike nuclear weapons — that is, weapons that are highly accurate and are targeted on an adversary's weapons, and thus designed for first or pre-emptive use — are not intended simply to deter by threat of retaliation. Such weapons are intended, in times of crisis, to give political and military leaders additional nuclear options to consider.

Canada ought not to be in the business of expanding the nuclear options of the superpowers or any other powers. At a time when nuclear arsenals have reached obscene levels, the only sane or moral policy is one which is intended to reduce or limit nuclear options and the circumstances in which their use can be seriously contemplated.

Canada possesses a unique resource with which to pursue the objective of reducing nuclear options and contributing to international stability. That unique resource is Canadian territory. A reliable principle by which Canada should govern what happens in its territory is the principle that Canadian territory should not be made available in peacetime to any other country for the purpose of attacking or threatening to attack a third country. Central to this principle is the requirement that Canadian territory not be available for the operation, deployment, transit, testing or production of nuclear weapons (or elements of nuclear-weapon systems). In other words, Canadian territory can make an effective contribution to international stability, and to an environment conducive to nuclear disarmament, if it is made a nuclear-weapon-free-zone (NWFZ).

Indeed, some significant steps have already been taken toward this end. Nuclear weapons are not permitted to be deployed or stored on Canadian territory and Canadian nuclear fissionable materials, in principle at least, are not to be used here or anywhere in the world for the purpose of building nuclear warheads.

It is time now to go further. It is time to devise a policy which rejects the nuclear-weapons system in all its manifestations. The first step is to complete the denuclearization of Canadian territory, thus creating a concrete base from which to pursue innovative and energetic strategies to liberate the rest of the planet from the tyranny of nuclear weapons.

What is a Nuclear-Weapon-Free-Zone?

The concept is a simple one. *A nuclear-weapon-free-zone is a defined geographic area within which the possession, deployment, storage, transit, manufacture, testing or other support of nuclear-weapons systems is prohibited.* An area can become nuclear-weapon-free as part of an international zone established by treaty (the United Nations has developed some guidelines for this type of zone) or by national declaration and policy. On a symbolic level, provincial, municipal and other locations can also be declared nuclear-weapon-free. Although symbolic, these declarations can be given some legal force by, for example, municipalities prohibiting nuclear-weapon-related activities through their zoning regulations.

Almost since its beginning, the United Nations has urged the creation of NWFZs as a form of "confidence-building measure" that would help to create an international climate in which more comprehensive arms limitation could be undertaken. NWFZs exist by international treaty in five regions — outer space, the seabed, Antarctica, Latin America and the South Pacific. However, the South Pacific nuclear-free-zone, which was established only in 1985, has not yet been recognized by three of the five main nuclear powers. There are proposals for regional NWFZs in the Nordic countries, the Balkans, other parts of Europe, the Middle East, the Indian Ocean, Southeast Asia and Africa. In addition, a large number of nations have declared themselves nuclear-weapon-free unilaterally, including Austria, Japan, New Zealand, Sweden and (to varying degrees) a number of NATO countries. By symbolic declaration, there are now thousands of NWFZs worldwide — including more than 150 in Canada — expressing the wishes of people all around the world to withdraw support from the nuclear arms race.

What is the Purpose of a NWFZ?

The point of any state becoming a NWFZ (or joining an international NWFZ) is not to seek immunity from nuclear war. Once war breaks out, all bets are off; any country, nuclear-weapon-free or not, will be vulnerable to direct attack — the relevant circumstance being whether the nuclear combatants will consider it to their advantage to attack or not to attack — and all will suffer the post-war devastation. Treaties count for little in war, and they certainly count for nothing in the sharing of the effects of war. Although a Canadian NWFZ would eliminate any willing Canadian role in nuclear war-fighting, this also is not the point of a NWFZ; after the war few Canadians would either be around or inclined to celebrate the virtues of non-involvement in global self-immolation.

The real purpose of a NWFZ is to influence national and international behaviour before war breaks out, thus helping to reduce the likelihood of war. *A NWFZ is a peacetime measure to restrict the spread of nuclear weapons, to withdraw political and technical support from the nuclear arms race, and to build trust between nations and regions of the globe.* NWFZs signal to nuclear powers that their prerogatives are not limitless, and thus serve to withdraw legitimacy from the possession of, and the threat to use, nuclear weapons. By keeping the nuclear forces of the superpowers widely separated, such zones (particularly those in strategic locations) can also serve as "confidence-building measures" and act as stabilizing factors during a nuclear crisis. In these ways, NWFZs can contribute to the prevention of nuclear war.

The Broad Requirements for a Canadian NWFZ

Canadian governments have traditionally supported the idea of establishing nuclear-weapon-free-zones. Canada voted in favour of the treaties to establish NWFZs on the seabed and in outer space, Antarctica, Latin America and the South Pacific. Canada has also voted in favour of similar initiatives related to Africa, South Asia and the Middle East. At two special sessions of the United Nations General Assembly on disarmament (1978 and 1982), Canada supported final declarations which encouraged the establishment of NWFZs. All this support, however, has not yet been manifest in support for a Canadian NWFZ.

There is no single, internationally accepted definition of the detailed requirements of a national nuclear-weapon-free-zone. The requirements widely accepted by proponents of a Canadian NWFZ can be outlined in four broad categories:

- No nuclear weapons on Canadian soil;
- No transit for nuclear weapons through Canadian territory;
- No production in Canada of components for nuclear weapon systems; and
- No support systems (or testing) for nuclear weapons, whether based in Canada or operated by Canadians outside Canada.

Some significant changes would be required in Canadian policies in order to meet these criteria, but such changes would not be as extensive as initially might be thought. Many parts of the policy, as the table shows, are already in place.

Policy Changes Needed

According to Prime Minister Brian Mulroney, "we do not have a nuclear dimension to our policy. Canada does not have nuclear weapons on its territory, nor shall it during the life of this Govern-

Present Status of Canadian Nuclear Weapons Policies

1. NO NUCLEAR WEAPONS

a) for Canada	Policy in place
b) deployed in Canada	Peacetime practice must be made policy
c) stored in Canada	Policy in place

2. NO TRANSIT OF NUCLEAR WEAPONS

a) nuclear-armed aircraft	Peacetime practice must be made policy
b) nuclear-armed naval vessels	Must be banned
c) other	Must be banned

3. NO PRODUCTION OF NUCLEAR WEAPONS

a) nuclear weapons	Policy in place
b) nuclear-delivery systems	Must be banned/ Requires definition

4. NO SUPPORT OF NUCLEAR WEAPONS

a) nuclear-weapon testing	Policy in place
b) delivery/support testing	Must be banned
c) nuclear-weapon training	Must be banned
d) nuclear-support systems	Must be banned/ Requires definition

ment."[1] Unfortunately, it is not quite that simple. It is true that Canada does not have nuclear weapons on its soil. It is also true that this is a very good start. But there are some additional and rather important changes that have to be made if Canada is truly to have no nuclear dimension to its policy.

The following sections look at some of those changes in the context of each of the major provisions for a Canadian NWFZ.

No Nuclear Weapons

Nuclear Weapons for Canada

Canada does not possess any nuclear weapons of its own, and it does not possess foreign nuclear weapons for Canadian use. Under current arrangements, however, Canada might assume operational command of certain U.S. nuclear-capable naval forces (and therefore of nuclear weapons) during a conventional or nuclear war. In a NWFZ, such command over nuclear forces would have to be foregone.

Nuclear Weapons Deployed in Canada

No nuclear weapons are currently deployed in Canada for the use of other states. According to the research of U.S. policy analyst William Arkin, the U.S. does plan to place thirty-two nuclear depth bombs at two Canadian locations and to disperse armed B-52 bombers to Canadian airfields in time of war or crisis.[2] However, government statements indicate that Canada has no existing commitment to accept such contingency deployments of nuclear weapons and that Canada retains the right to refuse requests for such deployments at all times.[3] As a NWFZ, Canada would formalize this right and exercise it at all times as a matter of policy.

Nuclear Weapons Stored in Canada

No nuclear weapons are stored in Canada.

No Transit

In order to become a NWFZ, it will be necessary to prohibit visits to, or transits of, Canadian territory by nuclear-armed aircraft, ships and submarines, or any other carriers.

Nuclear-armed Aircraft

Although nuclear-armed aircraft do not overfly Canadian territory in "normal peacetime" conditions, in an atmosphere of heightened tension the U.S. would probably request permission for nuclear-armed flights over Canadian territory. Canada has approved such flights in principle already, but as with nuclear weapons deployments, Canada retains the right at all times to refuse permission for armed overflights. Under current policy, permission for such flights would likely be granted almost immediately; under a formal NWFZ policy, such permission would be denied in advance.

Nuclear-armed Naval Vessels

Port visits and transits of territorial waters by U.S. and British nuclear-capable warships, many of which are carrying nuclear weapons, are currently accepted by Canada. Canada is traditionally associated with the Northern Flank members of NATO — Denmark, Iceland and Norway — but of these four countries, only Canada accepts the transit of nuclear weapons on naval vessels through its territory. (Although there is little doubt that their policies have been violated on numerous occasions, each of the other three officially prohibits such transits.)

Part of the worldwide controversy surrounding the issue of naval nuclear-weapons visits is the policy of the NATO nuclear powers to "neither confirm nor deny" the presence of nuclear weapons on any particular aircraft, naval vessel, or other carrier. In the case of Canada, this policy denies the Canadian government knowledge of what nuclear weapons are present in Canadian ports and territorial waters. Canada accepts this policy as it applies to naval vessels even though it does not accept it for any other transit of nuclear weapons through Canada (such as nuclear-armed aircraft), which all require specific Canadian permission. The Department of National Defence has failed to provide any explanation for this double standard.[4] Clearly, the "neither confirm nor deny" policy is not inviolable, although the U.S. has recently portrayed it as such in its disputes with New Zealand and other nations.

As long as Canada is not informed when nuclear weapons are being carried on naval vessels wishing to enter Canada, it will be necessary — once a NWFZ is established — to prohibit visits by all nuclear-capable warships (about 85 per cent of warships in the U.S. case) in order to prohibit the entry of naval nuclear weapons. If the NATO nuclear powers would disclose which vessels were carrying nuclear weapons (which need not tell the Soviet Union anything it does not know), fewer visits would have to be curtailed.

Naval nuclear weapons represent a growing danger to world peace. Increasingly, these weapons are becoming war-fighting weapons designed for use during a conventional or nuclear war. As such, they are widely recognized to be one of the most likely causes of a nuclear war.

The majority of naval nuclear weapons coming into Canada are anti-submarine and anti-aircraft weapons, designed for fighting a war. The addition of nuclear-armed Tomahawk cruise missiles to U.S. Navy ships and submarines means that a growing number of these vessels are also equipped to fight "limited" or "protracted" nuclear wars.[5] What Canada is supporting, by allowing vessels with these various nuclear weapons into Canadian ports, is a naval nuclear war-fighting strategy. This fact underlines the importance of withdrawing current Canadian support for these weapons.

Other

The government has confirmed that on rare occasions nuclear weapons may be moved through Canada as part of peacetime logistical moves, subject to prior permission. Such movements would be forbidden in a NWFZ.

No Production

Nuclear Weapons Production and Export

Consistent with Canadian obligations under the letter and spirit of the Non-Proliferation Treaty, Canada does not manufacture nuclear weapons and Canadian policy forbids the export of fissionable materials, tritium and nuclear technologies for use in the development or production of nuclear explosive devices. There is serious concern, however, about the effectiveness of the regulations enforcing these policies. Research conducted by the Saskatchewan Inter-Church Uranium Committee and others suggests that Canadian uranium exports are making their way into the atomic bomb programs of a number of countries. Concern also exists that the waste products of the CANDU nuclear reactor could be reprocessed to produce the material required for a nuclear weapon.[6] NWFZ status would demand that Canadian exports of uranium, tritium, nuclear reactors and related technologies not be used, directly or indirectly, to facilitate the nuclear weapons programs of other nations. If these strict conditions could not be met, then such exports would have to cease. As noted above, Canadian policy already forbids the facilitation of nuclear-weapon programs — it is now time to make sure the policy is followed meticulously.

Nuclear-Weapons Delivery Systems Production and Export

Current Canadian policy places no restrictions on Canadian industrial involvement in the production of U.S. nuclear and nuclear-capable delivery systems. Canadian nuclear-weapons production extends beyond the already well-known Litton cruise missile component contract. Canada is a regular producer of components for an arsenal of nearly thirty different nuclear-weapons-related missiles, aircraft, and other weapons systems — including at times MX missiles, Trident submarines, and B-1B bombers — as well as Air-Launched Cruise Missiles and B-52 bombers, the instruments of the recent U.S. violation of SALT II.[7] The components Canada produces for these systems are exported to the U.S. under the terms of the Defence Development and Production Sharing Arrangements. These arrangements, which have created a kind of common market in military goods between Canada and the United States, make no distinction between nuclear and non-nuclear weapons or between types of nuclear weapons which may be more or less destabilizing and provocative.

Canada also produces components for some of the nuclear systems of its other allies, such as the British nuclear-capable Tornado aircraft.

While it is clear that the production of components for weapons systems used primarily or exclusively for nuclear-weapons delivery would be banned in a NWFZ, the production of components for nuclear-capable delivery systems that are primarily conventional weapons, such as fighter aircraft, is an ambiguous activity. Nuclear-capable weapon systems are those which can carry nuclear weapons but which exist primarily to serve other purposes. As an example, the F-18A Hornet aircraft can deliver B57 or B61 nuclear bombs, but its primary purpose (and, as the Canadian CF-18, its sole purpose) is to be a jet fighter with conventional bombs and missiles. The question of nuclear-capable systems requires further thinking about the kinds of production which would be acceptable in Canada under a NWFZ.

Every year, the Canadian government provides large sums of money to corporations, through the Defence Industry Productivity Program and through tax breaks and other subsidies, to produce military products for export. These products sometimes include nuclear and nuclear-capable weapons system components. Subject to the definitions arrived at, production of such components would cease when Canada became a NWFZ, as would government subsidies of that production. Economic disruption caused by this policy should be minor: there is no evidence that any companies in Canada are dependent upon nuclear-related contracts and, by supporting industrial-conversion efforts, the government can facilitate — with minimal disruption to local jobs and economies — the transition to fully non-nuclear production by those companies which do have nuclear-related contracts.

No Support of Nuclear Weapons

Nuclear-Support Facilities

These facilities could be as important to the use of nuclear weapons as the weapons themselves. The nuclear infrastructure is a world-wide network that provides such services as research, development and testing of nuclear weapons; personnel training for nuclear-weapons use; and communications and other support facilities for controlling nuclear weapons.

This infrastructure is not maintained exclusively within the territories of the nuclear-weapon states. The infrastructure is global, and the nuclear powers rely on friendly states to host elements of the infrastructure on which the operations of nuclear weapons depend. To the extent that the nuclear-weapon states depend on other states for these facilities, the latter potentially have the capability to limit the operations of nuclear weapons by denying them a global infrastructure.

The Canadian government regards this network of nuclear-support facilities as part of a stabilizing deterrent to nuclear war. But a combination of the high numbers of nuclear weapons and the development of nuclear war-fighting technologies and doctrines calls this assumption into question. Such provocative goals as "prevailing" in "protracted" nuclear combat (in other words, fighting and coming out "ahead" in a nuclear war) suggest a willingness to consider nuclear combat as a real option, thus increasing the chances of slipping into a catastrophic war.

Among non-nuclear powers, Canada is second only to West Germany in the number of nuclear-weapon-related facilities it hosts.[8] However, this large number is accounted for mainly by northern and Pinetree line radar sites, none of which would have to be removed as a result of a NWFZ policy. The role of many of the remaining facilities could be modified to negate the nuclear-weapons connection; the others would have to be removed from a Canadian NWFZ.

Nuclear-Weapon Testing

No actual nuclear-weapon explosive testing is permitted in Canada.

Delivery/Support Systems Testing and Development

Nuclear-weapon-delivery-system testing is currently permitted. The existing agreement to permit the testing of the Air-Launched Cruise Missile (ALCM) in Canadian airspace could not continue in a Canadian NWFZ. This testing agreement comes under the umbrella of the Canada-U.S. Test and Evaluation Program agreement, which makes allowance for the cancellation of any such project if "any unforeseen imperative circumstances should so warrant."[9] Thus, Canadian withdrawal from ALCM testing is clearly feasible.

Other weapons tests would also be affected by a Canadian NWFZ. For example, cold-weather flight tests of U.S. 155 mm "neutron bomb" artillery shells have taken place in recent years in Canada; ASROC and SUBROC (nuclear anti-submarine weapons) have been and may still be tested at Nanoose in British Columbia; and Trident I submarine-launched ballistic missile flight tests over the Atlantic Ocean are supported by a "Remote Ranging Station" at Argentia, Newfoundland. The testing of all these weapons would be banned under a NWFZ.

Nor is this all. Nuclear-related testing and development activities in Canada that would not be permitted in a NWFZ include the simulated nuclear explosions conducted by the Defence Research Establishment at Suffield, Alberta, to study weapons effects. And studies of satellite transmissions in the Arctic related to the new U.S. MILSTAR communications satellite, which is intended to be the primary means of communication during a nuclear war, would also not be permitted.

Nuclear-Weapons Training

Nuclear-weapons training by U.S., and possibly other NATO forces takes place across Canada, from the Northwest Territories to the U.S. border, from Labrador to the Georgia Strait. U.S. Strategic Air Command (SAC) FB-111, B-52 and B-1B bombers train in alert procedures, low-level flying, penetration of air defences and electronic warfare in Canadian airspace on a weekly basis and in large-scale exercises several times per year. Canadian fighter aircraft often take part in these simulated battles. This training prepares SAC crews to conduct nuclear attacks on the Soviet Union.

Nuclear-related anti-submarine warfare training is conducted by U.S. ships and submarines at Nanoose. Training by nuclear-capable British Tornadoes in Labrador and by German nuclear-capable artillery in Manitoba may also include nuclear missions.

All nuclear-weapons training (but not conventional training) would be prohibited under a NWFZ.

Operational Nuclear-Support Systems

Command and control, communications and other support facilities are essential elements of operational nuclear-weapons systems. In this regard, the creation of a Canadian NWFZ will affect a range of institutions and policies:

- NORAD — Currently, NORAD does not involve the command and control of any nuclear weapons, with the possible exception of a small number of U.S.-deployed Genie air-to-air missiles facing retirement. Nevertheless, NORAD requires a close examination to determine how it would relate to a NWFZ policy.

  NORAD's primary peacetime functions are surveillance of North American airspace and early warning of nuclear attack. These are important functions that would have to be carried out in some form even after a Canadian decision to become nuclear-weapon-free. In order that Canadian territory act as a buffer between the superpowers, rather than as an avenue of possible surprise attack, it is important that Canada continue to monitor and control Canadian airspace, sharing this information with the United States (as it does now under NORAD) and with the Soviet Union.

  NORAD's existing air-defence forces are an integral part of the early-warning system and are not sufficiently large or survivable to play a significant part in a nuclear war-fighting exchange. However, the developing NORAD role in war-fighting must be taken seriously. Any move on the part of the United States to upgrade NORAD's forces into a comprehensive air defence, to integrate them with a deployed "Star Wars" defence system, or to do both, would clearly involve them in a war-fighting role. Under these circumstances, a nuclear-weapon-free Canada would be obliged to withdraw from all joint air-defence activities with the United States and concentrate on maintaining an independent early-warning surveillance system for Canadian territory. Barring future changes in the role of air defence, the NORAD relationship with the United States can continue largely unchanged in the context of a NWFZ policy, with either a modified NORAD agreement or a replacement agreement emphasizing surveillance and early-warning.

- Communications facilities transmit the information necessary to plan and order nuclear attacks. The only communications facilities in Canada clearly dedicated to nuclear weapons support are six "Green Pine" UHF radio sites intended to transmit attack orders to U.S. strategic bombers flying over this country on the way to the Soviet Union.[10] The Green Pine system would have to be removed from a Canadian NWFZ. The nature and extent of other Canadian links to the command, control, communications and intelligence-gathering for nuclear forces is the subject of continuing research. Many other communications networks in Canada could perhaps be used to carry nuclear orders, but it is probable that this could be prevented with little or no effect on the networks themselves.

• Canada supports nuclear weapons in several other ways: arrangements exist to allow SAC tanker aircraft, or other SAC support aircraft, to disperse to and operate from Canadian airfields[11] (since these are not nuclear-armed, they do not fall under the transit ban); Canada contributes money to NATO Infrastructure Funds for nuclear emplacements in Europe and participates in nuclear decision-making in the NATO Nuclear Planning Group; Canada may have military personnel serving on exchange in nuclear-weapons-related roles in other armed forces. All these kinds of direct nuclear-support activity would have to be eliminated in a NWFZ.

The status of other elements of the Canadian military as part of the nuclear-support infrastructure is ambiguous. For example: the LORAN-C long-range radio navigation system (used by missile-carrying submarines) is now primarily useful for civilian navigation; the communications support for the Ballistic Missile Early Warning System radars used by NORAD could conceivably support the use of these radars in nuclear war-fighting, but that is not their primary purpose; and, similarly, the land-based receiving stations (at Argentia, Newfoundland, and Shelburne, Nova Scotia) for the SOSUS underwater submarine-detection system have more of an early-warning function than a war-fighting function given that the sea-leg of the Soviet nuclear deterrent is no longer dependent on deployment in the western Atlantic. For the purposes of a Canadian NWFZ, it would probably be advisable to focus on only those support systems that are primarily or exclusively dedicated to the support of nuclear-weapons use.

NATO and a Canadian NWFZ

The current Canadian government position on Canada as a NWFZ is that "the Government does not support a declaration of nuclear weapon-free status for Canada because, while in fact Canada does not possess nuclear weapons, nor are such weapons stationed on Canadian territory, we continue to participate fully in NATO, a defence alliance which deploys a nuclear deterrent. The declaration of a nuclear-weapon-free-zone would be inconsistent with membership in that alliance."[12]

It is both technically and politically incorrect to argue that refusal to participate in or support the nuclear forces of other NATO members is incompatible with membership in the alliance. As France and Spain have demonstrated, even the refusal to take part in NATO's integrated military structure is not incompatible with NATO membership. Iceland, which has no armed forces at all, also remains a welcome member of NATO.

The nature and size of the commitments (even conventional) made by any NATO member are, in the final analysis, decisions for that state alone. The North Atlantic Treaty makes no reference at all to nuclear weapons. Article 5 of the treaty allows each of the sixteen members to take "such action as it deems necessary" for collective defence. This action may, or may not, include the use of armed force.

Canada demonstrated clearly that nuclear-weapon commitments are solely national decisions when it made the unilateral decision in the late 1960s to eliminate the nuclear-weapon roles for Canada in Europe.

Canada is not alone among NATO members in restricting or prohibiting its involvement with nuclear weapons. Excluding the United States, seven NATO members have U.S. nuclear weapons deployed in their territories. One of these, Greece, is publicly committed to creating a NWFZ in the Balkans and has pledged to remove U.S. nuclear weapons and bases from its soil by 1989. Every one of the remaining eight members of the alliance has some sort of restrictions or prohibitions on the deployment of other NATO members' nuclear weapons in its territory. For example:

- Spain succeeded in having all nuclear warheads removed from its soil in 1979 and its parliament has voted to ban all storing, transit or installation of nuclear weapons in Spanish territory.
- Denmark prohibits the entry of nuclear weapons during peacetime and has refused to pay its share of NATO infrastructure costs pertaining to U.S. cruise missile and Pershing II missile bases in Europe. The entry of naval nuclear weapons is prohibited, but this policy, apparently, is not enforced.
- Norway and Iceland also forbid the entry of nuclear weapons to their territory in times of peace. Both of these countries have recently reaffirmed that this policy does apply to naval nuclear weapons.

These eight countries — Canada, Denmark, France, Iceland, Luxembourg, Norway, Portugal, and Spain — comprise just over one-half of the non-U.S. membership of NATO (of course, France is a nuclear-weapons power in its own right). *Including Greece, the percentage of non-U.S. NATO members that have policies directed at partially or completely prohibiting involvement with other NATO members' nuclear weapons is a solid 60 per cent.* Clearly, national policies that prohibit nuclear weapons are entirely consistent with NATO membership.

Currently, Denmark, Iceland and Norway are actively examining the prospects of creating a regional Nordic Nuclear Weapon-Free Zone that would expand and codify their existing nuclear prohibitions and which might also include Sweden, Finland, and perhaps the Baltic Sea. Greece is attempting to negotiate a similar Balkan zone. These countries intend and expect to remain members of NATO even if they should become full nuclear-weapon-free-zones. There is no reason why Canada could not also become nuclear-weapon-free while remaining a member of NATO.

The idea of Canada as a NWFZ is proposed as a general framework for Canadian policy towards nuclear weapons. This framework would replace Canada's current uncritical acceptance of the alliance's nuclear-weapons policy with a Canadian-defined policy rejecting any Canadian role in support of nuclear weapons. Such a stance need not be in conflict with alliance membership, although there is no doubt that the alliance "leadership" would loudly oppose a Canadian NWFZ and would characterize it as a threat to "alliance solidarity."

Conclusions

The Case for Consistency

Although significant changes in Canadian policy are required to make Canada a nuclear-weapon-free-zone, these changes are not as extensive as one might have expected. In many cases, the policy changes that are required are simply logical extensions of policies that are already in place. If Canadian policy already prohibits the export of fissionable materials for nuclear warheads, it is only logical and consistent to insist that Canada also prohibit the export of systems and components that help to guide and transport those warheads to their targets. If airborne nuclear weapons are not permitted in Canadian territory, it is only logical and consistent that shipborne nuclear weapons also be prohibited. Canada, having divested itself of all operational nuclear roles for Canadian forces, should now extend this principle and refuse to host nuclear roles in Canadian territory for its allies — even more so since some of these activities are in direct violation of Canadian arms-control and disarmament objectives and policies (e.g. SALT II violations and the development of nuclear war-fighting doctrines).

A Political Message

By declaring itself a NWFZ, and by taking the measures necessary to make this policy a reality, Canada would also be sending a clear and compelling political message — a message that the continuing cycle of nuclear deployments, expansions and modernizations must be stopped. Nuclear weapons ultimately must be eliminated, but until that happens all states have a responsibility to adopt policies and practices that will reduce the likelihood of these weapons being used. This is the true function of a NWFZ in Canada. A Canadian NWFZ, by denying access to Canadian territory for elements of nuclear war-fighting systems, would reduce the nuclear options available to the superpowers and thus contribute directly to greater global security. Contrary to the charge that a NWFZ represents "unilateral disarmament," a Canadian NWFZ would in no way jeopardize the legitimate security interests of our allies.

By becoming a NWFZ, Canada would also be telling the world that it expects major progress in disarmament by the nuclear weapons states. To be most effective, Canada should twin its NWFZ declaration with high-profile international advocacy in support of such measures as a comprehensive test ban, a ban on flight testing of new nuclear-weapon delivery systems, adherence to the ABM Treaty, "no first use" declarations, radical reductions in nuclear arsenals and ultimately the abolition of nuclear weapons. Canada's unilateral initiative in becoming a NWFZ would help it to become a credible catalyst for global disarmament. A leader of the Netherlands Interchurch Peace Council has made a very succinct case for such unilateral initiatives:

> This is not to be seen as an element of an approach towards complete unilateral disarmament, but as a first step, which is unilateral and independent, but fit to evoke a bilateral and multilateral process towards disarmament. [This is] a step, which should be drastic enough to be a clear expression of an alternative approach, but at the same time small enough to enable allies and others to respond to it on the military and political level.[13]

A Canadian NWFZ initiative would be true to Canadian foreign-policy tradition. While Canada has placed itself, often uncritically, in the camp of one of the superpowers, it has also been willing to advance progressive alternatives. A Canadian nuclear-weapon-free-zone is one of the most important initiatives Canada could now undertake in that tradition.

Endnotes

Chapter 1

1. Ralph Earle II "America Is Cheating Itself," *Foreign Policy*, Winter 1987, pp. 3-16.

2. See the Center for Defense Information "Soviet Compliance With Arms Agreements: The Positive Record," *The Defense Monitor*, Volume XVI, Number 2, 1987; Gloria Duffy "Study finds treaty compliance," *Bulletin of the Atomic Scientists*, October 1987, pp. 30-32; and Allan Krass & Catherine Grirrier (eds.) *Disproportionate Response: American Policy and Alleged Soviet Treaty Violations* (Cambridge, Massachusetts: Union of Concerned Scientists, 1987).

3. Simon Rosenblum, *Misguided Missiles* (Toronto: James Lorimer, 1985), pp. 77-101.

4. U.S. Department of Defense, *Fiscal Year 1987 Department of Defense Program for Research and Development* (Washington, D.C. 1986) p. 11.

5. Michael T. Klare and Peter Kornbluh, (eds.) *Low Intensity Warfare: Counter-insurgency, Pro-insurgency, and Anti-Terrorisim in the 80s*, (New York: Pantheon, 1988).

6. Alva Myrdal, *The Game of Disarmament* (New York: Pantheon, 1978).

7. Allan B. Sherr, "Sound Legal Reasoning or Policy Expedient?," *International Security*, Winter 1986-87, pp. 71-93.

8. Herbert Lin, letter to the Editor, New York *Times*, October 26, 1987. The writer of the letter is identified as a postdoctoral research fellow at M.I.T.'s Center for International Studies.

9. John Tirman (ed.), *Empty Promise: The Growing Case Against Star Wars* (Boston: The Union of Concerned Scientists, Beacon Press, 1986).

10. Johan Galtung "The Real Star Wars Threat," *The Nation*, February 28, 1987, pp. 248-250.

11. Quoted in Robert S. McNamara, *Blundering Into Disaster* (New York: Pantheon, 1986) p. 102.

12. Quoted in Elizabeth Drew "Letter from Washington,"*The New Yorker*, October 27, 1986, p. 134.

13. Freeman Dyson, *Weapons and Hope* (New York: Harper and Row, 1984).

14. Ulrich Albrecht "Revive the Reykjavik Dynamism," *Bulletin of the Atomic Scientists*, March 1987, pp. 40-41.

15. *F.A.S. Public Interest Report*, November 1986, p. 7.

16. Hearings of Senate Armed Services Committee, *The Washington Post*, February 6, 1987, p. A 16.

17. John Pike "ABM Treaty: New Quantitative Limits" *F.A.S. Public Interest Report*, March 1987; and Raymond L. Earthoff "Refocussing the SDI debate," *Bulletin of the Atomic Scientists*, September, 1987.

18. John Pike "Goals of the ABM Treaty," *F.A.S. Public Interest Report*, September, 1987.

19. Michele A. Flourney "A Rocky Start," *Arms Control Today*, October 1987, pp. 7-13; and Michel Tatu "Real Signs of Progress in Nuclear Arms Reductions" *Manchester Guardian Weekly*, January 31, 1988.

20. Leon V. Sigal "Stability and Reduction of Nuclear Forces" *Bulletin of the Atomic Scientists*, Volume 16, Number 3, 1985, pp. 233-239.

21. Christoph Bertram "US-Soviet Nuclear Arms Control" in *SIPRI Yearbook 1987*, pp. 323-337.

22. Canadian Institute for International Peace and Security, *Nuclear Weapons, Counter-force, and Arms Reduction Proposals* (Ottawa, 1987).

23. Robert S. McNamara, *Blundering Into Disaster*, (New York: Pantheon, 1986).

24. Richard Garwin "Mad is Sane — Interview with Dr. Richard Garwin," *The Cornell Review*, September 1986; and Harold Feiverson, Richard Ullman and Frank von Hippel "Structure of a Minimum Deterrent" *Bulletin of the Atomic Scientists*, August 1985.

25. Freeman Dyson, *Weapons and Hope* (New York: Harper and Row, 1984), p.313.

26. Jonathan Schell, *The Abolition* (New York: Knopf, 1984).

27. Gwynne Dyer, "On Alliances," *CPPNW Quarterly*, Summer 1987.

28. Bruce Birchard and Rob Leavitt "A New Agenda," *Nuclear Times*, October, 1987.

29. Richard J. Barnet "The Four Pillars" *The New Yorker*, March 9, 1987.

30. Independent Commission on Disarmament and Security Issues, *Common Security: A Blueprint For Survival* (New York: Simon and Schuster, 1982).

31. Randall Forsberg "The Freeze and Beyond: Confining the Military to Defense as a Route to Disarmament," *World Policy Journal*, (Winter, 1984).

32. Randall Forsberg "Ending Intervention: The Global Stakes" *Defense and Disarmament News*, September-October 1987; and Robert Johansen "Global Security Without Nuclear Deterrence" *Alternatives* XII (1987).

33. John Lewis Gaddis "How The Cold War Might End" *The Atlantic Monthly*, November 1987, pp. 88-100.

34. Andrei Sakharov, *Time*, March 16, 1987, p.32.

Chapter 2

1. Quoted in S.F. Wise, *Canadian Airmen and the First World War*, (Ottawa: Minister of Supply and Services, 1980), p. 279.

2. *Ibid.*, p. 280.

3. Quoted in Ronald Schaffer, *Wings of Judgment: American Bombing in World War II*, (Oxford University Press, 1985), p.21.

4. Sidney Axinn, "Honor, Patriotism, and Ultimate Loyalty," in *Nuclear Weapons and the Future of Humanity*, edited by Avner Cohen and Steven Lee, (Rowman and Allanheld, 1986), p. 275.

5. Quoted in Burns, Lieutenant-General E.L.M., *Megamurder*, (New York: Pantheon Books, 1966, 1967), p. 54.

6. Robert W. Malcolmson, *Nuclear Fallacies: How We Have Been Misguided since Hiroshima*, (Toronto: McGill-Queen's University Press, 1985).

7. John P. Holdren, "The Dynamics of the Nuclear Arms Race," *Nuclear Weapons and the Future of Humanity*, edited by Avner Cohen and Steven Lee, (Rowman and Allanheld, 1986), p. 42.

8. Joel Kovel, *Against the State of Nuclear Terror*, (Boston: South End Press, 1983), p. 35. See also Malcolmson, 1985, and Holdren, 1986.

9. Holdren, p. 61.

10. Holdren, p. 61.

11. The International Institute for Strategic Studies, *The Military Balance, 1984-1985*, (London, 1984), p. 13.

12. Michael Wallace, Brian L. Crissey, and Linn I. Sinnott, "Accidental Nuclear War: A Risk Assessment," *The Nuclear Time Bomb, Peace Research Reviews*, Vol 10, No.3, (Dundas: Peace Research Institute, May 1986), p. 113.

13. Crissey, cited in *The Nuclear Time Bomb*, op cit. p.7.

14. General Bernard Rogers. SACEUR, "Improving Public Understanding of NATO Objectives, *The Atlantic Community Quarterly*, Vol 20, No. 4, Winter 1982-83.

15. Jocelyn Coulon, "New Zealand's Nuclear Allergy," *Peace and Security*, Vol 1 No. 4, Winter 1987/87, (Ottawa: Canadian Institute for International Peace and Security).

Chapter 3

1. Theodore A. Postol, "Possible Fatalities from Superfires Following Nuclear Attacks in or near Urban Areas," in *The Medical Implications of Nuclear War*, ed. by Frederic Solomon and Robert Q. Marston, Institute of Medicine, National Academy of Sciences, (Washington: National Academy Press, 1986), pp. 15 to 72; p.51. I have depended heavily on this excellent book which is the published proceedings of a conference sponsored by the Institute of Medicine, in Washington, September, 1985. Hereafter, the book itself will be referred to as I.O.M.

2. For some interesting reflections on firestorms caused by conventional weapons in World War II, see Thomas Powers, "Nuclear Winter in Nuclear Strategy," *The Atlantic*, November, 1984, p. 53f.

3. *Hiroshima and Nagasaki: The Physical, Medical, and Social Effects of the Atomic Bombings*, (New York: Basic Books, 1981), p. 420 f. Hereafter referred to as H&N.

4. H&N p. 504. See also *Time*, July 29, 1985, p. 36.

5. Personal conversation with Dr. Kiyoshi Kuramoto, Vice Director of the Red Cross "Atomic Bomb" hospital in Hiroshima.

6. H&N, pp. 508 and 512.

7. See, for example, Lester Machta and Kosta Telegradas, "Radioiodine Levels in the U.S. Public Health Service Pasteurized Milk Network from 1963-1968 and Their Relationship to Possible Sources," *Health Physics*, 1970, 19:469-485.

8. "Ethno-Epidemiology: The Marshall Islanders Twenty-Five Years After Exposure to Radiation," Transcript of Symposium for American Association for the Advancement of Science, San Francisco, January 7, 1980, p. 5. The speaker was Dr. Hugh Pratt of the Brookhaven National Laboratory.

9. *Ibid.*, passim.

10. Two recent books have covered the subject extensively: Richard L. Miller, *Under the Cloud: The Decades of Nuclear Testing*, (New York: Free Press, Macmillan, 1986), and Howard Ball, *Justice Downwind: America's Atomic Testing Program in the 1950s*, (New York: Oxford University Press, 1986).

11. Lord Penney, who, as Sir William Penney, was in charge of British nuclear tests in Australia in the 1950s, told a hearing on the subject in January, 1985, that he would welcome a proper survey to discover the effects of all the tests on the Australian servicemen! *Manchester Guardian Weekly*, January 27, 1985. See also, "UK Secrecy Irks Australians," *Globe and Mail*, January 7, 1985. Information pertaining to French secrecy in Polynesia was obtained from a transcript of a speech by Dorothee Piermont, Member of the European Parliament for the Green Party, in Cologne, May, 1986.

12. Zhores A. Medvedev, *Nuclear Disaster in the Urals*, trans. George Saunders, (New York: Vintage Books, 1979).

13. "Radioactive leftovers," *Globe and Mail*, January 17, 1987; "Chernobyl legacy: Radiation levels high in Soviet tea, nuts, envoy says, " *Montreal Gazette*, April 4, 1987. For a medical assessment of the accident, see Robert P. Gale, "Immediate Medical Consequences of Nuclear Accidents: Lessons from Chernobyl," *Journal of the American Medical Association*, 1987, 258: 625-628.

14. Eliot Marshall, "New A-Bomb Data Shown to Radiation Experts," Science, 1981, 212: 1364 f. See also letters to the editors, *ibid.*, 213: 6-8 and 602-604.

15. "Acute Radiation Mortality in a Nuclear War," in I.O.M., pp. 233-250.

16. Letter to the editor by Frank von Hippel in *Science*, 1985, 230: 992.

17. William Daugherty, Barbara Levi, and Frank von Hippel, "Casualties Due to the Blast, Heat, and Radioactive Fallout from Various Hypothetical Nuclear Attacks on the United States," in I.O.M., pp. 207 to 250.

18. T. Postol, *op. cit.*, in I.O.M., p. 69.

19. What follows is from David S. Greer and Lawrence S. Rifkin, "The Immunological Impact of Nuclear Warfare," in I.O.M., pp. 317 to 336.

20. W. Daugherty, *et al*, in I.O.M., p. 214.

21. Quoted in W. Daugherty *et al*, in I.O.M., p. 29, where the story that follows appears.

22. von Hippel, letter to the editor, *op. cit.*

23. See, for example, the lampooning editorial, "Where Were You When the Lights Went Out?" *Globe and Mail*, November 22, 1986.

24. *Maclean's*, January 4, 1988, pp. 46-47.

25. For a general survey of the subject just before the environmental effects began to come before the public, see Don G. Bates, "The Medical and Ecological Effects of Nuclear War," *McGill Law Journal*, 1983, 28: 716-731.

26. For two studies that tried to address the environmental consequences in 1965 and 1966, without success, see *The Effects on the Atmosphere of a Major Nuclear Exchange*, Committee on the Atmospheric Effects of Nuclear Explosions, National Research Council, (Washington: National Academy Press, 1985), p. 185f.

27. John W. Birks and Sherry L. Stephens, "Possible Toxic Environments Following a Nuclear War," in I.O.M., pp. 155-166; p. 163.

28. Paul J. Crutzen, "The influence of nitrogen oxides on the atmospheric ozone content," *Quarterly Journal of the Royal Meteorological Society*, (1970), 96: 320-325.

29. Paul J. Crutzen and John W. Birks, "The Atmosphere After a Nuclear War: Twilight at Noon," in *Ambio*, (1982), 11: 114-125.

30. For a brief overview of this history, see "The Effects on the Atmosphere ...," *op. cit.*, pp. 185 to 188.

31. To the chagrin of many scientists, it appeared first in public in the Sunday newspaper magazine *Parade*, under the authorship of Carl Sagan, October 30, 1983.

32. R.P. Turco, O.B. Toon, T.P. Ackerman, J.B. Pollack and Carl Sagan, "Nuclear Winter: Global Consequences of Multiple Nuclear Explosions," *Science*, (1983), 222: 1283-1292.

33. Paul R. Ehrlich, Carl Sagan, Donald Kennedy and Walter O. Roberts, *The Cold and the Dark: The World After Nuclear War*, (New York: W.W. Norton, 1984). Contains the published results of a conference of scientists on the subject that was held at the end of October, 1983, and which was dubbed "the Halloween Party."

34. See, in particular, the letters to the editors of *Nature* and *Science* over the ensuing few months. Particularly controversial was an article by Carl Sagan, "Nuclear War and Climatic Catastrophe: Some Policy Implications," *Foreign Affairs*, (1983-84), 62: 257-292. This sparked a lively debate in that journal as well. See Starley L. Thompson and Stephen H. Schneider, "Nuclear Winter Reappraised," *ibid.*, 1986, 65: 163-178.

35. *op. cit.*

36. Reported by Stephen Schneider at the annual meeting of the American Association for the Advancement of Science, Chicago, February 16, 1987.

37. M.A. Harwell and T.C. Hutchinson, *Environmental Consequences of Nuclear War*, Vol. II: Ecological and Agricultural Effects, (New York: John Wiley and Sons, 1985). The two volumes together are commonly known as the SCOPE/ENUWAR (Scientific Committee on Problems of the Environment/Environmental Effects of Nuclear War) Report.

38. Mark A. Harwell and Christine C. Harwell, "Nuclear Famine: The Indirect Effects of Nuclear War," in I.O.M., pp.117 to 135.

39. *Ibid.* See also *Nuclear Winter and Associated Effects: A Canadian Appraisal of the Environmental Impact of Nuclear War*, Report of the Committee on the Environmental Consequences of Nuclear War, The Royal Society of Canada, 1985, pp. 37 to 41. For a general study of the impact of nuclear war on Canada, done before the TTAPS report on nuclear winter, see D.G. Bates, D.P. Brisk in, L. Cotton, M. McDonald, L. Panaro and A. Poslon, "What Would Happen to Canada in a Nuclear War?" in *Canada and the Nuclear Arms Race*, ed. by E. Regehr and S. Rosenblum, (Toronto: James Lorimer, 1983), pp. 171 to 190.

40. What follows is taken from Harwell and Harwell *op. cit.*

41. Harwell and Harwell, *op. cit.*, p. 134.

Chapter 4

1. Ralph Earl III, quoted in *Arms Control Verification*, William F. Rowell (Cambridge: Ballinger, 1986) p.22.

2. U.S. Arms Control and Disarmament Agency, Verification: *The Critical Element of Arms Control* (Washington D.C.: 1976).

3. Government of Canada, "Verification in All Its Aspects: A Comprehensive Study on Arms Control and Disarmament Verification Pursuant to UNGA Resolution 40/152(0)," Government of Canada. April, 1986. p.2.

4. Sidney Graybeal, quoted in Roger Bungham, "The Politics of Mistrust," *Science 85*, December 1985, p.36.

5. "Nuclear Disarmament by the Year 2000," Statement by Mikhail Gorbachev, General Secretary of the CPSU Central Committee, January 15, 1986. Reprinted in *New York Times*, February 5, 1986, p.5.

6. See for example, Leslie Gelb, "A Practical Way to Arms Control," *New York Times Magazine*, June 5, 1983, pp.33-42; David Hafemeister, "Advances in Verification Technology," *Bulletin of the Atomic Scientists*, January 1985, pp.35-40.

7. U.S. Arms Control and Disarmament Agency, *op. cit.*, pp.17-18.

8. John A. Adam, "Verification: Peacekeeping by Technical Means," *IEEE Spectrum*, July 1986, p.76.

9. Louis C. Finch, "Verification of Arms Control Limits on Land-mobile ICBM Launchers," *Congressional Record*, April 7, 1983, p.E1424.

10. John Horgan, "Underground Nuclear Weapons Testing," *IEEE Spectrum*, April 1986, pp.32-43; Lynn Sykes and Dan M. Davis, "The Yields of Soviet Strategic Weapons," *Scientific American*, January 1987, pp.29-37.

11. J.F. Evernden, C.B. Archambeau, and E. Cranswick, "An Evaluation of Seismic Decoupling and Underground Nuclear Test Monitoring Using High-Frequency Seismic Data," *Reviews of Geophysics*, May 1986, pp.143-215.

12. Herbert Lin, "Military Capabilities, Technology and Arms Control," *Issues in Science and Technology*, Summer 1987, pp.73-80.

13. S.M. Meyer, "Verification and Risk in Arms Control," *International Security*, Spring 1984, pp.111-126.

14. Glenn Buchan, "The Verification Spectrum," *Bulletin of the Atomic Scientists*, November 1983, pp.16-19.

15. Harold Brown, prepared statement to the U.S. Congress, Senate Committee on Foreign Relations, "The SALT II Treaty" (Part 2), 96th Congress (Washington D.C.: 1979), p.241.

16. Noel Gayler, quoted in Glenn Zorpette, "Monitoring the Tests," *IEEE Spectrum*, July 1986, p.66.

17. Allan Krass, "The Politics of Verification" *World Policy Journal*, Fall 1985, p.742.

18. United Nations, "The Implications of Establishing an International Satellite Monitoring Agency," U.N. document A/AC.206/14. (New York: 1983), 110 pp.

19. United Nations, "Monitoring of Disarmament Agreements and Strengthening of International Security," Report of the Secretariat, 27 August, 1979, U.N.G.A. A/34/374. p.28.

20. Right Honourable Joe Clark, Secretary of State for External Affairs, Statement to the House of Commons, January 23, 1986.

21. "The Verification Research Programme," *The Disarmament Bulletin* (Department of External Affairs, Canada), Spring-Summer 1985, p.12.

22. David Cox and Mary Taylor (ed.), Steve Baranyi, Jane Boulden and Mary Goldie (researchers), "A Guide to Canadian Policies on Arms Control, Disarmament, Defence and Conflict Resolution 1985-86," Canadian Institute for International Peace and Security. (Ottawa: 1986), 285 pp.

23. Government of Canada, "Verification in All Its Aspects: A Comprehensive Study on Arms Control and Disarmament Verification Pursuant to UNGA Resolution 40/152(0)," Government of Canada. April, 1986. p.41.

Chapter 5

1. See: "Disarmament: The Problem of Organizing The World Community." Ottawa: Department of External Affairs, *Statements and Speeches* No. 78/7; and "Technological Momentum The Fuel That Feeds The Nuclear Arms Race." Ottawa: Department of External Affairs, *Statements and Speeches* No.82/10.

2. Pierre Trudeau, "Disarmament: The Problem of Organizing The World Community." Speech given to UNSSOD I, New York, May 26, 1978.

3. As cited in Robert Reford, "UNSSOD II and Canada." *International Perspectives* July-August 1982, p.8.

4. Standing Committee on External Affairs and National Defence, *Report on Security and Disarmament*. (Ottawa: 9th Report to the House of Commons, April 1, 1982).

5. *Ibid.*, p.78.

6. Department of External Affairs, "Supplement," in: *International Perspectives* July-August 1982, pp. 17-18.

7. As quoted in: David Cox, "Trudeau's Foreign Policy Speeches." *International Perspectives* November-December 1982, pp. 8-9.

8. Pierre Trudeau, "Technological Momentum: The Fuel That Feeds The Nuclear Arms Race." Speech given to UNSSOD II, New York, June 18, 1982.

9. Toronto *Star*, May 8, 1982.

10. As quoted in: Department of External Affairs, "Supplement," in: *International Perspectives* September-October 1982, p.19. See also: "New Initiatives in Arms Control and Disarmament." *The Disarmament Bulletin* (Ottawa: Department of External Affairs, September 1982), p.5.

11. Mark MacGuigan, "Arms Control and Disarmament Agreements Essential to World Peace." Ottawa: Department of External Affairs, *Statements and Speeches* No. 82/17.

12. See: "Committee on Disarmament," in: *The Disarmament Bulletin*. (Ottawa: Department of External Affairs, February 1983), p.3.

13. Allan J. MacEachen, "Mutual Security: Negotiations in 1983." Address to the Committee on Disarmament, Geneva, February 1, 1983. Ottawa: Department of External Affairs, *Statements and Speeches* No. 83/1.

14. Pierre Trudeau, "Canada's Position on Testing Cruise Missiles and Disarmament." May 9, 1983. Ottawa: Department of External Affairs, *Statements and Speeches* No. 83/8.

15. Pierre Trudeau, "Reflections on Peace and Security." Notes for remarks to the Conference on Strategies for Peace and Security in the Nuclear Age, University of Guelph, October 27, 1983. Ottawa: Department of External Affairs, *Statements and Speeches* No. 83/18.

16. Michael Pitfield, "Problems of Preserving Peace and Security." Notes for a Statement before the First Committee of the UN General Assembly, New York, November 1, 1983. Ottawa: Department of External Affairs, *Statements and Speeches* No. 83/22.

17. See, for example: Adam Bromke and Kim Richard Nossal, "Trudeau Rides The 'Third Rail'." *International Perspectives* May-June 1984; Geoffrey Pearson, "Reflections on the Trudeau Peace Initiative." *International Perspectives* March-April 1985.

18. See: Department of External Affairs, "Supplement," in: *International Perspectives* January-February 1984, pp. 14-16.

19. Pierre Trudeau, "Initiatives for Peace and Security." Remarks in the House of Commons, Ottawa, February 9, 1984. Ottawa: Department of External Affairs, *Statements and Speeches* No. 84/2.

20. Harald von Riekhoff and John Sigler, "The Trudeau Peace Initiative: The Politics of Reversing The Arms Race," in Brian Tomlin and Maureen Molot (eds.), *Canada Among Nations 1984: A Time of Transition*. (Toronto: Lorimer, 1985), p. 68.

21. See, for example: E.L.M. Burns, *A Seat At The Table: The Struggle For Disarmament*. (Toronto: Clarke, Irwin & Company, 1972); Peyton V. Lyon, *Canada in World Affairs: 1961-1963*. (Toronto: Oxford University Press, 1968), esp. Ch. 4.

22. See, for example, the report of the President's Commission on Strategic forces, as excerpted in *Survival*, 25:4 July-August 1983, pp. 177-186.

23. Toronto *Globe and Mail, October 1, 1984*.

24. Joe Clark, "Peace and Disarmament First Priority in Canadian Foreign Policy." Notes for a Speech to the UN General Assembly, New York, September 25, 1984. Ottawa: Department of External Affairs, *Statements and Speeches* No. 84/6.

25. Douglas Roche, "Canada and the Common Commitment of Peace." Notes for a Speech to the First Committee of the UN General Assembly, New York, October 30, 1984.

26. Among the reasons listed by Ambassador Roche for the government's decision to vote against the freeze resolutions were, *inter alia*, the following: freeze-type arms control agreements does not necessarily enhance mutual security; negotiation of a freeze "world detract from efforts to achieve real reductions"; mutual agreement is required on establishing rules for verification; the freeze resolutions tabled do not deal with the "potentially destabilizing" problem of peaceful nuclear explosions. See: Department of External Affairs, "Supplement," in: *International Perspectives* January-February 1985, pp. 21-22.

27. *Hansard* 128:35, pp. 1501-1502.

28. Arthur Kroeger, "The U.S. Strategic Defence Initiative and Canada's Role," June 7, 1985. Disclosed, with exemptions, under the Canadian Access to Information Act.

29. Special Joint Committee of the Senate and the House of Commons on Canada's International Relations, *Interim Report*. (Ottawa: August 23, 1985).

30. For the text of the prime minister's statement, as well as the text of Minister of National Defence Erik Nielsen's letter on the same day to U.S. Secretary of Defense Caspar Weinberger, see: *The Disarmament Bulletin*. (Ottawa: Department of External Affairs, Autumn 1985), p. 7.

31. Office of the Prime Minister, "Notes for a Speech to the Consultative Group on Disarmament and Arms Control," Ottawa, October 31, 1985.

32. See, for example *Soviet Non-Compliance*. (Washington D.C.: United States Arms Control and Disarmament Agency, February 1, 1986); and "'Pattern of Soviet Noncompliance' with Arms Accords Seen." Text of the Report by the President to the U.S. Congress, as released by the United States Embassy Press Office, Ottawa, December 24, 1985.

33. Representative of this view is: Julian Robinson, Jeanne Guillemin and Matthew Meselson, "Yellow Rain: The Story Collapses." *Foreign Policy*, 68, Fall 1987, pp. 100-117.

34. See, for example, "Canada and the Current Crisis in Arms Control." Ottawa: Canadian Centre for Arms Control and Disarmament, *Arms Control Communique* No. 24, June 5, 1986.

35. "Declaration by the Prime Minster of Canada and the President of the United States Regarding International Security." Quebec City, March 18, 1985.

36. Standing Committee on External Affairs and National Defence (SCEAND), *Canada-U.S. Defence Cooperation and the 1986 Renewal of the NORAD Agreement*, (Ottawa: February 14, 1986); and Office of the Prime Minister, "NORAD Renewal." Ottawa: March 19, 1986. The latter four-sentence communique issued by both leaders contained, *inter alia*, the following short and unelaborated remarks: "The Prime Minister and the President agreed to extend the NORAD agreement for a further five year period. They noted that the extension of the NORAD agreement is fully consistent with other U.S. and Canadian treaty obligations."

37. Indicative of this approach is the "breakthrough" attributed by the Ambassador for Disarmament, Douglas Roche, in getting the UN to focus on the issue of verification when the UN General Assembly adopted by consensus a Canadian-initiated resolution [40/152(0)] entitled "Verification in All Its Aspects." For more detail, see: *The Disarmament Bulletin*. (Ottawa: Department of External Affairs, Winter 1985-Spring 1986), pp. 4-5.

38. *Hansard* 128:212, p. 10101.

39. See text of statement in: *The Disarmament Bulletin*. (Ottawa: Department of External Affairs, Summer-Autumn 1986), p. 4.

40. Joe Clark, "Statement on SALT II Compliance," Ottawa, November 28, 1986. Ottawa: Department of External Affairs, *Statements and Speeches* No. 86/54.

41. Joe Clark, "Statement on the Summit Preparatory Meeting at Reykjavik," Brussels, Belgium, October 13, 1986. Ottawa: Department of External Affairs, *Statements and Speeches* No. 86/54.

42. This proposal and its origins was explained by Max Kampelman, chief of the U.S. delegation to the Geneva arms control talks, in a press conference held in Paris, France, October 23, 1986. See: "'Real Tough' Questions Remain at Geneva Arms Talks." Transcript of Kampelman Press Conference. Ottawa: United States Information Service.

43. *Hansard* 129:15, pp. 553-554.

44. Standing Committee on External Affairs and International Trade, *Minutes of Proceedings and Evidence*. Issue No. 10, January 21, 1987, p. 9.

45. *Ibid.*, p. 24.

46. Standing Committee on National Defence, *Minutes of Proceedings and Evidence*. Issue No. 10, April 28, 1987, p. 13.

47. For a description of the place of the "transition to defence" in the U.S. negotiating position at Geneva, see *Arms Control Chronicle*, (Ottawa: Canadian Centre for Arms Control and Disarmament, Number 8, June 1985), pp. 7-8.

48. *Hansard* 129:48, pp. 2133-2134.

49. Office of the Prime Minister, "Notes for an Address Before the North Atlantic Assembly," Quebec City, May 23, 1987.

50. Office of the Prime Minister, "Prime Minister Brian Mulroney's Statement on the Reagan-Gorbachev Summit," Ottawa, December 10, 1987.

51. Department of National Defence, *Challenge and Commitment: A Defence Policy for Canada*, (Ottawa, June 1987), p. 19.

52. *Ibid.*

53. Robert S. Norris, William M. Arkin and Thomas B. Cochran, *START and Strategic Modernization*, (Washington, D.C.: Natural Resources Defense Council, NWD 87-2, December 1, 1987), pp. 21-24.

Chapter 6

1. This is based on the report of the Stockholm International Peace Research Institute that at the beginning of 1987 five and one-half million soldiers from 41 countries were involved in 36 armed conflicts. *SIPRI Yearbook 1987: Armaments and Disarmament* (Oxford University Press, 1987), pp. 297-320.

2. Based on a tabulation of all wars this century in the *1987-88 World Military and Social Expenditures* by Ruth Leger Sivard (World Priorities, Washington, 1987).

3. In 1984 a SIPRI study reported the dramatic increase in the number of countries regularly supplying arms to the two sides after the start of the war: in the case of Iraq from 3 to 18, and in the case of Iran from 5 to 17. *SIPRI 1984 Yearbook* (London: Taylor and Francis, 1984), pp. 195-201.

4. See Chapter 8.

5. Ruth Sivard's study of *World Military and Social Expenditures 1986* (Washington: World Priorities, 1986), pp. 24-25, shows that of the 57 governments identified as military-controlled, none had not exercised repression or used official violence against its citizens (i.e. torture, brutality, disappearances, and political killings).

6. Daniel Deudney, "Whole Earth Security: A Geopolitics of Peace," *Worldwatch Paper 55*, (Worldwatch Institute, July 1983), p. 8.

7. Ruth Leger Sivard, *World Military and Social Expenditures 1986* (World Priorities, 1986), pp. 25ff

8. This longstanding Canadian objective was repeated in the Tory Government's foreign policy green paper, *Competitiveness and Security: Directions for Canada's International Relations* (Department of Supply and Services, 1985; Catalogue No. E2110/1985), p. 14.

9. Robert C. Johansen, *Toward an Alternative Security System*, p.44.

10. Daniel Deudney, "Whole Earth Security: A Geopolitics of Peace," *Worldwatch Paper 55*, (Worldwatch Institute, July 1983).

11. Bruntland Report

12. ICC presentation to the Ambassador for Disarmament's Consultative Group on Disarmament and Arms Control, October 1-3, 1987.

13. *Common Security: A Programme for Disarmament*, Report of the Independent Commission on Disarmament and Security Issues (London: Pan Books, 1982).

14. *Foreign Affairs*, Vol. 51 (1973), p. 267.; quoted in Robert C. Johansen, *Toward an Alternative Security System: Moving beyond the Balance of Power in the Search for World Security* (World Policy Institute, World Policy Paper No. 24, 1983), p. 2.

15. American Bishops' reference

16. Jeff Sallot, "PM Warns U.S. on offensive use of Star Wars," *Globe and Mail*, May 25, 1987.

17. Douglas A. Ross, "Coping With 'Star Wars': Issues for Canada and the Alliance," *Aurora Papers 2*, The Canadian Centre for Arms Control and Disarmament.

18. Committee of Soviet Scientists for Peace, Against the Nuclear Threat, "Strategic Stability Under the Conditions of Radical Nuclear Arms Reductions" (an abridged report on the study), April 1987, p. 31.

19. John M. Lamb, "Canadian-American Defence Relations and the Cruise Missile Problem," *Arms Control Communique No. 31*, The Canadian Centre for Arms Control and Disarmament, November 11, 1986.

20. Lamb, p. 3.

21. Johansen, p. 46.

22. Randall Forsberg, "Nonprovocative Defense and the Abolition of Nuclear Weapons," *Defense and Disarmament News* (Brookline, Ma: Institute for Defense and Disarmament Studies, undated).

23. Johann Galtung uses the term transarmament to describe the restructuring of national defence forces from offensive to more defensive postures. See Johan Galtung, *There are Alternatives: Four Roads to Peace and Security* (Nottingham, England: Spokesman, 1984), pp. 172 ff.

24. Johansen, p. 45.

25. The term, "commons," as used here is, borrowed from Daniel Deudney, "Whole Earth Security: A Geopolitics of Peace," *Worldwatch Paper 55*, July 1983: "With the advent of planetary warmaking, security strategy has been based on the militarization of the commons — the ocean depths, the atmosphere and orbital space. With the enclosure of the planet by warmaking systems, security itself has become indivisible, a commons in its own right." p. 6.

26. On October 31, 1985, Prime Minister Mulroney told the Consultative Group that "the Government's research priorities were judged to lie more in the investigation of outer space verification technology than in feasibility studies of space-based weapon systems." And, as already noted, Mr. Mulroney warned the Atlantic Assembly in May of the dangers of strategic defence combined with counterforce weapons (see Note 2).

27. References to the Defence White Paper, *Challenge and Commitment: A Defence Policy for Canada*, are indicated by page numbers in the text.

28. To affirm the mutuality of deterrence is not to counsel political neutrality or to claim that there are no political or moral distinctions to be made between the two sides — it is only to acknowledge that as long as both sides have chosen weapons of global annihilation as their last resort, both must be subject to the discipline of deterrence.

29. *Legion Magazine*, May 1987.

30. Douglas A. Ross, "Coping With 'Star Wars': Issues for Canada and the Alliance," *Aurora Papers 2*, The Canadian Centre for Arms Control and disarmament, 1985, p. 2.

31. The feasibility of such systems was argued by Rear Admiral Charles Thomas, chief of Canada's Maritime Doctrine and Operations, in testimony before the Standing Committee on National Defence, January 28, 1987.

32. Bill Robinson, "US and NATO Maritime Strategy in the Arctic," Project Ploughshares, 1987 (paper prepared for Consultative Group, October 1-3, 1987).

33. *Globe and Mail*, December 20, 1987.

34. Purver, *Arms Control Options in the Arctic*, p.20.

35. Independence and Internationalism — incomplete

36. "Notes for an intervention by Douglas Roche, Canadian Ambassador for Disarmament to the United Nations Disarmament Commission," May 5, 1987 p. 6.

Chapter 7

1. Daniel Deudney, "Whole Earth Security: A Geopolitics of Peace," *Worldwatch Paper 55*, Worldwatch Institute, July 1983, p. 20-21.

2. William Arkin and Richard Fieldhouse, "Focus on the nuclear infrastructure," *Bulletin of the Atomic Scientists*, June-July 1985, p. 12.

3. Both the United States and the Soviet Union developed and deployed crude ground-based anti-satellite (ASAT) rockets in the 1960s. These systems lacked reliability and flexibility,however, and neither was effective against satellites in high orbits (where the most important communications and early-warning satellites are based). The U.S. ASAT system was retired in 1975. Since that time, the US has been developing a small ASAT weapon launched from a fighter aircraft, but it is not yet operational. Research is also being done by the US on lasers as ASAT weapons and, of course, Star Wars weapons would have potential as ASAT weapons. The Soviet ASAT system is still nominally operational, but it has not been tested since 1983, when the Soviet Union began a moratorium on all ASAT testing in the hope of negotiating a treaty banning ASAT weapons. Although it is calling for an ASAT ban, the Soviet Union is also conducting research on new ASAT weapons.

The United States and the Soviet Union also developed and deployed crude ground-based anti-ballistic missile (ABM) interceptors in the 1960s and 1970s. These systems were limited in 1972 by the U.S.-Soviet Anti-Ballistic Missile Treaty to deployments of no more than 200 (now 100) ABM interceptors. As a result, the US decided to retire its ABM system in 1976. The Soviet system, consisting of 100 interceptors around Moscow, remains in service, although it is not considered to be very effective. In addition to intercepting ballistic missiles, it has a theoretical capability to destroy low-orbit satellites. (Both countries also have a theoretical capability to destroy low-orbit satellites with their nuclear-armed ballistic missiles. However, simple countermeasures by the target satellites, such as hardening and evasive manoeuvring, would protect most of the satellites that are within range of these existing systems.)

4. U.S. President Ronald Reagan, televised speech of 23 March 1983.

5. Quoted in Simon Rosenblum, *Misguided Missiles*, (Toronto: Lorimer, 1985), p. 195.

6. Union of Concerned Scientists, *The Fallacy of Star Wars*, (Random House, 1984), p. 162-163.

7. Quoted in Willis Witter, "Reagan denounces Soviet SDI 'charade'," *Washington Times*, 17 November 1987.

8. Office of Technology Assessment (US Congress), *Strategic Defenses*, (Princeton University Press, 1986), p. 11-12. (Originally released by the OTA as "Ballistic Missile Defense Technologies," September 1985.) Emphasis in original.

9. Union of Concerned Scientists, *Space-Based Missile Defenses*, Briefing Paper, September 1984, p. 2.

10. Office of Technology Assessment, *Strategic Defenses*, p. 125. Emphasis in original.

11. Paul Nitze, speech to the Philadelphia World Affairs Council, 20 February 1985.

12. Unnamed SDI official, quoted in Douglas Waller, James Bruce and Douglas Cook, "Star Wars: Breakthrough or Breakdown?," *Arms Control Today*, May-June 1986, p. 10

13. Quoted in Rosenblum, *Misguided Missiles*, p. 194.

14. Waller, Bruce and Cook, "Star Wars: Breakthrough or Breakdown?," p. 10.

15. Office of Technology Assessment, *Strategic Defenses*, p. 33

16. *Ibid.*, p. 22. Emphasis in original.

17. *Ibid.*, p. 190.

18. "Star Wars Lasers," Wire News Highlights, *Current News*, 13 January 1986.

19. Peter Zimmerman, "SDI, a Two-Edged Sword: Defense or Destruction?," Los Angeles *Times*, 28 December 1986.

20. Ashton Carter, "Satellites and Anti-Satellites," *International Security*, Spring 1986, p. 68.

Chapter 8

1. Charles W. Corddry "At least 13,500 nuclear warheads in Europe will be untouched by pact" *Baltimore Sun*, December 8, 1967.

2. Strobe Talbott "The Road to Zero" *Time*, December 14, 1987, pp. 20-35.

3. Simon Rosenblum, *Misguided Missiles*, (Toronto: James Lorimer, 1985), pp. 102-140.

4. Jack Mendelsohn "Wending Our Way to Zero" *Arms Control Today*, May 1987, pp. 4-9.

5. Horst Ehmke "A Second Phase of Detente" *World Policy Journal*, Summer 1987, pp. 363-382.

6. Quoted in *Maclean's*, March 16, 1987.

7. Daniel Charles "NATO looks for arms control loopholes" *Bulletin of the Atomic Scientists*, September 1987, pp. 7-12; and John Pradas, Joel S. Wit and Michael J. Zagurek "The Strategic Forces of Britain and France" *Scientific American*, August 1986.

8. David N. Schwartz *NATO's Nuclear Dilemmas* (Washington, D.C.: The Brookings Institution, 1983) pp. 136-192; and Daniel Charles *Nuclear Planning in NATO* (Cambridge, Massachusetts: Ballinger, 1987).

9. Desmond Ball "Can Nuclear War Be Controlled?" Adelphi Papers, Number 169, The International Institute for Strategic Studies, London, 1981.

10. McGeorge Bundy, George Kennan, Robert McNamara and Gerard Smith "Nuclear Weapons and the Atlantic Alliance," *Foreign Affairs*, Spring 1982, pp. 753-768.

11. *Globe and Mail*, February 1, 1984.

12. James M. Garrett, "Theatre Strategic Deterrence Re-examined," *Armed Forces and Society*, Fall 1983 (Vol. 10, No. 1), p. 32.

13. Egbert Boeker "Defence In a Peaceful Europe" *ADIV Report*, March-April 1987, pp. 1-4.

14. Quoted in Leon V. Sigal "Conventional Forces in Europe: Signs of a Soviet Shift" *Bulletin of The Atomic Scientists*, December 1987, p. 16.

15. "West German Leader Urges Reagan to go Slow on Modernizing Missiles," Ottawa *Citizen*, February 20, 1988.

16. John Mearsheimer, "Why the Soviets Can't Win Quickly in Central Europe," *International Security*, Summer 1982, p. 38.

17. Quoted by Center for Defense Information, "US-Soviet Military Facts," *The Defense Monitor*, Vol. 16, No. 6, 1984, p.5.

18. Quoted in Lee Feinstein "What's in a Number? Annotating the Conventional Balance in Europe" *Deadline*, May-June 1987, p. 9.

19. Horst Ehmke "A Second Phase of Detente" *World Policy Journal*, p. 376. See also Thomas K. Longstreth "The Future of Conventional arms Control in Europe" *F.A.S. Public Interest Report*, February 1988.

20. Bernard Trainor "NATO troops likely to deter Soviet Attack, Pentagon says" *Globe and Mail*, December 1, 1987, p. 14.

21. International Institute for Strategic Studies, *The Military Balance, 1986-87*, 1986, pp. 224-227.

22. Alternative Defence Commission, *The Politics of Alternative Defence* (London: Paladin, 1986) pp. 224-227.

23. Quoted in Frank Blackaby "Agenda for European Security" in Marek Thee (ed.) *Arms and Disarmament* (New York: Oxford University Press, 1986) pp. 243-246.

24. Jonathan Dean, *Watershed in Europe: Dismantling the East-West Military Confrontation* (Lexington, Massachusetts: Lexington Books, 1987) p. 259.

25. Jonathan Dean p.85.

26. Mariano Aguirre and Conrad Miller "Low-Intensity Conflict: The European Front" *Defence and Disarmament News*, November-December 1986, p.4.

27. Jonathan Dean p. xiii

28. Mary Kaldor "The Imaginary War" in Dan Smith and E.P. Thompson (eds) Prospectus For A Habitable Planet (London: Penguin, 1987) pp. 72-99.

29. Christopher Donnelly "The Development of the Soviet Concept of Echeloning" *NATO Review*, December 1984, pp. 9-17.

30. Michael McGwire "Update: Soviet Military Objectives" *World Policy Journal*, Fall 1987, pp. 723-731.

31. Bjorn Moller "The Need for an Alternative NATO Strategy" *Journal of Peace Research* Volume 24, No. 1, 1987 pp. 61-72.

32. Alvin M. Saperstein "An Enhanced Non-Provocative Defense in Europe" *Journal of Peace Research* Volume 24, No. 1, 1987, pp. 47-60.

33. Mikhail Gorbachev, quoted in *Globe and Mail*, April 11, 1987, p.3.

34. C.A. Namiesniowski, The Stockholm Agreement: An Exercise in Confidence Building (Ottawa: Canadian Institute for International Peace and Security, 1987)

35. Robert Neild and Anders Boserup "Beyond INF: A New Approach To Nonnuclear Forces" *World Policy Journal* Fall 1987.

36. Frank Barnaby and Egbert Boeker, Defense Without Offence: Non-Nuclear Defense for Europe (Bradford, U.K.: Bradford University School of Peace Studies, 1982)

37. John Galtung, *There are Alternatives!* (Chester Springs, Pennsylvania: Dufour Publishers, 1984).

38. Ben Dankbaar "Alternative Defense Policies and Modern Weapon Technology," in Mary Kaldor and Dan Smith *Disarming Europe* (London: Merlin Press, 1982) pp. 163-184.

39. Leon V. Sigal "Conventional Forces in Europe: Signs of a Soviet Shift" *Bulletin of Atomic Scientists*, December 1987, pp. 16-20.

40. Alternative Defence Commission, *The Politics of Alternative Defence* (London: Paladin, 1986).

41. Dan Smith and E.P. Thompson (eds.) *Prospectus for a Habitable Planet* (London: Penguin, 1987).

Chapter 9

1. "No nuclear arms on Canadian soil, PM tells U.S. TV," Jeff Sallot, *Globe and Mail*, 16 March 1985.

2. Nuclear depth bombs: "Canada to get 32 nuclear bombs if war breaks out, analyst reports," Paul Knox, *Globe and Mail*, 10 January 1985. B-52 bombers: *Nuclear Battlefields*, William Arkin and Richard Fieldhouse, 1985, p. 78.

3. See, for example, "Clark denies U.S. told us to take arms," Joel Ruimy, Toronto *Star*, 16 February 1985.

4. "Inert NERTS: Missing Alerts," Bill Robinson, *Ploughshares Monitor*, December 1986.

5. "Tomahawk Sea-Launched Cruise Missile," Factsheet, Greenpeace Nuclear Free Seas Campaign, July 1987.

6. See, for example, "Canada's Nuclear Industry and the Myth of the Peaceful Atom," Gordon Edwards, *Canada and the Nuclear Arms Race*, Ernie Regehr and Simon Rosenblum, eds., (Toronto: James Lorimer & Co., 1983), p. 122-170.

7. "More Bucks for the Bang," Ken Epps and Bill Robinson, *Ploughshares Monitor*, December 1986.

8. *Nuclear Battlefields*, p. 216-219. Supplemented with research by Project Ploughshares.

9. Exchange of notes on Canada-US Test and Evaluation Program, 10 February 1983, para. 23 c.

10. "The Green Pine Network: Radio-Activity in the North," Bill Robinson, *Ploughshares Monitor*, March 1988.

11. *Challenge and Commitment: A Defence Policy for Canada*, Department of National Defence, 1987, p. 18.

12. "Canada's Position on Nuclear Weapon Free Zones,"Department of External Affairs, *Disarmament Bulletin*, Summer/Autumn 1986.

13. "Canada responds to the peace movement proposals," Ernie Regehr, *Ploughshares Monitor*, September 1982.

Index